THE HOLOCAUST
IS OVER;
WE MUST RISE
FROM ITS ASHES

THE HOLOCAUST IS OVER; WE MUST RISE FROM ITS ASHES

Avraham Burg

palgrave
macmillan

THE HOLOCAUST IS OVER; WE MUST RISE FROM ITS ASHES
Copyright © Avraham Burg, 2008.

English language translation © Israel Amrani, 2008

All rights reserved.

First published in Hebrew in 2007 by
Miskal-Yehidoth Ahronoth Books and
Chemed Books under the title *Victory Over Hitler*.

First published in English in 2008 by
PALGRAVE MACMILLAN®
in the United States—a division of St. Martin's Press LLC,
175 Fifth Avenue, New York, NY 10010.

Where this book is distributed in the UK, Europe and the rest of the
world, this is by Palgrave Macmillan, a division of Macmillan Publishers
Limited, registered in England, company number 785998, of Houndmills,
Basingstoke, Hampshire RG21 6XS.

Palgrave Macmillan is the global academic imprint of the above companies
and has companies and representatives throughout the world.

Palgrave® and Macmillan® are registered trademarks in the United States,
the United Kingdom, Europe and other countries.

ISBN-13: 978–0–230–60752–1
ISBN-10: 0–230–60752–7

Library of Congress Cataloging-in-Publication Data

Burg, Avraham.
    [Le-natseah et Hitler. English]
    The Holocaust is over; we must rise from its ashes / Avraham Burg.
        p. cm.
    ISBN 0–230–60752–7
    1. Burg, Avraham. 2. Political activists—Israel—Biography.
  3. Jews—Identity. I. Title.

DS126.6.B87A3 2007b
940.53′18092—dc22   2008012577

A catalogue record of the book is available from the British Library.

Design by Newgen Imaging Systems (P) Ltd., Chennai, India.

First edition: November 2008

10 9 8 7 6 5 4 3 2 1

Printed in the United States of America.

In loving memory of my late parents:
My mother and educator, the noble Rivka Burg (née Slonim),
who integrated her childhood in the heart of Hebron
with her adult poem of Jerusalem.
My father and mentor, Shlomo Yosef Burg,
who never hesitated to take the journey from Dresden,
Germany to Jerusalem, Israel and back.

In dedication to the cornerstones of my ever-growing
house of love: Yael, Itay, Roni, Nathan, Dan,
Avital, and Noam.

To the person who managed to grasp before
any of us what is concealed behind the walls of fear
and pain, who dared to give it the voice it needed
so badly, and who succeed in articulating this voice
better than anybody else—Hannah Arendt.

CONTENTS

ACKNOWLEDGMENTS

ALL MY LIFE I HAVE HAD THE GOOD FORTUNE TO MEET PEOPLE who shared their treasures with me. Many of them left their imprint on my own soul. Some became my closest friends and a handful were even willing to accept me always, and unconditionally, for who I was. Each and every one of them became a part of me—true soul brothers and sisters. We do not always share the same views, and they often refrain from indulging in the self-criticism I am so drawn to, but they are always there for me, with me, and I wholly believe that they shall forever continue in this way. They are all an extension of my *self*. And I try hard, very hard to be theirs. I thank them dearly, and am grateful for the privilege to be able to mention a chosen few of them:

The elder of the tribe, Edgar Bronfman (Yehiel Moishe on my mailing list), who opened my eyes to the possible syntheses of Jewish and Universal voices.

Brian Lurie, my first non-orthodox rabbi, a deeply courageous and creative man who has a heart big enough to care for us all, especially those who are less fortunate. Brian is my personal prophet.

Johnny Jacoby, who was and still is my scout, at all times one step ahead, looking for new paths and discovering the farthest and widest of horizons.

Israel and Evelyn Singer and all their children—we were summoned together many years before we were even born, never to be separated.

Helain and Marvin Lender, our family away from family, my home when I'm not at home—unconditionally committed, always concerned, and never short of love for humanity at large and for Jews in particular.

I shall always cherish the comforting and firm shoulder offered to me by Joel Tauber whenever I needed it, both personally and professionally. Ian Davis, my friend, my partner, and my guide. You are always so Jewish and so concerned. A true English gentleman. Thanks for the togetherness, friendship, and inspiration.

The maestro of my overseas affairs and good friend Clive Lessem, without whom none of this could have happened.

And to Alessandra Bastagli and her team at Palgrave Macmillan. You are my multicultural partners and you give me the energy to continue and accomplish my current mission.

The spirit of these soul-mates of mine is a beautiful reflection of the deeper self I'm longing to become. This spirit is best expressed by two individuals who I have never met, but who left a huge personal mark on me: the late Mordechai Kaplan and the late Avraham Yehoshua Heschel. I see them as the two pillars of the modern Jewish bridge: among Jews as well as between Jews and the rest of Creation.

And finally, last but in no way least, my Jewish places on earth; my home Kehila, the most beautiful place in Israel, Nataf and its beloved people and my Mikdash Me'at, the Bnei Jeshurun congregation in New York, a place which expresses so fully the realm I am dreaming of and the vision I am striving toward.

FOREWORD TO THE ENGLISH EDITION

B Y ITS VERY NATURE, THE EMERGENCE OF A BOOK INTO THE world is a slow process. Ideas are initially groomed in thought and imagination. Form is conceived by reason, and the words deliver the fruits of the mind—a book brimming with expression. Then it is laid on the table and awaits the verdict: Will they buy it? Will they read it? Will they agree? Will they object? And perhaps, God forbid, the worst will happen—they will ignore it.

This book tells of pain and, only in part, of hope. It tells the story of my parents and of their destroyed worlds, of the state of Israel, of Jewish and human society in which eyes are still shut, where people dream of distant stories as though they were concrete reality; about me and those dear to me, who live in Israel and try to establish for ourselves a new Jewish universe that is different from the travails of Jewish history.

Fear and concern were my close companions during the writing of this book. Throughout the process of converting my thoughts into words, I relied on, conversed, and consulted ceaselessly with Yael, my spouse and life partner. When the time came to release the book in Israel, I told her that if it did not cause a fierce backlash, then Israel must already be dying. The book makes harsh criticisms; it challenges old-fashioned ideas, questions existential foundations, argues with sanctified truths, attempts to replace rigid national dogmas with new universal paradigms. And Yael, with her wisdom and patience that is so Jewish, sought to mitigate my tempest and bade me to wait. Anxious just like I was, anxious for me.

We both knew that a towering wave awaited us. After all, it is not every day that a man who was once at the heart of the Israeli establishment gets up and thinks aloud. A man who was accompanied by heavy security because he was one of the Israel's "symbols of the state" does not ask questions, certainly not ones that are too tough. It is customary upon reaching these lofty echelons to provide only answers, to offer sedatives to dampen a painful reality, a verbal placebo. From the moment that the word "former" is attached to your title, you are eternally obliged to represent a plethora of things that you do not necessarily agree with or wish to represent. You become a passive memorial; presentable and dignified—yes, but doubting the present path and its justness? Never!

This is how many perceive a never-ending public service. Whereas I, having many "formers" hanging on my name, perceive my service in an entirely different way, one that does not part with my internal truth even when this truth it is not shared by the majority. Even today, when its foothold remains limited, and tenuous. Because its day will come. These thoughts were burning inside me.

For too many years I lived in the warm embrace of institutionalized elusiveness and was a part of it. I was very comfortable there. Comfortable, but not necessarily responsible.

One of the deepest reasons I chose to leave Israeli politics was the growing feeling that Israel had become a kingdom without prophecy. On the face of it, everything is working: decisions are being made, actions executed. But where are we headed? No one knows. The tired oarsmen are rowing in the ship's hold but remain in the dark. The junior officers are looking up to the senior captains who cannot see beyond the next waves, as they charge, crest, crash, and wane. Because even the lookout at the crow's nest has climbed back down long ago, and we have no one to watch and relentlessly search for the next Israeli and Jewish continent.

My perception of the Jewish people and the essence of Judaism forbid me from leading such a life—without a compass and direction. I was taught from infancy that the Jewish people never existed merely in order to exist, we never survived just to survive, we never just carried on in order to carry on. Jewish existence has always been directed upward: not just to the Father, the King, up in the heavens, but up toward the great human calling. We sought freedom in the days of Egyptian slavery, the constitution of justice and equality in the days of Sinai and the journeys in the desert, and universal humanism in the days of the great prophets; the Great Eagle, Maimonides, optimistically strove to put an end to conquests and subjugation of the Jewish people in the Middle Ages.

Even the Zionist idea was not merely a fascinating quest for saving the Jewish people from a wrathful and violent anti-Semite persecutor, but a heroic attempt to establish a model society that would prove to us and everyone else that there is a viable, alternative political reality, based, in a nutshell, on the principle: "What is hateful to thee, do not do unto thy fellow." This great call has become mute and silent in Israel of recent years. Concern for a secure livelihood and material welfare from within, and the bloodshed and existential threats from without have halted public discussion about social values and pulled the curtains on the horizons of thought and vision.

I wrote this book in order to open up the heart, mouth, and eyes for a new vision. I have tried to touch on our maladies and afflictions and to offer preliminary directions of cure and recovery on the road to a new national and global vision for the Jewish people. Many have already accepted my words with much love. They read the book, sent me letters, embraced me on the street. Others, who are many more, have come forward with vociferous objections: protesting, angry, assailing, and aggressive.

A few days after this book came out in Israel, I was standing in line on a city street. An old man approached me from across the velvet rope and told me with a sullen face:

"Burg, I'm very angry with you!"

"Why?" I asked.

"Because of what you wrote."

"And what did I write?"

"You wrote against the Holocaust!"

"And you?" I wondered aloud, "would you write in support of the Holocaust?"

Our exchange ended in silence. He went his way and I went mine, and the question remained unanswered and unresolved. What had angered that honest man when he approached me gave an insight into his mind and those of many others. I had placed harsh truths and mirrors before the face of Israel. I wasn't always gentle. At times I lacked the greater compassion that is essential for packaging painful messages. We have many wailers among us and I did not wipe all their tears. My voice was loud and dissonant because the noise and commotion have, for too many years, prevented us from hearing anything.

This is how I explain the fierce public debate that broke out immediately after my musings were published.

Mine is a testimony to Israel's ailments and a response to its cry for help. These days Israel has no guide for the perplexed; values have been blurred, mutual support is disintegrating and becoming riddled with holes, the diplomatic road to peace is blocked and gloomy. From the outside, Iran, Gaza, and the realities of demographics and population loom, and a public debate on the future of our tormented state barely exists. The political system is fatigued and remains outside of the piercing discussion on the fundamental questions of our lives and of the quest for new answers. This is why I wrote this book.

It took several years. My opponents were not always careful to present my ideas in full. Perhaps the book and its argument were too much for them to bear. This is natural, because we always find it easier to stick with what we know rather than trying to find new alternatives, like the ones that I propose in this book. My hopes are for a new humanism, a rejuvenated Judaism, for less traumatic interfaces of trust with the world; my positions and suggestions are ways to emerge from national trauma and turn weakness into strength, by offering alternative quests to high school students and proposing changes in the school curriculum and a different, more Jewish, way to commemorate the destruction of European Jewry—I understand these things will take time to catch on. They await the slower, moderate, and deep reaction that is still to come. Through the thicket of daily hardships and the screaming headlines it is not easy to imagine my vision for Israel as a generator of a large global peace process, and my belief that our entire existence should be motivated by a perpetual responsibility for the world's well-being. I strive toward a Jewish people that say, "Never again" not just for us Jews, but for every suffering victim in the world today, who I hope will enjoy the support and protection of the Jews, yesterday's victims who defeated Hitler. This is not yet the majority opinion in Israel. Not yet.

These issues go beyond the classic dichotomy of right and left. The Israeli right has nothing to offer but sword and messiah until the day of peace comes, and in general, once peace is achieved, the left will have

nothing to offer in terms of new spiritual content. In my books and statements I join the rising Israeli voices who are attempting to outline the future
Israeli landscape. We seek to add humaneness and universalism to the old
equations and new dimensions of value-based content and national existence. We propose a life of trust, not a reality composed of nothing but endless trauma. All those who are prepared to ask the tough questions, even if
our answers are utterly different, and those who, with hand on heart, confess, "We are anxious," are my partners. And there are many of us.

When President George W. Bush declares a war that may seal my fate
for better or worse, I must openly defend myself from him and the manipulations of an Israeli lobby that encourages dual loyalties. When force is used
in France to prevent an essential dialogue with second-generation immigrants, this is also my concern. And when I have influence, I do my best to
exert it. Because this is also part of my Jewishness. This is my dual responsibility, as a human being and as a Jew.

I have been asked time and again what my father, Shlomo Yosef Burg,
would have said. My beloved father was utterly different from the image
that people had constructed of him in their hearts and memories. I have
no doubt that he would agree with most of what I say. Where we might disagree (particularly in relation to his position that supported the religious
character of the state), he would argue with me like a Jew, not like an Israeli.
The Israeli would raise his hand to strike and hiss: "Who do you think
you are?" and once I was disqualified (by personal veto) he would exempt
himself from my questions. The Talmudic Jew, on the other hand, would
try to understand: "What is it that you are trying to argue here?" He would
follow me to the root of my argument and decide whether to adopt my
suggestions and change his mind, or whether to return to his initial position. He would always leave the opposing position intact, documented, and
respected, knowing that today's opposing opinion may become tomorrow's majority vote.

In the meantime, I would tell him, my father, this book's protagonist:
There is room for hope. People ask, argue, and seek answers. And I, with
them, am looking for the solution to the current Israeli frustration. This is
how we will truly defeat Hitler.

In my life I have been involved in many disputes and controversial confrontations. Polemic is not foreign to me. I am a great believer in dispute as part of the act of creation. Indifferent or subservient people and lame or worn ideas do not fertilize or bring to life new worlds. Only debate is capable of giving birth to humanity and humaneness. This is how I understand the culture of Jewish debate, a debate for the eternal renewal of the world. But never before have I witnessed a debate with such a precise characterization of supporters and opponents as I have this time. The vast majority of the angriest opponents were in their fifties or older, and most of the supportive and interested readers were young—in their teens, twenties and thirties. Israel's well-to-do and smug elders were unable to contain their anger at me for having dared to question and examine the sanctified axioms of the life that they have established at such a dear price with their bodies, souls, and sacrifices. Whereas the young, sensing that something is amiss, hollow, or fake in the "canonical" Israeli being, sought me out, and they were many. They came to see me of their own accord, not necessarily to hear my answers, but always out of a wish to partake of the questioning process. Maybe the message is that they are of the generation of hope, precisely because they take nothing for granted and they are constantly searching for openness, believe that there is a different, better way. Better than my parents' way and even mine. The members of my children's generation are the source of infinite optimism, I feel, in relation to my people and homeland.

For many long weeks the debates resonated in various Israeli arenas. There were blunt rejections and warm receptions—indifference was the only missing reaction. Israel emerged, assuaging my initial anxieties. I did not have to wait long, as Yael had predicted, to see it. Israel, as I learned once more to my delight, is still a very healthy society that responded with great emotion to its reflection on the mirror I placed before its face. True, we suffered harsh childhood illnesses as a young state while battling the symptoms characteristic of a 4,000-year-old nation, but all in all, hope is still here.

Now, the book has been published in other languages and I am once more ridden with anxiety. Can a foreigner understand Israeli intimacy? Is it possible for someone who is not part of the Jewish family to perceive the loving tension that characterizes family members who sometimes do not see eye to eye with one another and yet remain whole? Will there be people who take my words, distort them and use them as weapons against me, against my nation? Probably. Because those who hate never take into consideration the wounds of those who love. But is this reason enough to keep silent? Isn't silence a greater threat and risk? And generally, the new and old enemies of the Jewish people coexist with the current reality, whereas I, the son of national sovereignty and its independence, am no longer willing to allow the anti-Semite from without or the coward and conformist from within to define for me the boundaries of public discourse and discussion.

I pray that among my readership abroad, those of my kin and those who are not, there will be some who would understand that Jewish and Israeli society is among the most incredible on earth. Not only is it an open society where one is allowed to think and say everything, people are free to do this excess. Today's Israel is the microcosm of the entire world in the same way that the world is Israel's macrocosm. If you wish to understand the world, try to decipher Israel, and if you wish to understand Israel, examine the world within which you live. This is why this book is not only a constructive criticism of Israel. This is a book about the whole of humanity, about people good and bad, about human beings who are haunted by trauma and their brothers who are searching for trust. This is a book filled with tears, some of which are shed with great sadness for what has been, and some from happiness about the good that can and will come. And what will become of the world? It is all in our hands. So treat the world and us, Israelis and Jews, with understanding. Because we are two sides of the same coin.

CHAPTER 1

MY ROOTS

I WAS BORN IN JANUARY 1955 IN GERMANY, SO TO SPEAK. REHAVIA IS the "Little Germany" of Jerusalem, where I was born and raised. It was a literary place, and bore the promise of prosperity. The streets were named after Moshe Ben Maimon, Maimonides, Avraham Ibn Ezra, and Shlomo Ibn Gvirol, the medieval scholars and poets of the Iberian Golden Age. The glory of that period was renewed half a millennium later in Germany's modern age, which produced Moses Mendelssohn, Heinrich Heine, Walter Benjamin, Franz Rosenzweig, and the wonderful Else Lasker-Schüler. This grand but slowly dying German-Jewish tradition found its way to Rehavia, its final refuge. At the time, there were few places like this, in Israel or elsewhere, where modern Bauhaus architecture distinguished houses on the outside and heavy, leather-bound German libraries filled the inside.

As a young boy, I often would see Martin Buber pacing softly up and down the street. I used to think that all streets had Martin Bubers of their own. The Nobel laureate writer S. Y. Agnon visited our home, and I was sure he visited everybody in our neighborhood. Akiva Ernst Simon once complimented me as a child, and I thought everybody had a Professor Simon to compliment them. Even the skinny chimneysweep, Mr. Arnheim, who rode his noisy Sachs scooter with his blackened brooms, provided a connection to Germany. There were many others: The Schocken Library was across the street, and Rehov Ben Maimon, the street of my childhood, was fondly called Ben Maimon *Strasse*. Judges and senior officials called Rehavia home in those days.

Only much later did I come to understand that what I was witnessing as a child was really lost glory on its way out. I saw it from its back; I did not have the privilege to see its face. Indeed, the immigrant German-Jewish community had been magnificent. They erected factories and neighborhoods. They built the foundations of the Hebrew University, supporting its research and enriching the cultural landscape. But then Israel turned away from them and they, being refined and cultured, did not push or elbow their way forward. Now even though their memory is almost gone and modern Israel is different from their dreams and my own naive childhood expectations, I wish to hold on to them; to delay their departure just for another moment. It's not just them I wish to understand, it is also myself, and us as a people.

For many years I have lived an Israeli life: sheltered childhood, youth movement, schools, military service, studies, and a long public service. I was an Israeli in full, a strictly kosher *sabra* (a native-born Israeli Jew). Only much later in life did I understand the miracle that my parents had fulfilled. They did not allow tragedies and traumas to take hold of our lives. At the same time, they succeeded in bequeathing to us many of the values of a world that is now gone forever.

My mother survived the Hebron massacre of 1929, and my father was a stateless refugee, a German native who did not relinquish his gravitas or his heavy accent in his new home country, Israel. They did everything they could to ensure me and my siblings would have happy lives. The secret language between them was Heine's German; not the Holocaust German of the survivors. My parents often said that certain things should be done a certain way, as it was done "back in Saxony." If the loud demonstrations in Jerusalem against German reparations and diplomatic relations, even the well-publicized Eichmann trial, entered our homes, they did so only faintly. I do not remember a single conversation on these matters. The

Shoah industry that would develop in Israel in later years would be foreign to me. I am not a psychologist and do not know whether my parents successfully repressed the atrocities they experienced in their youths, the horrors that erased their happy childhoods. Perhaps they built a new reality of their own and created a new world. Either way, as a child I was never exposed, emotionally or practically, to "Shoahization," though this cultural movement has become second nature to us Israelis.

When I finished writing my first book, *God Is Back,* I was left with a sense of great loss. Although I had tried to describe the foundation of my identity, the religious aspect of world conflicts was largely lacking in my book. The Shoah is another pillar, a heavy one that defines modern Jewish identity. It became clear to me that in *God Is Back* I focused on what seemed most important, but in fact I was ignoring one of Israel's major illnesses. I tried to superimpose the healthy mentality that my family enjoyed on an Israel that is essentially different from my natural habitat. To many, the Shoah was and will forever be an incurable wound. To others, the Shoah is the nucleus of their identity. To everyone, the Shoah is a present, tangible experience wherever we go. For many months after the publication of *God Is Back* I tried to find my place in a different reality that had erupted into my life. It was as if suddenly, and retroactively, a new light had been cast on my childhood. The world of my father, who had since died of old age, was changing before my eyes.

In 2003 I was asked by the editors of the *Haaretz* book review to write a piece on Rubik Rosenthal's memoir, *22 Flowers Street*—the story of the Rosenthal family, which began with traumatic events in Germany and continued with bereavement in Israel's wars. For many days I was unable to write. The editor was impatient but my hand refused to budge. Even Rosenthal called me, to no avail. It wasn't until I met two close friends of mine that I finally was able to begin. He is a kibbutz native and the son of German immigrants from the 1930s. She is a sabra with roots, the daughter of a famous army man, whereas I am the son of German and Israeli Zionism. Three of us were sitting together—three Israelis who came from different and distant worlds.

"Our dads never kissed us," all three of us said.

"Why? Because of the Shoah?"

"No." We laughed. "Because he was from Germany."

And, the cork popped, and I was suddenly able to write. True, every father is different and every family is different. My father was warm, his love was inexhaustible, but something of the German tradition was at the foundation of all our lives, and since then we have been yearning for that extraordinary culture that was destroyed forever. Germany committed suicide—killing herself and us—and significant parts of our Jewish identity perished in smoke, together with the cultural models to which we could and should subscribe.

+≻━≺+

My bottle opened and many genies, bad and good, came out.

I wrote this book in two years, writing and deleting, sometimes deleting before writing. When you touch such pain, you must be very careful. On the one hand, I did not want to bring more pain to those who suffered. On the other hand, I knew very well that I must not pretend. When you deal with such matters, you must tell the most accurate inner truths. Many months of painful writing separated the dignity of the victims from my own inner truth. In the end I withheld many issues whose time had not come. I wonder if it will ever come. Our sages said: "It is a *mitzvah* to say a matter to be heard, just as it is a *mitzvah* to not say a matter not to be heard."[1]

When I began writing this book, I called the document *Hitler Won*. I felt that the wounds and scars were so deep that the modern Jewish nation had no chance to heal. Our Shoah-inflicted trauma seemed like an incurable disease. I was angry at the fact that we continued to miss the opportunity to live normal lives, and at the sourness of life here in Israel, which seemed to be our fate for generations to come. Exactly because of the desperation that seemed to take a hold of me, I struggled to beat back the overflowing tide of callousness. Then, a miracle: as I wrote, these issues took on a new dimension. Cautious optimism was born from the ashes and smoke. And as it is Jewish custom to give the sick person a new name to facilitate his healing, I changed the book's title in Hebrew to *Defeating Hitler*. It is still possible; there is still a chance. We must win; we have no choice, lest we stop living. I walked alone a long way but I am already optimistic. We will get there. And now the book travels abroad. The strong Hebrew title reads differently in English, with too much of a military maneuver and too little of its core humanity. So here is the third name, not really a name but a message: The Holocaust Is Over; We Must Rise from Its Ashes.

It was my mother, who died days before the book was published in Israel, who gave me the opportunity to cross over to optimism. We celebrated her last birthday together, children, grandchildren, great-grandchildren, and spouses. There was much joy. On the way home, just the two of us were in the car, driving slowly through the streets of Jerusalem.

"Avraham, God probably loves me very much," she said, radiant with happiness.

I had heard her say that more than once over the years. Now, taking advantage of the intimate moment, I asked her what I had dared not to ask. "But Mom, how can you say such a thing? At the age of seven you lost your mother. At eight, half of your family was slaughtered in Hebron. At fourteen, your father died of heartbreak, and in recent years you lost Tzviya, your eldest daughter."

"True," she replied after a moment of contemplation. "But all my life I was surrounded by love." Then she added, "Everybody loved me."

For many days to follow, thoughts on the power of the love that saved my mother were spinning inside my head. A short time later, we spoke again and the conversation turned to the news. The Israeli Air Force was bombing and killing innocent people in Gaza, on its beaches and streets, and in Lebanon's villages and cities. My mother's grandson is an IAF pilot, the captain of a transport plane.

"I'm so glad he's not a combat pilot," she commented.

"Why?" I asked, surprised.

"Would I want my grandson to drop bombs on innocent people?"

I was silent in the face of the courage of love that shone from her. As someone who lost her childhood in Hebron in 1929, she could afford to be a bit less tolerant, maybe even show some glee, with respect to the suffering of "the Arabs" as enemies of Israel, wherever they were. But it seemed that the same love that surrounded her had also seeped into her. She became for me an embodiment of the ultimate Jewish heroine. Who is the hero of heroes? Jewish tradition teaches, "One who turns one's enemy into a loved and beloved friend." If my mother could defeat her own personal inferno with sheer love and hope, then we all have a positive future.

Like my mother, who has lived beside me all my life, Lucien and Janine, the wonderful parents of Yael, my partner for life, were also *there*—she as a young woman in love who supported combat, and he as a brave partisan of France's Jewish Resistance. When many of their friends turned to the right in the middle of the last century, to the path of Jewish redemption and separatism, they turned to the left, toward the ideas of universalism and humanism. They dedicate the current chapter of their lives to revealing the goodness that shone through in the sea of evil of those days. Lucien, historian of France's Jewish struggle, spends his days and nights trying to locate and decorate "The Righteous Among Nations." The Righteous are the non-Jews who risked their lives to save our persecuted brethren, thus preserving the image of God by which humanity was created. The spirit of my in-laws hovers over every abyss to which the book and my thoughts took me. Without them I could not have known that there is an alternative, positive belief in the goodness of humans.

This is not a history book. I am not an interpreter of the past, just a consumer of the news that it produces. I touch the past only to understand the conditions of the present. This is not another indictment of Hitler and his henchmen. They are forever guilty in my court. This is our story beyond the evil of their crimes. The Shoah and the atrocities that the Nazis committed against us are an inseparable part of the active Israeli present. Since I want to repair the present for a better future for my children and their friends, I had no choice but to face the post-Shoah routine of the present; to try to understand, to change and to be changed. The following pages were written with awe and reverence. If I hurt anyone, I apologize. If the truth hurts, I too suffer.

From the time of its conception through to the birth of this book, the issue of a nuclear Iran was on the agenda, and it still is today. As usual, politics and history are paired: an atom bomb and anti-Semitism, dictatorship and hatred of Israel. President Mahmoud Ahmedinejad works energetically on his nuclear program and at the same time calls for wiping Israel off the map. Is history repeating itself? Is a second Shoah on the way? We still do not have answers, but the panic is back. What does it mean for me? Should I pack away my optimism, my faith in the nations of the world, and my hope for a better future for my children and replace them with classic Jewish paranoia? This is the response of many, but it is not mine. I understand contemporary Judaism differently. Something amazing happened to the Jewish people of this age, something that has happened only a few times to our forefathers in our tortured history. The world has changed in nature and character. World superpowers, most of the Christian churches, and a significant part of world citizenry vowed sixty years ago "never again," and this time they meant it. We are not facing a great menacing enemy alone. The upheavals of Arab nations, Islamic zealotry and its dangers, directed at us for years while we were on our own, have become the concern of many good nations. Our personal enemy has become the common enemy, and an expansive international coalition stands against it. This is a vastly different world than the one we have known. The world's stand and our own capabilities provide hope and faith. This is a world that I trust.

The last few words of this book were written during an incredible trip that I shared with my youngest son, Noam. We went to Germany together to retrace the footsteps of my late father. We traveled far and I reached the deepest part of my inner self. Our flight home was delayed and we had a few unplanned hours to spend, so we strolled, father and son, through the Berlin Zoo. As Noam was walking around the habitats of exotic animals, I found myself sitting and watching the captive monkeys. All of them jumped energetically and playfully from one branch to another. Holding on with one hand, the other stretched in the air toward the next branch, up they went. But one monkey sat alone and did not mingle. I asked a passing staff member what was wrong. "He is different," replied the veterinarian. "He can't climb because he's afraid to let go of the branch. If you hold a branch with both your hands, you cannot move up. This is his fate," he commented sadly. "He sits on the floor all day like a person in mourning, isolated from the life around him."

I thought about the poor monkey, and not just about him. I asked myself, Is this the fable or the moral? Is this the monkey or is it us? Since those days in Germany, we have been holding on painfully to the little that we have, not letting go. We hold the memories and the traumas and they do not leave us. We cling to the tragedy and the tragedy becomes our justification for everything. We sit on the branch of past mourning, not taking off to the heights of humanity and humanism where we belong.

Noam returned and I got distracted. I forgot to ask the veterinarian if there was a cure for the disease. We bought ice cream and headed for home.

CHAPTER 2

THE HOLOCAUST, EVER-PRESENT

THE CONSTANT PRESENCE OF THE SHOAH IN MY LIFE FEELS LIKE a buzz in my ear. Although none of the horrors affected me personally, I feel that this darkest period in human history is always present, everywhere, and its reminders are many. Children prepare for the "Auschwitz trip." World leaders are now celebrating six decades since liberation. And while the Shoah's tenth anniversary was hardly commemorated, and the fiftieth anniversary was pathetic, suddenly, in 2005, the world was holding extravagant ceremonies, pyrotechnics, and Hollywood-style productions for the sixtieth anniversary of our deaths. Not a day passes without a mention of the Shoah in the only newspaper that I read, *Haaretz*. The topics are varied: reparations, compensation, anti-Semitism, a new analysis, an interesting book, an insightful interview. Shoah is like the hole in the ozone layer: unseen yet present, abstract yet powerful. The more I think about it, the more I am certain that the Shoah has become a theological pillar of the modern Jewish identity and that it is one of the Jewish people's greatest challenges in modern times.

One day my daughter came home from her high school in Jerusalem. "Today," she said, "we had a lesson to prepare us for 'the trip to Poland.'" Over our family dinner, I asked her about the lesson. "The school principal said we are all Shoah survivors," she replied. Eventually she and her friends, in what has become the custom for many Israeli teenagers, traveled to Poland and returned as changed Israelis. Only my youngest son, Noam, did not join the trend. He, like me, does not want to base his Israeli, Jewish, and universal identity on the worst trauma in human experience. The silence surrounding the topic of the Shoah at my parents' home was now being replaced with its popularization. In this way, a link of memory was missing between my children and my parents. I see this book as a conversation between my father, Dr. Yosef Burg, a native of Germany who never lived a survivor's life, and my children, the offspring of an independent, sovereign Israel, who studied in a school that taught them that "we are all Shoah survivors."

⊹╾═╾═╾⊹

For many years I have been living a double life. Most of the time, it is an Israeli life, but a substantial part of it, in terms of quality, happens abroad. I spent many years networking and developing contacts to facilitate relationships between Israel and the international environment, the nations of the world and the Diaspora communities. In Israel I live in one language, that of tensions and traumas, conflict and confrontation. Outside of Israel I use a different language, of building bridges, understanding, forgiveness, and of concession. In Israel I live according to the Talmudic self-defense rule "Rise early to kill that which rises to kill you." It means, "Either I defeat you and you die or I die." When I was abroad, I learned the "win-win" concept: "I want to win, but not at your expense." It is possible for two parties to benefit from the same outcome.

As the years pass, the schism between the two languages I use deepens and tears me apart. I am increasingly convinced that the language of my land—not the spoken Hebrew but what is practiced—is based on a false premise. Israel accentuates and perpetuates the confrontational philosophy that is summed up in the phrase, "The entire world is against us." I often have the uneasy feeling that Israel will not know how to live without conflict. An Israel of peace and tranquility, free of sudden outbreaks of ecstasy, melancholy, and hysteria will simply not be. In the arena of war, the Shoah is the main generator that feeds the mentalities of confrontation and catastrophic Zionism.

Our reality is profoundly surprising. For the first time in our existence, the great majority of Jews live without an immediate threat to their existence. Except for a few thousands Jews in Iran and Morocco, a few hundred in Syria, and a lone Jew in Afghanistan, most Jews live in democratic societies. In less than a century-and-a-half, the living conditions of the Jewish people have changed beyond recognition. More than three-quarters of the Jewish people live in two relatively new societies: the State of Israel and the United States. Europe had been almost completely emptied of Jews through genocide and emigration. But it was not only the Shoah that was to blame. The liquidation process had begun years before the crematoria were built. Shalom Aleichem documented in doleful words the mass exodus from the regions of the Pale to the United States of America. S. Y. Agnon wrote *Yesteryear*, the stunning foundation of pre-state Hebrew literature, on the topic of an exodus from the land of Israel. The Zionist pioneers, together with religious immigrants, believers, and redemption-seekers, willfully left their Diaspora and built the new world of the modern Jewish people.

The State of Israel was built as a safe haven for the Jewish people, yet it is today the least safe place for Jews to live. Ask yourself, where is it safer to live? In holy Jerusalem, the city of bombs? Or in New York, where fundamentalist evil downed the twin towers of the World Trade Center? It seems that many more view New York as a safer place to live than Israel, regardless of how many atomic bombs the Jewish state allegedly stores in her arsenal.

An automatic Zionist answer to allay my fears would be that Israel is the safest place for Jews because anti-Semitism lurks everywhere, even behind the polite facade of American Christianity. Or they might argue that only in the land of our forefathers will our children and their children remain Jewish. I do not think that anyone can truly believe such arguments. We must admit that present-day Israel and its ways contribute to the rise in hatred of Jews. The responsibility for anti-Semitism is not ours, yet the mere existence of Israel is a thorn in the side of those who do not like us and requires more serious investigation and discussion than the shallow notion that "the world is against us no matter what we do." Such beliefs are suicidal, desperate, and defeatist. I do not subscribe to them.

⊹⊱━⊰⊹

Israeli society in the Holy Land is rich with a wide range of both religious and nationalistic expression. You have the ghetto ultra-Orthodox in the inner cities of Jerusalem and Bnei Brak; Hills Youth and stone-and-wood worshippers in the West Bank; New Age and Buddhist experimenters in Tel Aviv. They are all Jews, all spiritual, yet alien to one another. And an aura of ignorance surrounds them all. This is not only at the level of the simplistic question: "Who is Jewish?" but at the more sophisticated, intricate level that asks: "What is a Jew?" What does it mean to be a Jew? What does it require? Where has the elusive Jewish morality gone? We have erected a fortified haven but extinguished the flame of our "light onto the nations."[1]

The crisis is already here. When I study the components of my identity and the cause of my identity crisis, I recognize only one common thread that connects us all: the thick shadow, the unbearable heaviness of the Shoah and its horrors. It is the source of all, and it absorbs all. So much so that sometimes I want to rewrite the Bible to begin: "In the beginning there was the Shoah and the land had become chaos."

The Shoah is more present in our lives than God. The *Musaf* prayer says of God that "his glory fills the world"—here is no place in the world without the presence of God. Listening to the Israeli, Jewish, and even wider world's discourse today reveals that the Shoah is the founding experience not just of our national consciousness, but that of the western world as a whole. Army generals discuss Israeli security doctrine as "Shoah-proof." Politicians use it as a central argument for their ethical manipulations. People on the street experience daily the return of the horrors, and newspapers are filled with an endless supply of stories, articles, references, and statements that emanate from the Shoah and reflect it back into our lives. The Shoah is so pervasive that a study conducted a few years ago in a Tel Aviv teaching school found that more than ninety percent of those questioned view the Shoah as the most important experience of Jewish history. This makes the Shoah more important than the creation of the world, the exodus from Egypt, the delivering of the Torah on Mount Sinai, the ruin of both the Holy Temples, the exile, Messianism, the stunning cultural achievements, the birth of Zionism, the founding of the state, or the Six-Day War. This message comes from teachers to be! Add to them the scores of thousands of students who visit Auschwitz annually. The program is called the *March of the Living,* also called *The March of Remembrance and Hope,* an educational program that brings students from all over the world to Poland, where they explore the remnants of the Holocaust. On Holocaust Memorial Day (*Yom Hashoah*), participants march silently from Auschwitz to Birkenau, the largest concentration camp complex built during World War II. [2] This is the solemn Jewish ritual of death.

I have no doubt that memory is essential to any nation's mental health. The Shoah must therefore have an important place in the nation's memorial mosaic. But the ways things are done today—the absolute monopoly and the dominance of the Shoah on every aspect of our lives—transforms this holy memory into a ridiculous sacrilege and converts piercing pain into hollowness and kitsch. As time passes, the deeper we are stuck in our Auschwitz past, the more difficult it becomes to be free of it. We retreat from independence to the inner depths of exile, its memories, and horrors. Israel today is much less independent than it was at her founding, more Holocaustic than it was three years after the gates of the Nazi death factories opened.

CHAPTER 3

THE SHOAH
EPIDEMIC

WHERE TO BEGIN? HOW DO YOU START CLIMBING A MOUNTAIN so high without supplies, without experience? Those with experience, the survivors, claw their way out of the pits and mass graves, holding on to their memories as if they were ladders, passing their tortured legacies on to the next generation. Sometimes their anguish is silent, sometimes wet with their tears at night. They are ordinary Israelis, Americans, or British by day and Jews at night, forever persecuted. Researchers and historians rely on piles of documents, on archives, testimonies, analyses, and scientific insights. An observer like me, being neither a researcher nor a survivor, who lives life in full and senses the Shoah's unabated energy, must also start somewhere.

I try to begin with the past, returning to the future, and finally circling back to reconstruct the life of my family. I read and try to listen to other people's memories, and yet find myself at square one, at the observer's point of view, that of the curious outsider who looks into the reality of our lives and tries to decipher its code. I try to find the source of our tension and breaking points, the principles of motion that make present-day Israel what it is and the Jewish people what we have become. It becomes evident then that all aspects of our life are consequences of the Shoah of the European Jews.

+‑‑‑‑+

Mandatory for official guests to Israel is the visit to Yad Vashem, our state's most important Shoah museum and memorial. Every nation has a monument commemorating the Unknown Soldier, usually portrayed as an individual. We have a memorial to all the victims, for all of us, and all our visitors must come and mourn with us. It is a ritual of the new Israeli religion. If you are an official guest, you land at Ben-Gurion Airport, stop briefly in your hotel to refresh yourself, then you don a black suit and tie, perhaps a large velvet skullcap like that of a rabbi or a cardinal, and you are whisked to Jerusalem, to Yad Vashem.

A solemn face, a bouquet of flowers in hand, head lowered. Then a cantor chants the awe-filled *God Full of Mercy* prayer for the dead. Three steps backward and everyone gets back in the limos, off to the real business of politics and diplomacy.

From time to time an especially interesting guest appears and his speech draws momentary attention and camera flashes. Such a guest might be a German president or the head of a state that collaborated with the Nazis. Yad Vashem is the storefront and the gateway to the Israeli experience.

The Shoah is woven, to varying degrees, into almost all of Israel's political arguments. Unlike other events of the past, the Shoah does not recede but is coming closer to us all the time. It is a past that is present, maintained, monitored, heard, and represented.

Speaking shortly after the Six-Day War, one of Israel's most remarkable doves, the foreign minister Abba Eban, brilliantly argued that Israel must never return to its prewar borders. He coined a term that is still used today, defining Israel's boundaries, the 1949 Armistice Line, as "Auschwitz borders,"—tight boundaries that compelled Israel to act. In retrospect, he associated the miraculous war of wonders and redemption to the dark period that ended a quarter of a century earlier, contrasting the bright Israeli light with the pitch-black darkness that covered the stateless Jews. Six days of redemption against twelve years of oppression.

Of all people, Eban, the ultimate peace-seeking statesman, rendered legitimacy to the worst argument of the right, as empty rhetoric sometimes carries nations to unwanted destinations. Years later, in the midst of evacuating the Jewish occupiers of Gaza in the 2006 disengagement, this argument came full circle. According to the right, and Eban, if the 1967 boundaries are Auschwitz borders, then we will wear an Orange Star, a version of the infamous yellow star. It made sense emotionally. They were effectively saying: the Six-Day War removed the virtual ghetto fences between Israel and Auschwitz. Now that we are herded back into a ghetto, we will act as if we were in a ghetto, wearing stars and all. Thus a modern political move, the realignment of the occupation to a more logical border, had become another post-Shoah injury.

The list of Shoah manifestations in daily life is long. Listen to every word spoken and you find countless Shoah references. The Shoah pervades the media and the public life, literature, music, art, education. These overt manifestations hide the Shoah's deepest influence. Israel's security policy, the fears and paranoia, feelings of guilt and belonging are products of the Shoah. Jewish-Arab, religious-secular, Sephardi-Ashkenazi relations are also within the realm of the Shoah. Sixty years after his suicide in Berlin, Hitler's hand still touches us.

I do not know of any other country that counts its citizens one by one at every opportunity. A million and a half, two million, four million, five—how many are still missing until we reach the magic number of six million? Every year, Israel naturalizes the Shoah victims who were dead even before we were born, embracing them into the bosom of the third State of Israel. This is the visible part of the Israeli rite of death. Almost every nascent nation sanctifies her fallen.

"In their death they commanded us life," as the Israeli saying goes, expressing the supreme effort to overcome a great collective guilt. Was all this loss justified? Is it right for a nation to sacrifice her sons on the altar of its resurrection? We can argue that these words are directed to mourners, so they do not feel deserted and dejected. You suffer all day, every day, and we are beside you collectively as we swore by the fresh grave of the deceased. Except that in Israel the number of deceased is so great in proportion to the living that it fills this hollow vow with an inescapable obligation. Add the six million on top of it. Then every victim of Israel's wars adds another layer to the highest pile of dead ever known to humanity. Our death counter has been ticking from the destruction of the First Temple through the Massacre of Betar. It doggedly counted the dead from the Roman purges, those burned alive at the stake, the victims of pogroms and of the Inquisition, and then it broke world and history records with the industrial slaughter of six million brothers, sisters, sons, and daughters. The continued bereavement of war in our life reinforces again and again all the deaths, destructions, and atrocities that were forced on us, and which we commemorated. Therefore our dead do not rest in peace. They are busy, present, always a part of our sad lives. Shoah and wars, death and eternity. Although we often win the battles, we carry with us a sense of defeat. A victor should not feel this way.

Because of the Shoah, Israel has become the voice of the dead, speaking in the name of those who are no longer, more than in the name of those who are still alive. As if it were not enough, war has become the rule rather than the exception. Our way of life is combative, against friends and foes alike. One might say that the Israeli only understands force. This arrogant Israeli phrase, "Arabs understand force only," originally alluded to the Arab inability to defeat us on the battlefield, and was used as an excuse for unjustifiable Israeli behavior. They only understand force, we said, patronizingly, as if we were educators. If "he who spares his rod hates his son"[1] then treating the Arabs with force is an effective policy. Every state needs a reasonable force at its disposal. Yet raw force is not enough, and a state also needs the confidence to restrain it. Indeed, we have force, a lot of force, and only force. We have no alternative to force, no special notion or will to hold back our use of force, as in the popular slogan "Let the IDF [Israeli Defence Force] win." In the end, we did what the rest of the world's bullies do: we turned an aberration into a doctrine, and we now understand only the language of force. It is true in relations between spouses and colleagues, and between the state and its citizens, and between politicians. A state that lives by the sword and worships its dead is bound to live in a constant state of emergency, because everyone is a Nazi, everyone is an Arab, everyone hates us, the entire world is against us.

Israeli belligerence and perception of force eventually leads to the question, to whom do the wars belong? This indeed is a major expansion of the Shoah narrative, yet it is essential to understand other aspects of Israeli life. Israeli novelist Eli Amir, with his sensitive, even provocative outlook on social matters, drew me into a new way of thinking. His novel *Yasmin,* a best seller in Israel, describes the impossible and tragic love affair between an Iraqi-born Israeli Jew and a Christian Arab woman shortly after the war of 1967. It sadly, almost mournfully, addresses the opportunities that the "Jews of Arabia" missed, to build a bridge between the New Israel and the old Middle East. There are many reasons these opportunities may have been missed and Amir's tragedy is another legitimate entry in what I call the Israeli "trauma competition."

CHAPTER 4

DEFEATING HITLER

MY NEIGHBOR RAMI'S PARENTS CAME FROM GERMANY. HIS wife Edna's father also came from Germany. Brakha lives two houses down from them and her parents also came from Germany. Her husband Yossi probably has German roots. All of us are sons of *Yekkes,* meaning Israelis of German origin, yet all of us are different. Under the microscope we are a caste society, some of us Brahmins, others untouchables. Rami's father is from a family that claims to have been in Germany for one thousand years. I shiver at his gaze.

Rami's father looks at me as if I were a Gypsy who soiled his well-groomed garden. He does not regard us as real *Yekkes, echte Yekkes,* purebreds. My father is only first-generation German-born. We are *Ostjuden,* Eastern Jews, I admit meekly. We came to Germany from a town in East Galicia that was once part of Austria, then of Poland, then of Ukraine. When I was a child, I was sure that *Ostjude* meant leper, an inferior creature that lived in the sewer. Adults pronounced the word "*Ostjude*" with contempt; it means the person is a cunning, primitive exploiter, an untrustworthy boor.

Years later, as a young officer in the paratroop brigade, I rode to the Sinai peninsula with one of the battalion's drivers. He was a young man from a Moroccan immigrant family. The drive to the Sinai was long, as was often the case during the Israeli empire of the 1970s. We picked up another soldier on the way, and the three of us talked about everything. The rider turned out to be a new immigrant from Georgia. Buskila, the driver, told him: "Since you *Gruzinim* [the new emigrants from Georgia, or *Gruzia*] came to Israel, we Moroccans started to go to [classical] concerts," meaning that the Moroccans had moved up in the pecking order. Later, when I came home for Shabbat, I recounted the incident to my parents. My father demanded an explanation.

"You know, dad," I said. "The *Gruzinim* are...you know."

"No. I don't know."

"Different...distant...Jewish Gypsies..."

I used many laundered words to avoid using the horrible stereotypes that were circulating at the time in Israel at the Shabbat table. Still, my father did not understand. So I told him everything I heard, about the look and the smell attributed to the Georgian Jews as they came off the planes. I told him about their leather jackets and their pendants, their square heads and their gold teeth. My father was astonished. He hadn't heard about these stereotypes. It couldn't be. Not in the state that he helped build. Not in the nation of the Jewish people. Not in the new state of the Jews where the rule should and must be, "Do not do to your friend what you hated being done to you during the Diaspora." It was his country, Yossel Burg's, whose passport had the word *Jude* stamped on it. Joseph Goebbels had compared him to a rat, called him a usurper, a gold dealer, Shylock.

This could not be.

He went to bed upset, mumbling in German, *Das ist unmöglich*, "This is impossible," and I knew he was not sleeping. He was turning over and over in his bed. I knocked on his door and asked if I could talk to him. His eyes were still closed as he responded, as if our conversation had never ceased, even in sleep.

Georgian Jewry is dated back to the First Temple, he proclaimed, from the encyclopedia in his head. They have been in Georgia almost 2,600 years. They are writers and artists, poets and financiers. It is absolutely forbidden to talk about them as you did. They have been in Georgia longer than we have been in Germany, he stated, invoking his ultimate test of Jewish existence. Then he fell asleep, into the *schlafstunde*—the German idiom of afternoon rest—literally the sleeping hour of the Shabbat. I left quietly.

When he woke up, he continued the conversation, determined to teach me.

"You mustn't talk like that about the Georgians."

"Dad, why are you making such a big deal?" I said, sensing that he was annoyed by something that my juvenile ignorance did not allow me to grasp.

"Probably," he sighed, "probably every Jew has his own *Ostjude*."

My father knew what he was talking about. For Rami's father, my dad was the *Ostjude*, a *gruzini*; and for my father, Polish Jews were *Ostjuden*. The Polish Jews had their *Ostjude*. For Buskila, the Georgian hitchhiker was the *Ostjude*.

Many years later I flew to Georgia for the first time, taking off from Moscow. Next to me sat a famous figure of the Russian immigration, an ex-prisoner of Zion, a freedom fighter, human rights activist, and media personality. Somewhere in the sky above the Caucasus, he turned to me in anger.

"Why are you even bringing them?" he asked.

"Who?"

"The *gruzinim*. Why do we need them in Israel?"

"Every Jew must have his own *Ostjude*," I replied indignantly, my father speaking from my throat.

Somehow the German Jews had acquired the arrogant German attitude toward all the Eastern people and had converted it into arrogance toward the Jews of the East. Later, when German arrogance proved fatal to our brethren in Poland and Hungary, it was too late to rectify. They all became *Yekkes*. Hitler melted us into one entity. He did not distinguish between first-generation Jews and tenth-generation Jews. The Israelis were not impressed by pedigrees either. Rami's father and my father were both contemptible for being part of a generation Hitler had turned into soap. Nothing German was wanted. German should not be spoken; Richard Wagner should not be played. Hitler and *Yekkes* were all *putzs*.

+⪼•⪻+

Most Shoah victims were European Jews, Ashkenazi. Israel's War of Independence was also mostly an Ashkenazi war, fought by sons of pioneers who had emigrated from Europe, and concentration-camp survivors who were shipped to battle in the new state joined them. The Six-Day War was different. The 1967 victory should have been a shared victory, a uniting one, belonging to both the veteran Israelis and the newer immigrants. Yet something went wrong. The old-timers and the religious Zionists snatched the victory and claimed it for themselves.

Most of the Jews from Muslim countries arrived here by surprise. It seems to me that the Zionist political and cultural preparation process skipped over most of the Jews who emigrated from Yemen, Morocco, Libya, Algeria, Iran, India, and other countries. While in Europe, especially in the east, national sentiments brewed for decades in newspapers, literature, language conflicts, uniting unions, and congregating conventions, Middle Eastern Jews went on living as usual. Messianic Zionism and political activism had always existed there, but not on the same scale as in Europe. I am not sure that the Jewish public in the Muslim world was as thoroughly politically prepared as the European Ashkenazis. Perhaps this was for the better.

In the three-year window between World War II and the creation of the state of Israel, it became obvious that the world had changed. The Zionist establishment realized that the major human reserves of the state-to-be had perished in the Shoah. The dream of founding the State of Israel with the human, cultural, social, and political forces of the Jews of the Pale of settlement—Poland, Russia, and Ukraine—had gone up in flames.

David Ben-Gurion and his colleagues in the Jewish settlements in Israel, the *Yishuv,* understood that the only replacement for human loss could be found in the Muslim world. The Middle Eastern Jews had become "spare parts"—vital substitutes without whom the Israeli state could not exist. At the same time, the War of Independence underscored the violent nature of Arab-Jewish relations. Although the alienation of Jews in the Muslim countries was already widespread—roused locally with European help—the war of 1948 established new rules. Many years of living peacefully alongside the Arabs ended. It became unbearable for Jews to live with the brethren of the enemy of his Jewish brethren. The Arabs expelled their Jews; the Ashkenazi Israeli community absorbed them willingly. Mass immigration took place.

As Middle Eastern Jews were reluctantly adjusting to the new reality, tremors shook the old Zionist leadership in the new state. The liquidation of Eastern European Jewry also liquidated the cultural and human foundation from which they drew their power. The local leadership of Ben Gurion and his colleagues in the Labor Movement suddenly became the leadership of a flock that did not resemble its leaders, like an island with no sea surrounding it. The implosion of the state's historic leadership was inevitable. A new leadership, with roots in agony and tragedy, would rise in its stead. It was this leadership that formed the coalition of victims that rules Israel to this day.

Someone in Jerusalem decided on the mass immigration of "our Sephardic brethren" and created ever-widening ripples of new immigrants. Unlike noted Sephardim of old, Yehuda Halevi, Haramban, and Maimonides, who emigrated or traveled privately, following their religious and spiritual yearning, this time there was a mass uprooting and transplanting. Every new immigrant paid a high price physically, financially, and socially. Jobs were lost forever, as was social status. Community structures formed over hundreds of years disappeared abruptly. It was like an amputation without anesthetic. Centuries of histories were wiped out. The new immigrants left behind their ways of life, cuisine, music, languages and dialects, fashions, and landscapes. The combination of hostility in their home countries, plus an inviting Zionism in Israel, sparked waves of immigrants. They came on rickety boats and "on eagle's wings," doubling and tripling Israel's population and staying power. The new state gained resilience as the newcomers ensured its future. But few at the time noticed the toll. In every other human setting, in a more repaired society, more attention would have been paid to the harsh manner with which this absorption took place and its psychological and sociological effects. Not in Israel, however. Apart from being young and patronizing at the outset, it was a secretive society that kept mum on matters of personal injury. Israel was developing muscles, not soul.

Nevertheless a silent dialogue must have taken place among all carriers of trauma. Nothing was said explicitly and no formal policy was written, but when unspoken traumas were compared, the Ashkenazi overpowered the Sephardic. "Is this real trauma? Ours is much more traumatic," Shoah survivors must have felt. Then, as today, nobody argues about the Shoah, since nothing compares to it. The obsession with the Shoah shoved aside any discussion on other Israeli suffering. The price paid by the Jews of Asia and Africa was never officially acknowledged, perhaps it was even denied. There was ambivalence, as on the one hand, it was said that the newcomers were religious, fulfilling their Judaism through Zionism. On the other hand, it was argued, the Ashkenazis did them a favor by rescuing them from the ghettos of Morocco and Yemen. Thus thousands of years of Sephardic history were deleted, erasing with them the social and cultural affinities to the neighboring Arabs and Muslims.

The old, proven familiar structure was destroyed and replaced by an empty "Israeliness" that was weak on spirituality. Therefore the literature of Middle Eastern Jewish immigrants should be read with attention. A bitter cry emerges from the pages: we suffer, we grieve, we beg for recognition for the price that we paid in our conversion from Middle Eastern Jews to Western Israelis. That recognition was never given.

Also lacking was the recognition that the end of Middle Eastern Jewry may be no less, and sometimes even more, meaningful to Israel than that of the European Jewry. Middle Eastern Jewry could have provided a reliable human bridge between Israel and its neighbors. The Shoah, winner of the trauma competition, cast a long shadow that hid Israel's internal distortions. It also influenced life in the most intimate ways, as in the case of Mr. D.

Mr. D. is an outstandingly successful businessman, a native of Israel in his early fifties. Some time ago we tried to set up a meeting but it was cancelled again and again. He told me that he had to go on a business trip to Poland and I expected the meeting to take place a few weeks later. But a few days later, his secretary called and said that he was available.

We met that same day, and I asked him what happened in Poland that cut his visit short.

"I couldn't bear it any more," he replied. "Everything came back to me. I landed in Warsaw and it was cold and snowy. The same day we traveled into the Polish hinterland to check on a few opportunities that I was being offered. The snowy plains blinded me. It was cold to the bone and all we saw were birch forests and shrubbery. We spent the night there and then continued on a night train. The train traveled for many hours. The wheels and the cars shook and the ticket conductor was aggressive. Then a sudden ticket control. I just couldn't bear it anymore. Polish trains are too much for me. Everything came back to me. The following day, I hopped on a plane and came back."

I called him in the evening at home. "Tell me," I asked, "where are your parents from?"

"From Iraq," he answered.

How could it be that everything "came back" to him, I wondered, if he or his parents had never been there? Did Hitler win over him, too? This to me was another case that showed that Middle Eastern Jews were embracing Israel's survivor narrative. The Shoah made us all one and the same.

The United States of America has always been a practical alternative to the Zionist idea—to assemble all the Jews under one national roof, independent and autonomous, thus removing once and for all the "Jewish problem" from the Old World's agenda. Solving the Jewish problem was not meant to be just for the sake of the Jews, but for the benefit of whole world. The Zionists wanted to transplant the hated, persecuted Jews into their historic homeland in the Middle East and thus rid Europe of them. A few thousand dreamers and pioneers came to Zion but a hundred-fold more left czarist Russia for the *Goldene Medina*, the golden state of America, as it was called by the Jewish emigrants of North America. The idealist few came to the Land of Israel, but the traditional wandering Jew, always optimistic, went to America. The Jew was reborn in Zion, but in America, against all expectations, the New Jewry was born. Israeli ideology was tough and head-on—"You can not conquer the mountain until you dig a grave on the slope," says the tombstone of Shlomo Ben Yosef, an Israeli terrorist from the 1930s. "It is good to die for our country" is inscribed on the roaring lion's monument to another Zionist hero, Yosef Trumpledor. The American Jewish spirit was less dramatic: Assimilate. Be American. Integrate into the spiritual and material life that America had to offer. As Israelis were developing collective separatism, American Jews wove themselves into the fabric of the general public. Being Jewish could be achieved in two different ways: isolation or integration; a ghetto of belligerent colonialism or Jewish universalism.

The difference between the integrative American Jewish approach and the re-creation of Jewish ghettos and *shtetls* in Israel is plain. Listen carefully to the Jewish voices of renewal; the seeds may have been planted in the Germany of Moses Mendelssohn, Heinrich Heine, and Abraham Geiger, but the fruits belong to American Jewry. The Jewish "churches"—Orthodox, Conservative, Reform, Reconstructionist and Secular—were made possible by America's religious freedom. The American Jewish Torah is a valid alternative to the Zionist national Torah and to Israel's fossilized religious Orthodoxy, the self-appointed "authentic Judaism." Unlike the wrathful prophecies of both the Orthodox, ultra-Orthodox, and Zionist preachers, there are and there will be alternatives.

One of American Jewry's most enlightened speakers was Rabbi Julian Morgenstern, who presided over the Hebrew Union College of New York from 1922 to 1947. He was born in St. Francisville, Illinois, in 1881, the year of the worst pogroms in Russia and Ukraine, called "Storms of the Negev." Those massacres unleashed the enormous waves of immigrants from the Pale to the shores of America, as well as the first emigrations to Israel.

Not coincidentally, Morgenstern was the son of Jewish immigrants from Germany. One must ask, how did German Jews lay the foundations of American Jewish autonomy when so many of them, my father included, emigrated to the Land of Israel? Similarly, how did the Jews of the Pale lay the foundations of the Jewish state when their majority emigrated to North America? Since then the small divide between the two Jewries—Israeli and American, Eastern and Western European—has deepened.

Morgenstern was a biblical scholar of the Reform persuasion and his research is a modern critical study. In 1915 he published his controversial thesis, *The Foundations of Israel's History.* He believed that the Reform movement's foremost duty is to reinterpret and rewrite the early history of the people of Israel. In his view, ancient Israel was one nation among other nations and civilizations of the ancient world, not a separatist, isolationist nation, as it is today. Even in the face of fierce resistance from his colleagues in the Reform leadership, his view prevailed and became central to the movement. Morgenstern was both a Jew and an American; a faithful Jew who did not make opportunistic compromises to smooth his way into the bosom of the non-Jewish world, yet he defined himself as an American for all matters. He was unwilling to isolate himself inside the Jewish ghetto of the mind. In his early work, Morgenstern viewed Zionism as an ideology of identity by negation. The Zionist reaction to assimilation, including the retreat to the Middle East, seemed to him an admission of defeat and acceptance of anti-Semitic values. Zionism was escaping Judeophobia instead of repairing Judeophobic societies and the world, so as to prevent future anti-Semitism. It was treason and dereliction of duty, in violation of the universal tenets of Jewish values of identity and inclusion.

+≻═•═≺+

As the Zionist movement aspired to create a new structure that would enable the Jewish people as a collective to join the family of nations, the Reform movement took it upon itself to create a standard for Jewish individuals to integrate as equals in non-Jewish societies. The revival of nineteenth-century scholarly Judaism—resembling the most important Diaspora, the Babylon Revival centuries earlier—started in Germany and the Austro-Hungarian Empire and continued unabated in the United States. For many years it opposed Zionism and the idea of a Jewish state. Few remember that the majority of the Jewish people opposed the creation of a Jewish state well into World War II. This opposition came from all sorts of Jews, Reform, ultra-Orthodox, communists, Bundists (members of the Jewish Labor Union, the Bund) and plain ordinary Jews. They opposed the Zionist minority and feared the consequences of a national and political revival. Each group had its own ethical and spiritual reasons, but all were united by the fear—which eventually materialized—that a Jewish political entity would create intolerant nationalistic sentiments that would drastically alter the historical character of the Jewish people.

All this was to change in a few years. American Jewry adopted the overt and covert messages of the Zionist movement and sought models for synthesis of national separatism and integration into the all-American society. In those days, the newly born socialist-secular political movement *Yishuv* renewed and reinvented the minor holiday of Hanukkah, turning it into a celebration of heroism and triumph. We all sang loudly, "Hear o, in those days in this time, Maccabee is the savior and redeemer...In every generation he will rise, the hero rescuer of the people..."

God was no longer the hero of the holiday; rather it was the Maccabee, the war hero. The Israeli myth designers freighted the nearly forgotten holiday with new symbols galore. A sacred date and a religious holiday commemorating the rededication of the Temple and its salvation from the Hellenists became a national holiday.

Hanukkah was altered unrecognizably and loaded with excess baggage. An emphasis was put on the military victory by the few, weak, and under-equipped over the many, well armed, and experienced. We were told of the Hasmonean state's status and acumen in the ancient world, about the reclaiming of land, expanding of boundaries, the expelling of foreign invaders. Hanukkah, in short, had become the symbol of Zionist revival. During World War II, Hanukkah also became the holiday of American Jewry.

It was not surprising, then, that even an important thinker like Morgenstern changed his views drastically. From viewing Zionism, as well as German nationalism, as expressions of dangerous ethnic selfishness and as antithetical to Judaism, he was compelled to unconditionally accept the new Israeli-Zionist reality. On the eve of the United States entering the war in 1941, he expressed, for the last time, the notion of an alternative:

> A twentieth-century Jewish state...will be no more than a passing nationalistic episode, a temporary retreat into Jewish history. Despite the pretentious Zionist claim of the benefit of rebuilding a Jewish national home...The undeniable lesson of Jewish history...teaches that Israel's ability and destination are expressed only by religion and only by Israel's role as the carrier of the religious spiritual legacy.[1]

Morgenstern never renounced his dream of reviving the Jewish spirit in the United States. Nevertheless, as a religious and community leader and scholar of Jewish history, he sensed that the Shoah was an event too great to ignore. His view of an independent Jewish state changed. It could be because he was convinced in his heart that this was the right idea, or he may have succumbed to the wishes of ordinary Jews and the Zionist ideas that enraptured the American Jewish population. From then on, he would look toward "that yearned-for day, the founding day of the Jewish state."

⊢⟩⟨⊣

The United Nations' 1975 resolution that "Zionism is a form of racism and racial discrimination" marked the beginning of the attempt to build a New Babel. Soon after the resolution was voted, the Reform movement decided to join the Zionist movement. Just as Zionism was losing its meaning in Israel, it became a defining element of Jewish American politics, especially in the Reform community. For me it is very clear: the American Jewry in the early days of the nineteenth and early twentieth centuries was supposed to be something else—the universalistic pole of the Jewish existence. Exactly like Morgenstern's early thoughts and writing. With the Holocaust, everything changed dramatically and even the reform movement joined the Zionist ideology and contributed to part of the national shell rather than the desired openness.

Thus the Shoah changed the course for American Jews. From a path of enormous potential toward becoming the rightful heirs of pre-war European, especially German, Jewish creativity, the Shoah narrowed the field of vision of American Jews. Anyone who follows the statements and actions of American Jewish leaders and organizations today would be unable to find anything that resembles Morgenstern's great spirit of universalism.

When the Jewish lobby in Washington, the Conference of Presidents of Jewish Organizations, and the other Jewish congresses and committees gather, only one issue is discussed: Israel. In the eyes of many Jews and non-Jews alike, the Jewish American community is a one-issue community. I regret this dangerous erosion of purpose very much. I fear a world in which the only Jewish voice speaks only of nationhood and nationalism. Such a world is bereft of the wisdom our father Jacob had when he prepared himself for the decisive encounter with his brother Esau.

Jacob was very much afraid, and justly so, of his redheaded brother who was a master hunter. Jacob had stolen Esau's birthright and robbed him of his father's blessing. Esau vowed that after their father Isaac died, he would "take care" of his devious brother. Jacob, distressed, "divided the people with him…into two camps. He said, if Esau comes to one camp and strikes it, the other camp will survive." This ancient story became the cornerstone of thinking for many generations.

This vision of "risk distribution" enabled the Jewish body to recuperate from blows while allowing the Jewish spirit to expand around the globe and to enrich it. It made Jewish contribution to the world possible, enabled adaptive thinking, and renewed Jewish civilization, which has a permanent backup system: if destruction happens to one Jewish organ—community—the other will survive.

For many years, three pillars supported the Jewish American structure from the outside: the memory of the Shoah, the founding of the State of Israel, and the struggle of the "Silent Jewry," the Soviet Jews who were imprisoned behind the iron curtain. As the years passed, two of these elements had weakened, but the Shoah element remained intact. The third is gone now: Jews from the former Soviet Union are completely free—thanks to American Jewry rather than to Israeli governments. Despite the artificial claims of fundraising campaigns, most of the Jewish people no longer need salvation. We have actually never been in better condition. As for the second element, Israel's centrality is eroded due to the constant embarrassments that it produces, which lowered its status in the eyes of many. Bitter identity struggles in the 1970s and 1980s, centered around the "Who is a Jew?" controversy, and the lasting attempts of the Orthodox and ultra-Orthodox to narrowly define a "Jew," did not bring hearts closer. The rise of the ultra-Orthodox to political power in Israel and the virtual ban on non-Orthodox streams of Judaism is how an unappreciative Israel reciprocated the warm embrace of American Jews.

In Israel and in America, the guilt complex over the Shoah created a national obsession of exaggerated securitism, the longing for power that often morphs into primitive belligerence. In America, the collective feeling of guilt that more could have been done if the U.S. government was prodded to act sooner is ever present. I do not know the details of the Jewish American experience, but I know the leadership pretty well. The Jewish masses are diverse and have a much more sophisticated agenda than presented and expressed by their leadership. The destruction of the Shoah seems to have been burned into the leaders' minds. One result is that Jewish American leaders tend to justify their government's wars and support the most right-wing foreign policies, especially vis-à-vis Israel and the Middle East. They are against everybody, including Germany, Russia, and the Arab countries. Furthermore, the official, organized Jewish voice is a power to reckon with in every election campaign. It is very difficult to be elected to high office in America against the wishes of the Jewish lobby. Financial and organizational resources, public support, legitimacy—and not least, the damage the Jewish lobby can cause to unwanted candidates—turn Jewish involvement in American politics into a factor with strategic international consequences.

Jewish influence sometimes causes American political candidates to sound like Shoah victims. "Never again" speeches, Auschwitz themes, and black skullcaps during memorial ceremonies, complete with *God Full of Mercy* prayers, are frequent. The inevitable outcome of this attitude is a feeling of power, and the further erosion of the Jewish idea of revival that was the basis for the American Jewish autonomy. American Jews, like Israelis, are stuck in Auschwitz, raising the Shoah banner high to the sky and exploiting it politically.

It seems natural then that the third supporting pillar, the Shoah and the vow "Masada will not fall again" becomes the central element of American Jewish identity. Masada was the site where allegedly Jewish warriors chose to commit suicide with their families rather than surrender to superior Roman forces. In one of my early trips in the United States I saw a poster in the offices of AIPAC, the America Israel Political Affairs Committee, that read: "Masada—A Living Memory." Is collective suicide the contemporary motto of American Jews?

Leon Uris's 1958 novel *Exodus* expanded the Shoah effect to justify the Israeli struggle one decade after the state had been established. It was a shallow, stereotypical story of a ramshackle refugee ship that was turned back at Haifa by the British authorities. The story is an important part of Zionist mythology. During the 1950s, the World Jewish Congress (WJC), whose power derives from the American Jewish community, led the charge to reestablish ties among Israel, the Jews, and the "other Germany." That is a classical Israeli expression meaning the non-Nazi, postwar Germany. The WJC navigated the intractable negotiations for the reparations, compensation, personal pensions, and the restitution of Jewish property that had been stolen in the Shoah. During the 1980s, the WJC targeted Kurt Waldheim, a former Austrian Nazi officer who had become Secretary-General of the United Nations. Waldheim was forced to resign, and the WJC thereby justified its existence. During the 1990s, then WJC director Dr. Israel Singer, with his president Edgar Bronfman and I, initiated and led the struggle against Swiss banks for the restitution of dormant deposits belonging to Jews who had perished in the Shoah. The campaign succeeded beyond expectations and the organization again justified its existence and gained strength.

In the 1990s Steven Spielberg, who directed the film *Schindler's List,* donated the film's profits toward the building of a world archive that would document all the survivors, wherever they are, for the memory of future generations. Thus he became an essential facilitator in the process, enabling several more years of recording live testimonies from firsthand witnesses, testimonies that would otherwise be lost forever. The Shoah is still the major forming experience of Jewish public life everywhere in the world.

It seems that more than six decades after his death, Hitler retains his influence over American Jews. Vulnerability can be felt in the most impressive community the Jews have ever built, a Jewry more glorious than those of Babel and Spain, even more so than German Jewry that existed between the time of Mendelssohn and of the Shoah. The potential is there for Jews to change the world for the better, if they only free themselves from the Nazi shackles.

Courageous Israel is a mini-America in the "Wild East." It faithfully represents the American spirit in a region that is very much in need of salvation. In Israel you find frontiers and pioneers with vision just like the early American West. Israel plays the cowboy, and the Jews of America provide the strategic support that compels every U.S. administration to support Israel. In turn, Israel supports the administration that is supported by the Jewish organizations that support Israel that supports them. What is wrong with mutual back-scratching?

There is a major weakness in this triangle of strategic alliance. Jewish voters traditionally cast their votes to the Democratic Party; Jewish Republicans are relatively few in number. Even in the heyday of Jewish support of Republican presidents—Ronald Reagan and George W. Bush—not more than one-third of Jews voted Republican. The American Jewish voter is apparently more concerned with domestic issues than with what the Jewish wheeler-dealers claim is good for Israel, namely a Republican president.

"Good for Israel" means different things to the Jewish masses and to their leaders. It seems that instinctively, millions of Jews understand that a White House that is good for Israel should not necessarily do everything that Israel requests, but rather do what Israel needs. Furthermore, an ordinary Jew, though he is affected by his family's memories and suffering for their traumas, wants his children to grow in a healthy society. He would rather integrate into a multicultural society and look forward to the future than linger, holding on to the past. He would want to preserve solidarity with the government, reducing its involvement to a minimum.

American Jews seek solutions both as members of the Jewish faith and as partners in the building of the American nation. The one-issue strategy does not address these goals as it deals with Israel and nothing else. Yet every time a strategic reevaluation concerning Israel is called for, the silencing voices are heard: Shoah, pogroms, self-hating Jews. Again anti-Semitism, swastikas, and Hitler decide the debate on Jewish identity and an opportunity for dialogue dies before it even begins.

So, three traumatized communities constitute the majority of the Jewish people today: American Jews, Ashkenazi Israelis, and Middle Eastern Israelis. The three communities are still Shoah-shocked, and they do not seek to mitigate the Shoah's burdensome weight. I still do not know what the role of the former Soviet Jewry will be in all this. It is too early to know whether they will fully assimilate into general society or create a niche for themselves. Until then, I compare the education and rise of Israel with the education of children, my own.

After the teenage rebellion comes reconciliation, acceptance, and even a partial adoption of the parents' ways of life; in the middle of our lives we find ourselves much more similar to our parents than we could ever have predicted. So it is with Zionism, the young rebellious daughter that declared itself independent from Mother Judaism. Authors, intellectuals, pioneers, and builders rebelled against the rabbis, their benefactors, and those they perceived to be part of Jewish religious degeneration. If the course of events had continued undisturbed, familial reconciliation would have come and Judaism and Zionism would have synthesized. Except that the Shoah happened in the fifth decade of Zionism, destroying history. Its shadow refuses to depart. The Shoah destroyed the Eastern European Jews, became the main argument for the Jewish state, accelerated its founding, and now it nourishes Israel's existence. The establishment of the third Jewish commonwealth indirectly encouraged Sephardic Jews to leave their centuries-old communities and come to Zion. On top of these obstacles, the Shoah prevents Israel from naturally reaching maturity, postponing the reconciliation of Judaism and Zionism. The overt result is that Israel and the Jewish people remain fully connected to the sick, malignant parts of the European experience. We are reliving with morbid intensity the most horrible twelve years of our history at the expense of Europe's Jewish millennia, the stunning ten centuries of mutual influences that changed their lives and ours. Instead, we sanctify our security doctrine, often expressed vengefully and belligerently. We have embarrassing politics that lack vision and resemble small-town wheeling and dealing instead of national leadership that grasps the burden of responsibility. We need to repair all this and more if we want a healthy, normal, and rational state. It is time for a sobering dialogue on the essence of this state and its ailments. How can it be cured?

Each year, two weeks after Sukkot, when we read the part of the Torah that tells the story of Noah's ark, I think of destruction. I try to imagine what Noah felt during the long days floating above the world that he had known and that had been annihilated. Did he ask himself who of his friends was still alive and who had already died? Did he feel sorrow? Did he miss them? What did he say to his dear ones? We will never know, for the Bible made Noah a silent hero. Unlike Adam, Eve, Cain, the Fathers, their wives, and their servants, Noah utters not one word on the topic of ethics. Even Balaam's donkey speaks, and stuttering Moses speaks volumes. Noah remains silent, drinks wine to escape the sorrow, and finds just a few words to curse his sons for seeing his private parts and maybe even for castrating him. It seems that destruction paralyzes and silences. The Hebrew words for blood and for silence, *dam* and *dmama,* have the same sound. The lesson is that the more blood is shed, the fewer words are spoken, until the ultimate silence. This is why we observe a minute of silence in memorial ceremonies.

What Noah saw upon disembarking from the ark was complete ruin; corpses, empty communities, and carcasses everywhere. All those who left the ark of Europe since 1945—my daughter's teacher insists "We all are Shoah survivors"—saw before them the ruin of the Jewish continent. All were affected, and worse, consumed by the Shoah's aftermath.

Hitler is no more. But we still suffer his evil legacy, and refuse to be comforted. It was easy for Hitler to take our lives away from us, and it is difficult for us to get Hitler out of our lives.

CHAPTER 5

REMEMBERING THE WEIMAR REPUBLIC

WHAT COLOR WAS THE HOLOCAUST? PROBABLY WHITE. The Angel of Death had white wings and a white cape. My grandmother sewed her own shroud in the Teresienstadt camp and it was white. The shroud looked like the white cloaks that my father and his friends would wear on Yom Kippur for the service at our *Yekke* synagogue in Jerusalem. Dr. Yosef Mengele wore a white coat in his "clinic." The Aryans were the white master race. Half the stripes on the camp prisoner's uniforms were white. The snow on the tracks from Auschwitz to Birkenau was exceptionally white and exceptionally frozen. My father never had a tan. The Shoah may have been all white. If not, at least the Shoah blindness was white, like in José Saramago's book.

Everybody thinks that blindness is black. "The patient sees black," the ophthalmologist in Saramago's book *Blindness*, notes. If the sighted see colors and hues, the blind should see the opposite, no color whatsoever and black is an absolute non-color. White, on the other hand, is all colors. The Shoah had all the human colors, from the worst of evil to the noblest of good. Shoah blindness, like the color white, is also all-encompassing. It is present in our lives everywhere, even when we do not see it and do not feel it.

My father was also struck with Shoah blindness. He knew the colorful components of the world in general and of the post-Shoah Jewish world in particular, but he did not see well. He was a fantastic observer, but the big picture was even more tremendous than his vision. A thick wall separated him from the real meaning of Israel that he had built and maintained. I almost never heard his positions on Israel from him directly. He did speak out on current affairs, endlessly—in his party's newspaper *Hatzofe,* from the Yiddish radio pulpit, or in the small Italian synagogue that we attended on Shabbat—but we almost never discussed existential matters. I had to search elsewhere for his positions. I had to go back to other places and other times, dig in the ashes, and dust my own memory in order to find my father of old, to connect with him and to bring his thinking to today.

He dismissed with a forgiving smile the messianic fanatics of Gush Emunim, the hardcore settler movement, who were growing like wild grass within his own party. He withheld his criticism. He knew that they were ruining his dream, but he did not confront them, as if waiting for the nuisance to go away by itself. What he did not realize was that they were here to stay and he was to go away. They lived in the political present, and he was stuck with the historical clock. His timepiece stood still when Hitler jammed its mechanism, but their clock changed Israeli history in an irreversible way. Perhaps he liked their values and only disagreed with their actions. It may have been one thing or its opposite; one could never know because for him everything was Talmudic and there was always more than meets the eye. At the same time, everything was German with him, meaning that everything was planned ahead of time. Did he see and keep quiet, or did he simply not see? I do not know.

My father was part of Israel's leadership and yet did not express his opinions, but my mother did, casually, as an aside. We stood on our porch, under the gaze of Jesus' mother from the Terra Santa monastery across the street. Down the street buses smoked and ambulances wailed. It was 1982, the first war in Lebanon. My dad was minister of the interior, a member of Prime Minister Menahem Begin's cabinet. I was an activist with the war protest movement. My father contained the conflict, absorbing it and not revealing his true feelings—an emotional feat, considering that he seemed to side with me and my friends. It was not just because his value system was mauled by his party colleagues, but because of his Talmudic approach, according to which a Jewish text must contain disagreement. You do not expel the challenger from the school; you contain him and his views. In the Talmudic tradition it is called "heavenly disagreement." Because today's minority view may be tomorrow's majority view.

My mother had a harder time, since she lived by the Book of Ruth, according to which a good neighborhood is an essential part of life. The question, "What would the neighbors say?" played an important role in her life.

We stood on the porch and had our respectful argument. I was furious with the government to which my father belonged, and she was trapped between the two of us, wanting yet unable to defend us both. "What do you need this 'Peace Now' for?" she asked gently of the peace movement I supported. Funny indeed, for a woman who had sacrificed everything in the name of the public life of the man she loved since youth, to ask me why I had chosen a public life. I almost said something harsh expressing my anger at my father, who was in a position he did not wish to be in. It was a warmongering cabinet, headed by Begin, a Jew with an exilic mentality and a childish prime minister.

"Mom," I said, "I would happily give up my struggle, but I want to pass on to my children a better country than the one you're passing on to me." My mother replied without hesitation, "This country is not the country that we built. We founded a different country in 1948, but I don't know where it's disappeared."

Our struggle for peace took place in the worldly Jerusalem. My parents built and lived in the heavenly Jerusalem. They did not want to come down to reality to see our suffering. I am convinced that they never spoke about this conversation, but through their tacit communication she knew his message. A great disappointment separated them from the reality in

Israel; they were almost dumbfounded. They saw a different reality, and they could not see ours because of Shoah blindness.

My partner Yael and I have been together since age fourteen. She is short and I am tall. She has abundant hair and I am balding. She stands upright like a dancer and I am a bit bent, in a Jewish way. She is olive-skinned and dark eyed and I am pale and blue-eyed. She is a native of France and very French and I am an Israeli with the brash roughness typical of Israelis. In short, we do not look alike.

But we are alike in many unapparent ways. Couples become similar. Friends and even rivals become similar over time, in their manners, speech, and body language. This is the result of years of mutual concessions and compromise. As people become similar, so do nations. Sometimes it is only the sound of their language, but often it is also in their inner worlds: values, narratives, heritage, and political actions. The traveler can see the similarities between France and the French part of Belgium. Switzerland has much more in common with its neighbors Austria and Germany than the spoken German dialects. They share fashion, customs, and humor, when it exists.

What does Israel resemble? In many ways Israel resembles no other country. In other ways, Israel is frighteningly similar to the countries we never wanted to resemble. In order to describe Israel, we will have to look at some of its prominent characteristics. No other country shares Israel's absolute freedom of speech. Great Britain decreed total blackout and media censorship during its foolish war with Argentina in the Falkland Islands in 1982. George W. Bush's United States will not show the caskets from the wars in Iraq and Afghanistan in the media. Israel, on the other hand, sets no limits on speech and expression. In Israel one can say everything about everything. People can call for the assassination of their prime minister and almost nothing will be done against them. Walls are covered with racist graffiti calling for "Death to the Arabs" and saying "No Arabs, no terror," and the police and other authorities do not even bother to erase the shameful slurs. In the ultra-Orthodox neighborhoods of Jerusalem, one can see more swastikas than on all the desecrated Jewish graves in the world. Freedom of expression in Israel crossed the line a long time ago and has led to a form of verbal anarchy that is very close to active violence. Our whole country is held hostage by a bunch of settlers who threaten civil war, call on soldiers to refuse orders, undermine the state's authority, and deny its right to carry out the majority's will—all this in the name of freedom of expression and affiliation.

So, with such a divided psyche, Israeli society is split to its core. What keeps this country together are the wars. Often we say that we are lucky to have the Arab as an enemy, otherwise we would have devoured one another a long time ago. Often we say that if our enemies were smart, they would lay down their arms, turn their swords into ploughshares and wait patiently for us to do the work for them. We may speak out against war, but in reality we are still over-armed and thus coalesce naturally with the surrounding enmity. In the high-school yeshiva I attended, I had an extraordinary Hebrew teacher. In the twelfth grade, he disappeared twice for a few days. The first time, he was arrested for the attempted arson of a Mount of Olives church; the second time, he chased someone—a non-Jew, naturally—with an ax in the Old City. He was detained on suspicion of membership in all kinds of extreme right-wing organizations. At that time these organizations were small and considered fringe groups. Since then they have grown, in the best tradition of right-wing ideologies.

As a schoolboy, I liked my teacher very much. I did not know his ideology well and did not understand it completely. I argued with him, trying to hone my values on his whetstone. The confrontation with him benefited me and I absorbed some of the most humanistic Jewish axioms that I treasure to this day. At the time I did not know how dangerous he was; just that he was a strong opponent, a unique, wise, and outstanding man in an otherwise rather mundane school. I remember his smile when he dictated the essay title for our final exam: "In Wars and Trials a People is Made." "This one is especially for you," he whispered to me.

As the years passed, he and his friends increased in numbers. The fringes became the center while on the left, we decreased in numbers and became marginal. Their insane narrative threatened to tear Israel apart. Concepts like expulsion, death, starvation, and persecution have become part of the political dialogue and not even the cabinet is exempt. Their voices are heard loud and clear, often from the Knesset podium, on Gaza, Judea, Samaria, and South Lebanon. The same spirit, the same words and the same logic: Jews and Israelis have become thugs. The rhetoric had its impact on policy. In the summer 2006 war in Lebanon, we crossed a line we had not crossed before when we bombed the enemy's capital city, violating Lebanon's symbol of sovereignty and national pride, not allowing room for reconciliation the day after. We did not do this to any capital city in 1967, or during the Yom Kippur War. In the first war in Lebanon, we stopped short of invading Beirut. Now we have removed all restraints.

It was a government in which both the prime minister and the defense minister were civilians, with no military careers behind them, that bombed parts of southern Beirut to dust, citing Dresden and Kosovo as precedents. Israeli arrogance in the sky above Beirut is the voice of the people at their worst. The guns blasted so loudly that we became used to it and we could no longer differentiate sounds. This noise is the result of the moral distortion in a victims' state, the country that permits itself to sacrifice the other. Victimhood sets you free. I have to confess, especially having rejected the position of victimhood, that my greatest surprise in writing this book was discovering that the political, social, and national structures that most resemble Israel's are those of Germany's Second Reich before the period of anarchy that facilitated the rise of National Socialism. I must emphasize, though: *before,* not *during.*

This is both embarrassing and frightening.

Otto Eduard Bismarck was the founding father of the second German empire, known also as the Second Reich. Early in the 1870s Bismarck fulfilled a two-decade-long dream. In a few months he crushed the French army of Napoleon III and founded the Second Empire in Versailles, France, of all places. With this act, he elevated Germany to the level of the other European powers. Most Germans, among them Jews, regarded the unification of the German lands as an act of historical, if not messianic, redemption. Friedrich Nietzsche, the doubting philosopher, was not amused. He tried to shake them, stating "such a magnificent military victory may cause much greater destruction and annihilation than was defeated in battle, especially if it is interpreted by the Germans as proof of their human and cultural superiority over the defeated French."[1]

The few who shared his views understood that German national revival at gunpoint was a poor substitute for true national revival, such as was needed to repair a decadent regime and society. Leopold Sonnemann, the Jewish publisher of the *Frankfurter Zeitung,* predicted that the new German unification "will come at the expense of freedom." He and others correctly saw that the new union was based on the strength of the German army. They understood that the new situation created tension between a military state and a civilian state. In such a situation, the military state would sanctify flawed values, such as nationalism, belligerence, and the idolization of a national security doctrine, above all others. Militarists know no other way of functioning but to manipulate people's prejudices against those perceived "others" through social and political toughness

When my initial courtship of Yael came to an end, I decided to invite her to my family's home. I needed to prepare my parents for this historic meeting. I told them that I had a new girlfriend.

My mother smiled, and my father seemed puzzled.

"So?" he said.

"She will come here tomorrow for the first time. Don't mess it up," I begged.

I knew my father's endless curiosity for other people's backgrounds, and occupations. At the time I did not understand why he stored so much information about the Jews he met, never to be forgotten. I was afraid that my young friend would be afraid of him and run away from me forever.

"Don't worry," my mother said, trying to ease my anxiety.

"Tell me, who is she?" my father asked.

I told them she was French, and that she had emigrated from France not long ago...

"Nu, nu," my father concluded, and returned to his business.

Yael came over the following day, nervous about meeting my parents for the first time, not to mention meeting a minister, a Jewish minister, for the first time in her life. As I feared, my father broke his promise and launched into his usual interrogation: "Who are you?" "Who are your parents?" "Where are you from?" Only the notorious KGB interrogation lamp was missing in that small room that seemed to grow smaller with every passing moment.

She finally confessed meekly, "I am from Strasbourg." That was the beginning of a great friendship between my father and Yael. "Why did you say she's French?" he snapped at me, "She's one of our own; she's from Alsace. Bismarck gave us back Alsace-Lorraine in the 1870s. Strasbourg is ours!"

So spoke the former German Jew, with a sudden burst of national pride. For a moment he relived his German identity, forgetting that it no longer existed.

Bismarck's victory and the repatriation of the Alsace-Lorraine province generated rhetoric and acts in Germany that may sound familiar to Israelis. Although the land had belonged briefly to Germany a few hundred years earlier, at the end of the nineteenth century most Alsatians were French. In a parliamentary debate in Berlin, Sonnemann said, "You will never be able to force them to be German." The patriotic press retorted by writing that the re-education of the Alsatians "would commence with the help of a whip. These alienated children should feel our fist. Love will follow the taming." The rhetoric of "the Arabs only understand force" was being composed. So it was then, and later, and so it is with us.

Service in the Israeli military is key to dignified life as a civilian, or so it was for many years. Despite the recent erosion of their status, the Israeli Defense Forces are still the foundation and launching pad of the Israeli civilian, and his service is part of his identity. Israeli Air Force pilots are still considered among the best in the world. Some intelligence and information technology units are the launching pads for those hoping to be part of the high-tech industry. Military service opens doors. Former senior officers are installed in key positions of the civilian administration and city government, and more than one-fourth of Knesset members of the Labor Party are former generals or colonels. I often hear teenagers deliberating where it would be best for them to serve, with a view to post-army life. Any debate on conscientious objection includes the sentence, "If you don't serve, it will hurt your career later on." Some elite units produce future army chiefs of staff, who then enter politics and sometimes end up in the prime minister's office. Moshe Dayan, Yitzhak Rabin, Ehud Barak, and Shaul Mofaz moved directly from the top army post to the ministries of defense or the interior or to prime minister as if it were the most natural path. In short, the military is where Israeli leaders are made. We did not invent this system; it is borrowed from Bismarck's Germany.

Both the German and Israeli militaristic regimes excluded entire populations. In Germany, thousands of Jews who were qualified to become officers, and who had served in the German army as early as 1880, were never com-missioned. In Israel, no Arab (more specifically, no non-Jew) will ever be made a chief of staff or the prime minister, nor in the foreseeable future will a non-Jew sit in the Knesset security subcommittees or on the Mossad, or on any committee that deals with nuclear capability. In this sense, Israeli Arabs are like the German Jews of the Second Reich. I must reiterate that the comparison is not between the status of today's Israeli Arabs and that of the Jews during the Holocaust, not even in the pre-war Nazi years, but only during the long incubation period that preceded Nazism and that gave rise to a public mindset that enabled the Nazis to take power.

How does one lead a people, an entire society, millions of people, to shut their eyes and block their ears to the events that surround them? Many Germans would later claim, and were prepared to swear, that they had no idea of what was going on, and yet we do not believe them. It's impossible, we tell their sons and daughters, that one day people sud-denly started to disappear and they did not notice. The sons and daugh-ters who come to talk to us insist vehemently, "but my parents did not know." Once in a while, an old resident near a former concentration camp says that he walked by it daily but did not see the obvious and did not smell anything unusual, like the ashes of our brethren. It seems that there are mechanisms of suppression and denial that cause us to shut our eyes to the distress of a battered woman or to turn a deaf ear to the cries of a helpless child that is abused near us. Studies have shown that viewing images of a car accident is not an effective deterrent against reckless driving. The notion "it will not happen to me" creates an iron wall between the individual and the vision of blood, body parts, and death. It is easy to incite a crowd, instilling fear, raising demons, and the rest will simply follow. When individuals testify that they did not see or hear anything unusual, it may be true because it was simply too much to perceive, too much to bear.

Hannah Arendt wrote in her book *Eichmann in Jerusalem:*

Lying became integral to the German national character...In wartime, the lie that was most influential on the German peo-ple was the slogan "The fatal struggle of the German people," coined by Hitler or Goebbels. The easy [lying] facilitated the self-deception in three manners. First, it hinted that the war was not a war. Second, that fate, not Germany, started it. Third, that it is a question of life and death for the Germans, who had to eradicate their enemies or be eradicated themselves.[2]

Our beloved Israel also fell into the fatality trap: us, "the good," against "them," the demons, the ultimate enemy. When every enemy is the absolute evil and every conflict is a war to the death, all is justified in our eyes. We do not distinguish between levels of hostility nor do we view our enemies as rivals with possibly legitimate needs: they are all against us all the time, and all we can do is defend ourselves. Even our armed forces, who specialize in attacking and taking initiative, are still called the "Israeli Defense Forces." Former Prime Minister Binyamin Netanyahu announced to the U.S. Senate a few days after 9/11 that the attack was a turning point. He said that a critical war was imminent, in which the United States, led by George W. Bush, would be the keeper of the gate.

Netanyahu is without doubt an expert (some say, a propagandist) on Israel in recent decades, and he aimed for his target. He was speaking in Washington, D.C., but his audience was his own party in Israel. The press release from his office reported that Netanyahu presented the Associated Press with photos that showed body parts strewn among pizzas from a suicide attack at a Sbarro restaurant in Jerusalem. "Fifty years ago we defeated the Nazis with the consensus that the Nazis should be condemned..."[3]

When Hamas won the Palestinian elections in January 2006, Netanyahu rushed to announce that we had a new *tzorer,* a term used to describe the very worst of Israel's historic enemies, like Hitler. All Netanyahu's enemies are super enemies, and he and President Bush lead the free world against these frightening creatures. Many years of propaganda like this, using historically laden terminology, have resulted in perpetual hysteria: everything is a sign of fate and we are hanging in the balance, between existence and annihilation. Propaganda tells us that we await total destruction or salvation, with nothing in between. The war of 1948 was as significant as the ones in 1956 and 1967. Who could deny the similarity between three weeks of anxious siege preceding the Six-Day War and the Shoah's ghettos and camps? Was the country's fate not hanging in the balance in the Yom Kippur War of 1973? When the Egyptians seized some Israeli posts on the Suez Canal in October 1973, defense minister Moshe Dayan, the great general, talked about the possible destruction of the Third Temple! Netanyahu operates on prepared, cultivated ground, saturated with absolute evil, where the Jews are perpetually fighting for their survival.

Netanyahu follows the footsteps of many other talented, emotional speakers. When we attacked Lebanon in 1982, launching a war of deceit, folly, and futility, Prime Minister Menahem Begin sent us out to fight Yasser Arafat, the "two-legged beast." It was the same expression he had used thirty years earlier to describe Hitler. He also liked to compare the Palestinian National Charter to Hitler's *Mein Kampf*. "Never before in human history was such a despicable, wicked, armed organization formed—except for the Nazis," Begin once said, referring to the Palestinian Liberation Organization. Following the attack on Arafat's headquarters in Beirut, according to the Israeli historian Tom Segev, Begin told President Ronald Reagan that he felt as if he had sent the IDF to Berlin to kill Hitler in his bunker. His cabinet secretary at the time, Arye Naor, testified that Begin persuaded his cabinet to launch the war in Lebanon with these words: "You know what I have done and what we have all done to avoid war and bereavement, but our fate in the Land of Israel is such that there is no choice but to fight and sacrifice. Believe me that the alternative is Treblinka, and we have decided that there will be no more Treblinkas." "Hitler is already dead, Mr. Prime Minister," novelist Amos Oz retorted in the magazine *Yediot Aharonot* two weeks after that unnecessary war broke out. "Again and again, Mr. Begin, you show the public your strange urge to revive Hitler in order to kill him anew in the form of terrorists. This urge to recreate and re-eliminate Hitler again and again is the fruit of distress that poets are obliged to express, but for a statesmen this might lead to dangerous results."

The political debate between Oz, the prophet of the left, and Begin, the icon of the right, was not about form but about substance, about the ways of influencing history. It was a struggle between the poet's distress and the politician's psychosis; it was a wrestling match between value systems, in the arena of words, over the use of language, in this case laundered language. A harsh reality needs harsh words to describe it, live it, and survive it. Laundered words allow us to perceive soiled realities as clean. We did not invent this method, but we improved it, as if we learned nothing from the evil ones who had laundered words before us.

The Nazi method was ingenious. Joseph Goebbels, the father of modern propaganda, knew how to spin the sickest ideas as if they were health itself. He and his henchmen sold these ideas, and the Germans bought them and looked away. In his brilliant essay, "The Future of Liberty," Thomas Gauly examined the Western concepts of freedom and liberty:

> In his film *Schindler's List,* American director Steven Spielberg presents an effective example of the danger that threatens freedom as the result of changing language values. The film tells the story of German businessman Oskar Schindler, who succeeds in saving several thousand Jews from death in concentration camps. When Schindler discovers that his closest worker, who is privy to all his secrets, is about to be sent to a concentration camp, he tries to encourage him:
>
> Schindler: I will see to it that you receive special treatment if you are sent to Auschwitz.
>
> Worker: I hope that by "special treatment" you don't mean what people say.
>
> Schindler: Do we need a new language?
>
> Worker: I am afraid so, Mr. Schindler.[4]

Many books and studies have been written about the Nazi reinterpretation of words, and the direct and indirect methods of brainwashing the German people. There are not many German documents that specifically use the words "destruction," "elimination," "murder," or "killing." The destruction process is described as "evacuation," "special treatment," "relocation," "work in the East," "residential relocation," and "final solution." This special terminology was developed to allay the fears of Jews so that they would go easily to the centers of death, believing they were going to work in the East. The destination was a "labor camp," because the word "camp" denotes a temporary stay, definitely not anything definitive (we, too, have yet to overcome this, since we still call the Nazi death centers "concentration camps"). Even when the victims arrived at Auschwitz they remained optimistic, since above the gate was the slogan "Work Makes You Free." Then there were the "showers" for them to cleanse and disinfect themselves after the long journey. Who would believe that they meant something else entirely? What was Zyklon B gas? Humans always believe words. Frantz Fanon wrote in the early 1950s. "To speak means to use a certain syntax, to have the morphology of a certain language. But the true meaning is to assume a certain culture, a load of civilization."[5] A civilization that employs laundered words uses a false language to represent a false culture and allows a state to wash itself clean of any responsibility for acts done in their name. "I didn't know," "I wasn't told," "It can't be, the newspapers didn't report it" are common manifestations of responses to laundered language. The reply should be, "They did tell you, but in words that allowed you to not acknowledge their true meaning. They told you, but in a way that enabled you to not know what you did not want to know."

Fanon is an expert witness worth listening to. He forced the old, bloated, and hollow France to stand up against the oppression of blacks and to assume responsibility for white crimes against nonwhites, and through France he reached the West. His book *Black Skin, White Masks* became one of the twentieth century's most important texts. It explains the origins and the extent of modern conflicts that involve racism, oppression, independence, and cultural liberation. Some considered Fanon the prophet of modern violence, because he opined that violence must be integral to struggles for liberation. Fanon deserves credit for being one of the first to argue that language is the white man's major tool of oppression, as the nuances of the white man's language express the profound belief that blacks are inferior and evil while reinforcing ideas of white superiority.

Some of the trials and travails that Fanon attributed to blacks can also be attributed to the Jews, who were considered inferior for hundreds of years, and most definitely to the innocent Jews who were slaughtered in the name of racist, Aryan policy. For this reason, it is much more difficult to confront the situation in Israel. Yet we must not ignore the fact that the modern Hebrew language employs word laundering to mask an arrogant, violent and even racist attitude toward the Arab enemy.

In everyday spoken Hebrew, the adjective *Arab* has a bad connotation. "Arab labor" expresses low-quality work. An "Arab worker" means a cheap worker. An "Arab army" is a derogatory term for a defeated army (the late president Ezer Weizman once told me that the "IDF was the best Arab army in the Middle East"). Such examples are plentiful. The derogatory connotation makes the Arabs the heirs of the Jews and blacks as perceived inferiors. Yet there are two exceptions to this rule, two terms that express much appreciation to the word Arab. "An Arab House" in the Jerusalem real estate market is a highly sought after property; it is a high quality home, beautiful, well-built, large, and spacious. It is a house that will last forever. The other term relates to food. An "Arab Salad" is a dish in the great family of Arab cuisine. It is authentic, local, fresh, and wholesome. Hummus and falafel are much more well regarded here than Ashkenazi *gefilte* fish or the Moroccan dish *hreime*.

The exceptions regarding the words for these two very basic personal necessities testify that Israelis accept Arab presence as a fact of life. The barbed-wire fences and walls will not change the fact that when we look for food and shelter, we look for the Arab. A good Arab, according to this language, is an Arab of home and food. It is not the Arab of scorn, contempt, incitement and death. Reality, as bitter as it may be, cannot erase this.

I do believe wholeheartedly that despite our malaise, we prefer to live with our neighbors in dignity and respect and not to turn into wild beasts and oppressors, like our persecutors just two generations ago.

Such an attitude was well noted by Israeli journalist and novelist Davide Grossman, who spent seven weeks leading up to the twentieth anniversary of the occupation-liberation traveling in Israel's occupied territories. Fluent in Arabic, he spent time in refugee camps, observed proceedings in military courts, and visited settlements and Palestinian cities and villages, where he was a welcome guest. The now defunct *Koteret Rashit* newsweekly published a special issue based on Grossman's soul searching. He later added a few new chapters and turned his experience into a haunting book, *The Yellow Wind,* about the corruption and squalor of the late 1980s.

The book saddened me. But I was wrong to think that we had reached rock bottom, from which we could only move up. Twenty years have passed and today those depths seem like humanistic utopia. Grossman writes about word laundering:

> A state in confusion rewrites a new vocabulary for itself. Israel is not the first state to do so…but…it is revolting to witness the slow defacing. A new species of recruited, traitorous words is developing slowly; words that have lost their original meaning, words that do not describe reality, but aspire to hide it.

Israel's word laundering is among the most advanced in the world, in part because the reality here keeps changing and requires new words every time. The reinvention of words started long ago with the good old boys from the Palmah, one of the militias that fought for Israel's independence. They never stole; they merely "pulled" from the chicken coop. In the army we did not steal, only "completed inventory." We never sexually harassed women, we only asked what exactly she meant by "no." We were educated to respect the "purity of arms," an oxymoronic term meant to cleanse the conscience, as if killing with a "pure" firearm legitimizes killing. In time, we advanced so much we reached the heights of self-deceit. When our armed forces, in which our children serve, kill people who pose no immediate threat, who are not about to commit an act of terror and are not considered ticking bombs, we stop reading, knowing, hearing, and caring, because the army uses the term "targeted prevention." How targeted could it be when it is carried out dozens, if not hundreds, of times? How targeted could it be if innocent bystanders are also maimed and killed? Targeted prevention sounds much better than "extermination," "assassination," or "liquidation." Are we becoming more like them? Has the enmity between us and the Palestinians already blurred the line between a good moral soldier and a predator? If I resemble them, the Palestinians, and they are the heirs of the Nazis, what does that then say about me? About us? We have no answer, as we have no proper words.

For some the word "expose" may denote the courageous revealing of the truth, but round here, for others the same positive word means something else entirely, as it does for those who are crying over an old orchard that is gone forever since it was "exposed" for security reasons. The fence near the home of former defense minister Shaul Mofaz in Kokhav Yair was cleared and exposed. The orchard that existed there before the arrogant Jewish community was built no longer yields fruit. The terrorists no longer have a place to hide in ambush for the minister, so they try to harm elsewhere. The minister and his family can enjoy their sleep, except that by "exposing," they planted another hidden seed of hatred.

A "crown" in Israeli military lingo is not a royal accessory or a dental procedure but a stifling siege that leads to hunger, thirst, and desperation. A crown is what is done in my name when my children surround enemy cities and trap their Arab peers inside them. A crown is a terrible, dispiriting act to those who experience it—no matter how benign the term may sound to those who do not want to know it, who bury their head in the sand that corrupts the holy language and turns it into a useful tool of the occupation.

It is very difficult in Israel to compare something or someone to Germany because here, Germany means Nazis, gas chambers, and the final solution. It is inconvenient to recognize that Hitler's Germany did not start with those images; it was not always murderous. Germany was different before, but it deteriorated. A word bred a phrase that bred a reality that enabled destruction. Nothing compares—and I pray that it will never compare—with Germany in the last stages of the Nazi regime, from *Kristallnacht* in late 1938 to the liberation of the victims from the death centers in Germany and the East in the first half of 1945. It is true that we do not have gas chambers here and that we have no official policy of deportation and annihilation. Yet those who will not open their ears and eyes should not be surprised when it becomes clear one day how similar Israel is to those early years in Germany, when the German people were deceived, misled. Certain moments in the Israeli experience are very similar to what happened in Germany between the insult of defeat in the Great War and the Nazi's rise to power in 1933. In the early days after World War I, in the new German democracy, respectable, decent people did not take Hitler and his men seriously. They were loud and provocative, but transparent. They were not really seen and not much listened to.

Ian Kershaw, one of the most authoritative voices on modern German history, presented new details about Hitler and Germany in a new biography of Hitler, adding pieces to this puzzle and hence to our own. He argues early in the book:

> The twentieth century is "Hitler's Century"... no one left a deeper mark in it than Adolf Hitler. Other dictators—especially Mussolini, Stalin, and Mao—conducted wars of occupation, enslaved other peoples, supervised immeasurable atrocities and left an indelible stamp on the twentieth century's character. But their rule was not etched in people's consciousness...the way that Adolf Hitler's rule was etched...Hitler's dictatorship was like the implosion of modern civilization—like a nuclear blast in a modern society. It showed what we are capable of...[6]

He includes us all, the whole of humanity, among those responsible. In order to prevent this from recurring, he states:

> No effort to fully understand Nazism will succeed without an adequate reference to the "Hitler Factor," but such explanation must not only take into account Hitler's ideological goals, his deeds, and personal contribution to the forming of the events; it must reveal the social forces and the political structures that enabled, designed, and promoted the growth of the system...Hitler was the focus...He was its head and spokesman, not its major factor.

Hitler came from the fringes of right-wing circles. Even though he was considered a lunatic, he went on to become the epicenter of the world's nightmares. In extremist circles, people dip into pools of hatred, and pass this onto their companions. Inflammatory language arouses passions but creates false warmth. They allow themselves to speak words that should not be spoken in respectable places. Extremism moves from the fringes of xenophobic nationalism to the more moderate right and from there on to the cultural and political mainstream. The circles of influence almost always parallel those of indifference.

At first extremists are viewed with disdain, as they are just a "tiny minority," "lunatics," etc. But disdain, unfortunately, does not stop them. The people at the center are too indifferent and self-indulgent to pay too much attention, and they become accustomed to the sights and sounds of extremism. Once the noises from the right are part of the public agenda, then it becomes impossible to uproot them.

In the 1920s and 1930s members of the German Right demanded prosecution of the "November Criminals," as they called the leaders of the democratic parties who had signed the armistice agreements in 1918 that ended the Great War and thus, in their eyes, betrayed Germany. In Israel, both the extreme right that loiters in the hills of the West Bank and the bourgeois right in suits and ties demand the prosecution of the "Oslo Criminals." This is what they call the Israeli leaders, the late Prime Minister Rabin and President Shimon Peres, who signed the Oslo Accords in 1993, and most members of Israeli society who supported them, bringing an end to the first Intifada. This must be understood as a call to bring the whole democratic process to trial. Is the similarity between Germany and Israel incidental?

Are the writings on the wall, "Arabs Out" and "Transfer Now," different in any way from *Juden Raus* [Jews out]? The speeches in the Knesset, filled with hate, fear, and obscenities that are stricken from the minutes, though not from the consciousness, what do they tell us? When a radio newsreader says "an Arab has found death," what does it mean? That he lost death and IDF soldiers helped him find it? What does it mean, "soldiers fired in the air and two boys were killed"? That Palestinian children fly in the air like Marc Chagall creatures, and are hit by our innocent bullets? The dozens of cases of unidentified, unaccounted-for killings, to whom do they belong? They belong to us, to you and me.

Words can grant life and words can exterminate, and words always reflect reality. "Death and life are in the tongue," is an old Hebrew saying, and a bitter Israeli truth. If we listen to the substance of words in our lives and not just to their melody, we must conclude that we are much closer to the language of death than to the language of life.

So wrote a wise woman, Hannah Arendt, on the Eichmann trial for the *New Yorker* magazine:

> German society with its eighty million sons was also protected from reality and facts precisely by the same means, the same self illu-sion, lies and stupidity...These lies were altered from year to year and often contradicted one another...The habit of self-deception became so prevalent, almost a moral condition for survival...[7]

Israel today does not stand at the gates of gas chambers. It is reasonable to assume that if the values of the Palestinians' transfer and Torah-style genocide will be in our government's agenda, I and many of my friends will no longer be free citizens of this state. We will struggle with all the legitimate means at our disposal to prevent our state from committing moral suicide. We will serve time in prison or leave Israel for good. I prefer conscientious imprisonment to lowly liberty, and will much prefer an honorable exile to official national evil. It must be said here that willful mass imprison-ment or exile, if widespread and ethical, will bring Israel to its end. There are terms under which I, as a Jew, must choose exile or imprisonment in my land if our sins, God forbid, will force us on this path. Meanwhile we must not dismiss the issue by saying "If this happens, I will know what to do." There is a wide range of options between liberty and destruction; all of them are bad and all are likely to become worse. The notion that this cannot happen to us because our history as persecuted people makes us immune to hatred and racism is very dangerous. A look inside Israel shows that the erosion has begun. The dose of inoculation may have been too great. *This* is not happening to us. Bad things are happening to us. They are frightful reminders of what was and must not happen again. They are invisible to us because our language is opaque. We see dim shadows, but we do not dare to break the shackles of language and look inside.

"Language is the medium that allows us to understand the world," Gauly wrote. "We see nature, society and human motives not as they are but as our language allows us to see. This is the foundation of our culture. For this reason, it is important how we treat our language and what our concepts are meant to express."

Is it a coincidence that the late professor Yeshayahu Leibowich, a native of early twentieth-century Riga, was educated in Germany? Did the lessons of Bismarck and the German empire resonate in his ears when he watched the Seventh Day destruction in 1967 and refused to be carried away by the messianic ecstasy that followed the war? If not, how did he know so early, in the very first days of the new Israeli history, to predict the following:

> The dilemma of whether to hold on to the territories or to evacuate them is not directly related to the problem of peace and secu-rity...We are destined to live a long period in a state of perpet-ual war...The inclusion of one and a half million Arabs within Jewish jurisdiction means undermining the human and Jewish essence of the state and the destruction of the social-economic order that we established...The destruction of the Jewish people and the corruption of the human in Israel...In the greater land of Israel [there] will not be a Jewish worker or a Jewish farmer. The Arabs will be the working people, and we will become a people of managers, supervisors, officials and policemen, and especially undercover policemen. That state will necessarily be a police state, and its central institution will be the General Security Services...This will surely influence the entire spiritual and moral atmosphere in the state and in society; it will poison education...And all this is in the Jewish sector of the state. In the Arab sectors the Israeli government will build concentration

camps and gallows. This will be a state that is not worthy of being and will not be worth to let exist.[8]

When I am forced to listen to the news, usually while I'm driving, I must overcome the urge to stop and spray-paint a huge graffiti sign that says "Leibowich was Right." Yeshayahu Leibowich had not heard of "targeted prevention," so he wrote of gallows. He did not know then that in the prison camp in Ktziot tens of thousands would be imprisoned, vile criminals alongside innocents. He did not read Amnesty International's reports that were later rejected without debate, under the pretext that the whole world is against us.

We ignore the facts because it is too difficult to know them, we do not read and do not know anything of the reality of our lives. We build a huge network of roads through the occupied territories to act as reality bypasses that spare us the need to face the ugliness of discrimination and humiliation. We turn a blind eye, and disregard. Leibowich, unlike us, did not imagine less than a year after the Six-Day War that the mass detention centers would become hothouses of hate and schools for terror and insurrection against the Israelis. But Leibowich was right, as the lesson of the Germany in which he grew up never escaped his mind.

The centrality of the armed forces in our lives, the role of language in legitimizing the illegitimate, the infiltration of a right-wing narrative into the mainstream and the indifference of the passive majority—these are the major players that allow racism to contaminate our world. Moreover, in the painful comparisons between Israel today and the Germany that preceded Hitler, we have not yet considered the importance that both nations placed on national mythology and blood-earth relationships. We have not delved into the role of youth movements in the forming of a new breed of youth, either in the reforming of German society or in Israeli society today, a youth that rejuvenates the face of Judaism, wears the new Zionist *sabra* appearance, the new Jewish person. We did not describe nature's rituals and holidays or the role of folktales in nationalism. We have not expanded on the roadblocks, property expropriations, land theft, prevention of marriage, settlers' violence, the army's capitulation, and the ever-present longing for a strong leader. Recent surveys show that one out of four Israelis has been a victim of violence. Anarchy is an important feature of the new coercive, violent and dictatorial order. The list is very long and shameful, and the similarities to the German situation persist. Do we still see the original Jewish point from which we evolved? Or are we too entrenched in our frightening similarity with those from whom we fled? In both cases, the national traumas and humiliation competed with the new spirit of liberty, freedom, equality, openness, and democracy. In Germany of the 1930s, the former ideas won. Will Israel choose the latter for the future?

I cannot end such a sad chapter without thinking of something optimistic. I reflect on the question in Psalms: "Where from will come my helper?" Some layers of the old language make me hopeful. There are words that will never be erased and concepts so strong that their very existence in everyday speech testifies to the existence of a healthy, undefeated consciousness. When my Israel still debates the Green Line (the 1949 Armistice lines established between Israel and its neighbors—Egypt, Jordan, Lebanon and Syria—after the 1948 Arab-Israeli War), with passion, forty years later, it means that people have not yet erased the invisible boundary. It is not drawn in a field, and you cannot see it when you drive along the Jewish reality-bypass roads. Since the Six-Day War, the state's population has more than doubled and the vast majority of Israelis were born here or emigrated after the war, therefore they should not know of the old border. Yet the line is still there. Billions of dollars were spent erasing it and thousands of homes were built in hundreds of settlements that are home to hundreds of thousands of Zionist invaders—yet most Israelis are looking for a political way out of the territories trap and are waiting for all of us to come home. The Green Line is where Israel will come together when it regains consciousness. It cannot be erased. It turns out that the historical circumstances during the nineteen years between the state's independence and six days in June 1967 settled in the hearts more than any messianic message of a greater Israel. The Green Line is not just a phrase; it is a cornerstone for a new language and a new Israeli imagination.

CHAPTER 6

LESSONS FROM THE HOLOCAUST

THERE WAS A TIME WHEN THE SUN NEVER SET ON THE BRITISH Empire. It was a political as well as a natural phenomenon—the territory was so vast that it included all the world's datelines. The new German Empire of Emperor Wilhelm II and Reichskanzler Otto von Bismarck envied Great Britain. The Germans also wanted a united kingdom, elevated international status, and colonies to enrich their domestic economy at the expense of distant peoples basking under an imperial sun. Thus the German empire developed a rhetoric that expressed its entitlement to a "place under the sun." This was thanks to a combination of an inferiority complex in the face of Great Britain's might, a dash of German hot-tempered quarrelsomeness, and, above all, a willingness to fight and sacrifice to get that place in the sun. When their rhetoric ripened and was ready for action, Germany launched occupation wars in Africa and elsewhere.

One generation later, there was no empire or emperor, just a weak and defeated Weimar Republic. The rhetoric remained, but the reasons had changed. Germany was feeling claustrophobic within its borders. The demagoguery of place fell on willing ears, and Germany felt compelled to create a *Lebensraum,* living space, for itself in the East. *Lebensraum* was one of Hitler's two obsessions; the other was the Jews. Poland, perceived as a thorn in Germany's side, was the challenge, a seductive prize for the Nazi hunters. Late in 1939 Hitler began his campaign to erase Polish "nationhood," including its intelligentsia, the standard-bearers of Polish nationalism. Hitler hoped to annex Polish lands to Germany and to populate them with *Volksdeutche,* Aryans, and ethnic Germans who lived in the Baltic States and Eastern Poland. "A place under the sun," in the Judeo-German lexicon, means something very specific and sinister.

Why, then, did former Israeli Prime Minister Binyamin Netanyahu, name his book (in Hebrew), of all names, *A Place under the Sun?* Is it because the narrative speaks of the rightist, paranoid belief in nothing but power and settlements to counterbalance the Arab demographic threat? Is this a subliminal admission that with the expansion to the east and the de facto annexation—an *Anschluss*—of Judaea, Samaria, and the Golan, an Israeli Empire was born? Is it a manifestation of claustrophobic pangs in the Jewish ghetto mindset that seeks relief by breaking out into a broader living space? It may just be literary insensitivity on Netanyahu's part, another instance of the endless paradoxical expressions that Hitler and the Shoah left us to struggle with.

During the Nazi regime and World War II, the leaders of the pre-state of Israel (*Yishuv*) did very little in response to the annihilation of Europe's Jews. There was little knowledge and awareness "here" about the events "there" in distant Europe. The local Zionist politicians, most of them Eastern European Jews, were also unable to act. Headed by the pragmatic David Ben-Gurion, they did not wish to waste emotional resources that could otherwise be channeled into building the Jewish state. "The answer to the disaster of Germany's Jews," Ben-Gurion told the Jewish Agency Executive in 1935, "must be Zionist: to convert the disaster into a resource for building the land, to save the lives and the property of Germany's Jews for the land. This salvation comes before anything else." During the early days of danger, before the violence became deadly, the Jewish Agency, representing the local Israeli-Jewish population, negotiated with the Nazis. It was a cynical meeting of interests: neither the Zionists nor the Nazis wanted the Jews to remain in Germany. The Nazis wanted them far away, and the Zionists wanted them in their own, not-yet born state. This dialogue produced economic agreements between the Zionists and the Nazis that enabled the transfer of funds and goods to the would-be state. This resulted in economic prosperity and the building of much of the infrastructure that served the pre-state Israel in the 1930s, some even during the Great Arab Revolt. Israeli historian and journalist Tom Segev writes on this topic in his book *The Seventh Million:*

> In the afternoon of August 7, 1933, a meeting was held in the ministry of economics in which the Germans agreed that every Jew who emigrates to the Land of Israel would be allowed to take 1,000 pounds sterling (about 4,000 U.S. dollars) in foreign currency as well as goods worth 20,000 marks (about 5,000 dollars), and maybe more, through trust companies. One thousand pounds was the sum required to settle in the country as a "capitalist," as this category of immigrants was then called. It was a significant sum in those days, when a family of four could live in bourgeois comfort on less than 25 pounds a month. The transfer agreement saved the lives of tens of thousands of Jews. In retrospect, the agreement with the Nazis was also another step leading to the establishment of the State of Israel... The transfer agreement was based on identical common interests between the German government and the Zionist movement: the Nazis were interested that the Jews leave Germany; the Zionists were interested that they come to the Land of Israel.[1]

It turns out that before the Nazis started to slaughter Europe's Jews, they enabled us to build the foundations of our state-to-be, Israel. After the Jewish head was decapitated and our limbs cut off in terrible suffering, this very foundation absorbed the emaciated surviving remnants of European Jewry. After Israel was born in 1948, the German reparations and compensation agreement of 1952 helped the state regenerate itself. Israel absorbed new immigrants and rehabilitated the war refugees, in effect resurrecting a new Israeli nation that was essentially different from the sum of the ragtag Jewish refugees. Thus, the Nazis, in their cruel way, were involved in promoting the idea of the Zionist state and fulfilling it in three ways: before the war with the transfer agreements, during the war and its aftermath with the tidal waves of refugee migration, and after the war with the great sums of money that the "new" Germany paid on behalf of the "old" Germany.

I often wonder if we could have a state at all if not for the Germans and their savagery. What would Israel have become if it were established not by the negative forces of displacement and tragedy but by the positive forces of national revival? How would Israel have been if it were built not by Theodor Herzl, compelled to act in anger over the Dreyfus Affair, but by his rival Ehad Ha'am (Asher Ginzburg) and the other Zionist intellectuals who sought to revive the greatness of the Jewish people, not to replicate its ills?

The leaders of the pre-state of Israel paid lip service to the calamity in Europe. Segev draws a horrific picture of indifference:

> *Haaretz* once published a news story on the atrocities of the occupation in Kharkov, Ukraine ("The Nazi oppressors pushed in front of them half-naked Jews and beat them along the city streets with whips and rifle stocks. Frail old people and children fell helpless on the way and died in purity…"). The story was run on page two of the paper, under a headline of one column. There were other stories in that column, and this was not at the top. Above it appeared a story on a great football victory of Maccabee Damascus…In time the newspaper editors would claim that they did not believe the information that reached their desks…Therefore they published, but with reservation, for safety. They often used question marks: "Half a Million Jews Annihilated in Romania?" (Minor headline in *Davar*).[2]

Who can believe this today, when every alleged swastika makes a big headline? There are a number of Jewish organizations that make a living of reacting to expressions of hatred that are not so terrible, not so important, sometimes simply accidental or the product of a deranged mind. Can we imagine, today, a question mark in a headline about the death of half a million people?

This downplaying reflected the leadership's position and was the filtered product of the political watchdogs at the news desks, and in any case it was the position of the majority of the people living in the pre-state Israel. The local population was even more distant from the events in Europe than their leaders. Yiddish, the language of the Shoah, was not theirs, nor were the places. Ponevezh, Lithuania, was by no means like Dgania, to the shores of the Sea of Galilee, and Lublin, Poland, was totally foreign to Nahalal in the Jezreel Valley. Their distant cousins were more distant than cousins, and in the Land of Israel people were busy, especially with themselves. Only when the gates of the camps were force opened, when the curtain lifted and the heaps of ashes became apparent to all, only then did the petrifying news penetrate. It was not just that their inaction was appalling, but also the realization that Eastern Europe's Jewish population, the human reserves who were to inhabit the land and build the state, had been liquidated. They were gone forever.

The Zionist reaction followed soon enough. Israel declared itself the heir of the victims, their sole official representative in the world, and appointed itself as the speaker of the slain millions. We naturalized six million dead citizens. Young Israel, which was meant to be the healthy alternative to the ailing Diaspora, had scolded the Holocaust victims, post-humously, "We told you so," and transplanted their severed organs into its young body. From a new alternative to the Diaspora in Eastern Europe, the young trailblazing Israel metamorphosed into a country with the same mentality of an old, small, Jewish town, forever persecuted, in the heart of the Middle East.

The Zionist movement and its daughter Israel, founded on revolu-tionary ideals, severed themselves from the Jewish past and created a new national entity, adopting the body and soul of the Shoah victims and sur-vivors. Soon enough they reconnected in full force not only to the pain and mourning of the victims, but also to the same exilic degenerative disease from which they had escaped just a few decades earlier. In the new and innovative Israel, the radical movement of total renewal that promised a spring of nationhood and a new society was compelled to redefine itself by memory and the past. Israel went beyond mourning; it was no longer a future-oriented state, but a society connected to its bleeding, traumatic past. The dramatic proximity of 1945 to 1948, the years of grief and of utopia, depression and mania, fused two monumental events, the Jewish massacre in Europe and the building of the Jewish state of Israel, into one single entity. They became intertwined and inseparable.

Processes like this are by nature lengthy and subject to modification, so I find it very difficult to point to the exact turning point when optimism and exhilaration turned into pessimism and grief. Melancholy, like ivy, climbs upward and covers everything, including the native-grown plants.

The songs of the war, the Jews' poems, the fighters' anthems and the songs of the dead invaded the Zionist hall of hope. They became slogans that pass from one generation to the next. Fifty years of an optimistic Israeli struggle—from Herzl to the stormy 1940s—were suddenly replaced with desperation and admonishment. The powerful lyrics of a Yiddish protest song that Hirsh Glick wrote in the Vilna ghetto in 1943, upon hearing of the Warsaw ghetto uprising, later became the hymn of the Partisans who fought the Nazis. Glick joined the Partisans, fought the Nazis and disappeared in 1944. "Say not that you are walking down your last path," means that someone said publicly that it was his last path. The poet and the singers rebuke him. Since then, along the slippery road, the Israeli mindset has changed drastically.

Israel adopted this legacy of insecurity characteristic of trauma victims. Since then, we live under constant pressure and in the contradiction of unceasing armament to compensate and atone for built-in impotence and existential anxiety. We have become a nation of victims, and our state religion is the worship and tending of traumas, as if Israel forever walks down its last path.

In recent years, the subjects of sexual violence, harassment, and abuse became public and several methods of treatment for the victims have developed. With these new tools, we can begin to understand the mind of Shoah victims and then approach that which is beyond human comprehension. Judith Loyis Herman's book *Trauma and Recovery* is a powerful and fascinating look at human suffering and desperation that offers hope for treatment and recuperation.

Herman attempted to understand the depth of the traumatic experience and to find in it the key for a spiritual recovery. She interviewed victims of post-traumatic stress disorder from battlefields and concentration camps and also victims of crimes, vulnerable family members (especially women and children), former hostages, prisoners of wars and rape victims. Her documentation is stunning and horrifying, but not without hope. The healing process that she proposes is long, slow, and requires patience, but it offers the hope of a future that is at least as good as the pre-traumatic past. I would like to borrow some of her insights in order to understand the Israeli paradox that pairs power with weakness, nuclear weapons with paranoia, solid international status with the-world-is-against-us mentality.

> The victim asks the bystander to share with him the burden of his pain…He demands action, involvement and memory. Psychiatrist Leo Atinger, who studied survivors of Nazi concentration camps, describes the cruel conflict of interest between victims and bystanders. "The community seeks to forget the war and its victims," he writes. "A veil of amnesia is drawn over everything painful and unpleasant. We find the two sides standing face to face; on one side are the victims, who, perhaps, want to forget but are unable to, and on the other side all the highly motivated ones who are often unaware, who seek as best they can to forget and even succeed in forgetting. The conflict…is very painful to both sides. The weak side loses in this unspoken dialogue."[3]

Like any victim of a violent crime or other trauma, Israel was transformed by its experience. It began small and young, but it was united, and recognized its own worth. The first Israelis absorbed immigrants in numbers that greatly exceeded their own, and they assimilated them into their young and not fully formed culture. It was a stunning national enterprise, never seen before and perhaps never to be seen again, an epic achievement on a mythical scale. Then, at some point, the roles reversed. At first the native minority, which was united and relatively homogenous, absorbed the immigrant majority, which seemed divided, broken, isolated and exhausted, and the newcomers appeared to blend in, adopting the values of the new Israel. But the absorbing Israelis despised weakness and frailty and lacked empathy for the arriving Jews. As the Israelis absorbed the Jews, they fused into one silent, insensitive society.

In time, Israel became a multi-trauma society, a coalition of all its victims that harnessed its worst experiences and turned them into its central existential experience. The founding generation exuded a confidence that often covered fundamental weaknesses, but the next generation, their heirs, represent the dimension of temporary existence and insecurity, hiding nothing. The result is a national doctrine, aptly defined in Yiddish by the late Prime Minister Levi Eshkol as *Shimshon hagibor der nebechkicker*, literally, "mighty Samson the weakling." The ironic genius behind this phrase can only be understood by our generation. This national condition includes two contradictory elements that are derived from our history: excessive power and desperate weakness. It makes sense to Israelis, but not to others, who may interpret it as something between hypocrisy and madness. The wisdom is self-evident in the nonscientific expression "a battered boy will be a battering father." Few succeed in breaking the vicious cycle of pathology in their relationships with their parents. Israel arms itself to the teeth like the weak boy who comes to class equipped with a bat, a knife and a slingshot to overcome his real and imagined bullies. In our eyes, we are still partisan fighters, ghetto rebels, shadows in the camps, no matter the nation, state, armed forces, gross domestic product, or international standing. The Shoah is our life, and we will not forget it and will not let anyone forget us. We have pulled the Shoah out of its historic context and turned it into a plea and a generator for every deed. All is compared to the Shoah, dwarfed by the Shoah, and therefore all is allowed—be it fences, sieges, crowns, curfews, food and water deprivation, or unexplained killings. All is permitted because we have been through the Shoah and you will not tell us how to behave. Everything seems dangerous to us, and our normal development as a new people, society, and state is arrested. Yet despite the terrible dimensions of the Shoah, it was not terminal, and it is a fact that we are here, after it, after all. Instead of developing an alternative to the Holocaustic soul, we are bogged down in it and fail to reach the riverbank of optimism that is necessary for our rescue and survival. We must realize that, while it was the tragedy of all tragedies, it is not and should not become our final path.

One of the paradoxical outcomes of the trauma's omnipresence is the relationships we share with Germany and the Middle East today. The hasty reconciliation with Germany is one paradox of the perpetual trauma of remembrance, which worsens our hostile relations with our immediate Middle Eastern neighbors. A great portion of our alienation and generation-wide embarrassment regarding modern Jewish identity is due to forgiving Germany much too soon. The negotiations, agreements, and diplomatic relations were decided on for cold and practical reasons and state interests, but they brought about emotional acceptance. Today we hear the German language everywhere. As Knesset speaker, I allowed the late German president

Johannes Rau to speak in German from the Knesset podium, for the first time in the House's history. German cars are coveted status symbols in Israel. German products are considered superior to other products, and even Germany's soccer championship has many fans and followers in Israel.

Yet we will never forgive the Arabs, for they are allegedly just like the Nazis, worse than the Germans. We have displaced our anger and revenge from one people to another, from an old foe to a new adversary, and so we allow ourselves to live comfortably with the heirs of the German enemy—representing convenience, wealth and high quality—while treating the Palestinians as whipping boys to release our aggression, anger, and hysteria, of which we have plenty. I witnessed this in person at a school in Jerusalem.

Shortly before resigning from the Knesset, I went to a meeting with high school students in one of the oldest and more prestigious schools in the capital. The visit took place early in the century, when Palestinian terror attacks tore Israel apart. Jerusalem was the target for killings and terrifying propaganda by Islamic militants. The conversation with the students was on various subjects, some of which were embarrassing. The children, like typical Israeli youngsters, argued heatedly in favor of deportations and transfer of the Palestinians. Revenge was an accepted philosophy for them and the killing of innocents a legitimate means of deterrence. Some of the more extreme speakers garnered the applause of their silent friends. The school principal, shaken, stood in front of them and spoke with a trembling voice: "But you are not listening to what you are saying. This is how they spoke about us sixty and seventy years ago. This is what they did to us." He admonished them and they fell silent in awe, but it was apparent they disagreed with what he said. Then one angry student threw out at me: "I will never forgive them. My friend was killed in a terrorist act and my cousin was injured in a terrorist act...and I will never ever forgive them. They are the worst thing that ever happened in my life," said the sixteen-year-old. "The worst thing that happened to the Jews is the Arabs," he continued, genuinely hurt.

A rational response was not in order. So I tried to change the flow of his river of wrath; I asked him what brand of car his father drove.

"A Volkswagen Passat," he replied.

"And your mom?"

"An old Audi."

"And you've forgiven the Germans?"

"Yes," he said. "They did nothing bad to me. They weren't as bad as the Arabs."

There was a bit of silence and the bell rang, marking the end of the class session. "You tricked me," he said. "You set a trap. You're a demagogue politician." He was in tears. He then turned away and left.

I did not mean at all to "trick" him. The Israeli nation's wounded psyche spoke the truth from both our throats. The political manipulation that turned the Arabs into the spiritual brethren of the Nazis, or worse, conveniently allowed us to move forward in life. Restored relations with Germany and the West enabled us to receive the German reparations and compensation money. At the same time, we continued to lament our bad fortune, to express anger, to remember and never forget, by reincarnating the Nazi spirit into the Arab body.

What can you say to a boy like this? What he and his friends experienced in Jerusalem no one in the West had experienced for years. A terrorist attack in New York almost brought the greatest superpower to its knees, unleashing from it frightening aggression. That despicable act caused the American president to lie to his people and to the world, to declare a war of deceit and treachery on a weak state like Iraq in order to satisfy his urge for revenge and maintain the "American way of life." If a president breaks down in panic, how can we blame the children of Jerusalem, Kiriat Shmona, or Sderot? What else could one expect to hear from a teenager who experiences fear on a daily basis over the course of several years? Exploding buses, cafés, pizza parlors, car bombs, potential death traps on the way to school and back home. There is a limit to the amount of forgiveness and compassion that you can expect from a teenager, whose blood is boiling anyway. I wished to plant a seed for thought. I followed him after class and tried to engage him. I told him about a nightmarish ride that turned to a magical one in Jerusalem many years before.

One evening before Rosh Hashanah, the Jewish New Year, I drove through Jerusalem. The traffic was heavy, as it usually is on the eve of holidays. Suddenly traffic went from slow to still. I heard on the news that there had been a terror attack. With me in the car were my father and my elder son, still very young. We listened to the news, sent our wishes to the victims and hoped we would arrive home on time. But as the traffic jam dragged on, my son asked: "How could you even begin to think of making peace with these Arabs?" *These Arabs* is an expression in spoken Hebrew—all Arabs, always generalized, always disdained. Our existential fear of the dark, hidden, unknown and foreign among us.

I thought of how I might answer him, without seeming annoyed by the question, the traffic, and this life in general, when my father replied from the back seat. "*Yengele* (boychik)," my father said, "When I fled from Germany in the early days of the Second World War, I did not know where the war would lead and what it would bring. When the war ended, I discovered that my mother died in Teresienstadt, my grandmother was murdered, shot in the Sobibor ghetto, many of my friends and family had perished, and the whole culture of my childhood had gone up in flames to the sky. I never thought I would ever forgive 'these Germans.' Now, look at our relationship with Germany and how we regard them. 'These Arabs,' as you call them, never did—and never will do—to us what the Germans did." Then he was silent for a few minutes before adding, "And, in your lifetime, you will witness peace between you and them."

I am not sure that my son remembers the story, and I am certain that the high-school student from Jerusalem would not at all be persuaded by my late father's perspective. I live by the faith of my father, and believe that when we free the Arabs from the Nazi role we assigned to them, it will be much easier to speak with them and to solve both our existential problems—the national mindset that is required to remember the Shoah and the constant warmongering between the children of Israel and the children of Ishmael.

Israeli leaders have never admitted to our responsibility for the Palestinian refugee problem. From a tactical point of view, no one wanted to open the Pandora's box of refugee recognition and compensation too soon, so as to avoid giving the Arabs anything tangible in return for nothing. At the same time, Israeli officials did not want to "lose points" in the muddy arena of international political wrestling. Another reason that lurked under a range of devious, tactical arguments: a heavy guilt complex. We could not admit to ourselves, much less publicly to the world, that "the Wandering Jews," a people of refugees, are the cause of the Palestinian refugee problem.

In the same years and under the same conditions by which the Palestinian refugee problem was created, we solved the problem of our displaced Jewish refugees who flocked to Israel from all corners of the world, including the Arab countries. The Palestinians also could—if they only wanted, despite Israel's guilt—solve their refugee problem on the outskirts of Damascus, in the camps in Jordan, and in the cities of Lebanon and Egypt. Unfortunately, the Arab leadership did nothing for their displaced brethren, but they exploited the refugees' misery to perpetuate the dispute with Israel. It is hard not to compare two societies of refugees that were created here six decades ago from similar starting points. Israeli society absorbed all its refugees, not always perfectly from the perspective of those absorbed, but from the perspective of the outsider, the absorption went well. In the 1940s and 1950s, there was no difference between one refugee and another, but there was the national will to muster the resources and the willingness to help and to build. We have not seen such mustering on the Arab and Palestinian side. Palestinian refugees remained bogged down in camps, poverty, distress, and hatred. Israel has become an intriguing mosaic of cultures intermingling to produce a synthesis, while Palestinian refugees continue to be the cause of constant political foment with their claims, albeit justified, of injustice. This, therefore, creates an emotional obstacle to every political process that would allow them to move forward to their salvation and our own.

Not long ago I went to a dinner in Jordan. A group of young and old Middle Easterners sat around the table. Three were Lebanese, successful and articulate, media and business people of the newer generation. Although we were from two sides of the divide in the Middle East crisis, as long as the conversation centered on neutral subjects, there was no sign of rivalry. We held the same opinions about George W. Bush and his father, about Clinton and Monica Lewinsky. We had all read *The Da Vinci Code,* downloaded mp3 files from the same sites, and did not even have many differences of opinion regarding Ariel Sharon or religious fundamentalists of any persuasion. Then, late in the evening, the topic of the refugees came up at the table. The smiles and easy atmosphere were gone. Each of us told his story, recalled his parents' unending poverty, and missed a city in which he had not been born: in Jaffa, Acre, or the Old City. Then the conversation ebbed and all eyes were on me. Why are you not taking responsibility? You've asked us to control terror, to rout religious extremism, to commit to democracy, to act for liberty and women's equality. And you are willing to give us only very little in return. Words and no more. Suddenly, "I saw that I was naked and I hid" (Genesis 1:9).

How could it be that I never thought of my responsibility for their suffering? I am responsible, and I have an arsenal of excuses and arguments. I had no choice this matter. This is what war is about and this is the price. I hadn't been born yet; it was another Israel. Except that when I am alone, as I was with them in Jordan, I cannot and must not escape the bitter truth. I must admit it.

We have our own accounts to settle with the world, which almost never assumes responsibility for issues that relate to us. There is only one argument we cannot claim: that we were not listened to and that our lesson was not heard. The world took responsibility for the Shoah, and it did so very seriously indeed. Without the Shoah, the United Nations resolutions that brought about the establishment of Israel would not have been passed. Neither would the immediate international recognition of the new state have been granted; nor the generous German economic assistance and almost automatic support of Israeli causes. The Shoah sensitized governments and organizations to anti-Semitism and other hate crimes. Even the Catholic Church's dogmatic change of attitude toward Jews and human rights everywhere happened because of the Shoah. In contrast, we have never done anything similar for the Palestinian refugees and their descendants. We did not fulfill what we demanded of others. Therefore we must stand on the tallest mountain and declare clearly and loudly: we know that solving the Shoah refugee problem directly and indirectly caused the Palestinian refugee problem. Only then can we give our excuses and explanations: we were drowning and grabbing at straws; we were busy saving ourselves. We will tell them of our Talmudic heritage, by which we live. For example:

> Two men are walking down the road and one of them has a bottle of water. If both of them drink, both will die. If one drinks, he will reach the city. Ben Petura argued: Better for both of them drink and die so neither sees his friend die. Then Rabbi Akiva came and taught: "And your friend shall live with you," which means that your life has precedence over the life of your friend.[4]

Ben Petura's position was rejected because of the waste of precious human life and therefore Rabbi Akiva's position was accepted as a norm. We have to admit that, post-Shoah, we valued our lives because we wanted to live after so much death. We were not sufficiently sensitive to the lives of others and to the price that they paid for our salvation. Please forgive us, and together we will put an end to the unhealthy refugee mindset that torments us all. Let us stand together for our common future. We want to live in peace. Therefore let us start anew, with memories but without anger, with knowledge of the past, but with a bigger hope for the future. Most will be understood and much will be accepted, as this is how a reasonable person behaves when fighting for his life and the lives of his dear ones. What is most important is the recognition of the suffering and assuming of responsibility, even partial and belated, for the distress of the Palestinian refugees. Only with recognition and sharing will it be possible to rebuild the relations between the two great refugee cultures that came to the same piece of land to build anew from the ruins.

Although the creation of Israel led to the problem of refugees, it does not mean that Israel's existence prevents the solution. Yet the refugee problem haunts us relentlessly and is used to justify the harshest criticism of Israel by its most unabashed attackers. The heirs and descendants of our old European persecutors, who had slaughtered us and expelled us from Europe beaten and injured, take advantage of Israel's toughness and insensitivity to continue persecuting us by other means. They use the refugee problem to denounce our leadership in every possible way and try to undermine the moral basis of the Jewish people's state. The Palestinian refugee problem, born when we fled from their fathers as surviving refugees ourselves, is their most powerful argument against us.

I believe that the world and its spirit develops gradually as a chain of contradictions that complement one another and create a new reality. The chain is obvious here. Israel could not have been born without the Shoah, which crystallized the world's will to solve the Jewish problem. The Shoah supplied the masses of refugees and survivors that became Israel's human base and enabled the conversion from a haphazard territory to a viable state. Conversely, without the family of nations' recognition of a Jewish political framework, and the Jewish resolve to rebuild their national home here, the Palestinian refugee problem would not have been created.

The state was born, some refugees were taken in and others were forced out. Sixty years later, we are a state, and the ousted are still refugees with almost no hope. The victims of this war became political persecutors, using propaganda as a weapon against us everywhere on the planet. They torment us in the major capitals, in the diplomatic arenas and in the media. They have taken our place as objects of identification and empathy by do-gooders and evildoers alike. In this reversal of roles, we now hide behind the inaction of Arab leaders, who use our culpability to shield themselves from criticism. We became Goliath and they became David. So much so that the world's guilt, which was indirectly responsible for their plight, creates a whole new culture of equations that are expressed in graffiti that simplistically equates the Star of David with the Nazi swastika and Sharon with Hitler. Only a comprehensive recognition by Israel, the Arab states and the international community regarding the moral responsibility for this necessary historical event will enable the opening of hearts and minds. Once recognition is granted, technical negotiations on compensation will ensue. Restitution will be discussed in lieu of the refugees' return to their properties. My mother will not return to her home in Hebron, which became the slaughterhouse of her family; the Zaken family will not return to their home in Zaku, Kurdistan; the Cohens will not return to Cairo; the Shertoks will not return to their home near Ramallah. Likewise the Naqbas and the refugees of 1948 will not return to Jaffa, Jerusalem, Majdal, or Acre. This is life and these are the facts of life. We will recognize them, draw a line in the sand between the present and ever-present the past, and try to build a better future together.

Here for you is Israel in all its conflicting colors, paradoxical and contradictory. Israel moves in panic between the pole of belligerence and the pole of real and imagined fears that drive it to curl up like a battered child or a traumatized puppy. This is the Israel that relied on the force of its founders, now bequeathed to their descendants, the sons of refugees, compensating for the power that they never had at the time. All of us now try to live the past without using it to build a new present. Right now we are stuck between the incredible vitality that pushed us forward and our unwillingness to return to the circumstances of the past. Since we possess both power and helplessness, we move neither forward nor backward, not into Israeliness and not into Jewishness. Torn asunder, we do nothing at all.

For years Israel carried on reminding the world of the Shoah. Speeches and policies demanded the nations of the world to ensure that what happened would not happen again. We meant that it must not happen to *us:* do not allow evil to raise its head again, to persecute *Jews* again, but the world heard something else. It is common in life, and in interpersonal communication: it is not so important what I say, but what the other person hears. We cried, please save us from another Shoah, and the world heard more: No Shoah, no Holocaust, no genocide must ever happen again. This awareness slowly penetrated and became a world standard. Every evil person is automatically tagged as a new Hitler for the rest of the world to fear and loathe. The world has internalized the lesson, perhaps not completely, but undoubtedly the awareness of persecution and war crimes is much higher today that it used to be. It is by no small measure a result of our constant Shoah nagging.

The International Court of Justice tried the former Serbian president Slobodan Milošević for war crimes. His country will not be admitted to the European Union until it turns in the last of its war criminals. Likewise, the international community embargoed and economically besieged racist South Africa, once Israel's ally, and imposed cruel sanctions until its government, the last white colonial regime, surrendered. Many in the world, including a few Israelis, did much—and they could have done more—to stop the genocide in Rwanda. Colin Powell, former United States secretary of defense, personally intervened to stop the mass killings in Southern Sudan.

Almost everywhere the Shoah serves as a backdrop and metaphor, a winning argument, a lesson and a symbol for something that should never be repeated. It does not always succeed, but the Shoah of the European Jews always serves as a beacon whose light reaches the darkness far away. It is the beacon of a lesson learned and an obligation. The world expects more from itself now, and therefore this is a national success story of the highest degree. The Israeli expression "in their death they commanded us life" is becoming a reality. It is unlikely that the world would have tried to embrace peace without first knowing how far human criminality can go, in this case as far as Auschwitz and Birkenau, Treblinka and Dachau.

Then why do Israelis feel bitter? Why do we think that the world is hypocritical and does not understand us? It conducts itself according to the norms that we demanded. Now that change is happening, we are still dissatisfied. The reason may be that the world is redirecting, reflecting back to us our demand. And this is inconvenient. Just when we discovered power, and the joy of using it, just when we discovered the sweet taste of revenge, the world becomes Jewish, repenting and righteous. This is unfair. We want to be rowdy a little longer. We deserve it. We earned it in the Shoah.

Alain Finkielkraut, one of France's most visible intellectuals, has been trying in recent years to understand the hidden dimensions of anti-Semitism and the "anti-" sentiment in general. Two of his recent articles on the subject were published in the Israeli periodical *Azure,* an open-minded, right-leaning magazine that provides a bold, original voice to public debates. Finkielkraut writes:

> It is the Holocaust, then, that makes the territories occupied by Israel *the* locus of crime; it is the trauma of the destruction of European Jews that inexhaustibly fuels international sympathy for the suffering of the Palestinians. I would even say that for my correspondent to have so readily dated the scandal of the "occupation" not from the Six Day War, but from the creation of the Jewish state, the post-Hitler impulse to ignore all that came after Auschwitz must be deeply ingrained indeed. [...] Indeed, it is on the strength of their disgust for colonial, collaborationist, and fascist Europe that they now defend those whom they call "the victims of victims." Their indictment of the Jewish state goes hand in hand with their denunciation of Europe's old demons.[5]

Finkielkraut, who is a professor at the École Polytechnique in Paris, assumes that he understands the source of criticism against Israel and then tries to cancel it, writing: "The Palestinian cause has provided Humanity, which is weary of apologizing for having abandoned six million Jews to their deaths, the unhoped-for opportunity to relieve itself of the burden of repentance."[6]

It seems like a right-wing position in left-wing disguise. Indeed there is much hypocrisy in comparing Israel and her deeds in the occupied territories to the ultimate evil, but to go all the way to granting Israel a clean bill of morality is going too far. There is a middle ground. The world is indeed hypocritical, shallow, and opportunistic in its attitude toward us, yet the criticism is justified simply because we are not right. We are not as bad as we are depicted by our critics, but we are not as good as we describe ourselves. The truth suffers because it is surrounded by lies. The Israeli leaders and people delude themselves, and we all collude in an attempt to deceive the world. But just because we no longer value truth, I cannot ignore Finkielkraut's opinions. His temporary blindness when he defends us unequivocally does not dim his insight. I accept this piercing statement:

> What astonishes the Jew...is not that he is not accused of being a Jew but the opposite, of his treason of Judaism...as if he were expelled from himself and was marked like Cain.

Israel's policy in the land of our patriarchs desecrates the heritage of our fathers Abraham, Isaac, and Jacob. True, we are no longer Abel, always being murdered by his brother, because we now have power of our own and because international norms have changed. Nor are we Cain, who kills just for the joy of killing. But can we agree that Cainism has increased recently in the Jewish psyche? The Shoah and the establishment of our state created a mechanism that necessitates force and obsessive defense at any cost for every Jew wherever he is. The three weeks of anxiety before the Six-Day War intensified and the 1973 was perpetuated the obsession with the destruction of the temple, which we carry with us since the year 70 A.D. When Abraham called out to God, "Far be it, shall the judge of all the land not do justice,"[7] he was sounding not only a protest to save Sodom and Gomorrah, the cities of crime and evil, from destruction and annihilation by the furious Almighty. It was a testament for generations. Today we are not just judges of the land but also its masters, but our judgment is harsh, unjust and merciless. We still indulge ourselves with the moral parity among the children of Abraham our father, Esau our uncle, and Jacob, our father and thief of his brother's birthright. "The voice is of Jacob and the hands are of Esau," we like to quote, as if to say that the voice of prayer and righteousness is ours, but the hairy hands fit for hunting and killing are not, as they are of the "non-Jews," those who are as evil as Esau. Therefore we must turn to the Midrash or comparative interpretation, which contrasts the qualities of the voice with those of the hands.

> The voice is the voice of Jacob: There is no beneficial prayer that does not have something of Jacob's seed; and the hands are

the hands of Esau: There is no war that wins that does not have
something of Esau's seed.[8]

In other words, the meaning of Jewish war ethics is critical: The more we
fight and win, the more our hands become like Esau's and our voice less like
Jacob's. So it was in the ancient Talmudic times and much more so today.
What is that moral voice that is disappearing? It is Jacob's inner voice on
his way to his last confrontation with his brother Esau. "And Jacob was very
afraid and he was distressed."[9] The verse tells us of human anxiety, so familiar to us, of the soldier on his way to battle. But the Midrash searches further, as it often does, for something beyond and between the words *afraid*
and *distressed* to expand the meaning: "*Afraid* lest he is killed and *distressed*
lest he kills the others." The Jacobean fighter, the historic Jew, bears responsibility not just to himself and his fears; his responsibility extends to the
lives of his enemies and rivals. Do we still feel this responsibility?

Again we have a paradox. We fight to break the vicious cycle, which was
our portion since Esau, Pharaoh, Goliath, Adrian, Vespasian, Khmelnytsky,
Hitler, and the rest of the supervillains. But the more we fight them, the
more we feel heavy handed, like them, like Esau. We have forgotten the
obligations that our earlier generations took upon themselves. We treat
"them" as if we have never vowed in Hillel the Elder's brilliant summation
of the Torah: Do not do onto others what is hateful to you. We hated it,
and we are doing it, sometimes much too joyously. Is it any wonder no one
wants to be our friend anymore when we practice expropriations, injustice
in the military courts, abuse, roadblocks, food shortages, and, worst of all,
contempt for Arab life.

We were so adamant in demanding that the Shoah never happen again
that we did not notice what was happening under our noses. The Bible and
later sources command us dozens of times to treat the non-Jews among us
with sensitivity. The Midrash compares mistreatment of the resident to the
taboo on eating pork: "And you shall not harass the resident stranger nor
pressure him as you were strangers in the land of Egypt. Do not harass him,
in words, and do not pressure him, in money…And you have pig in your
mouth and still speak words against me?"[10] This means that the commandment to treat the minorities among us fairly and sensitively is as important
as the ban on eating pork.

Is it possible that we can be "Jewish" only when we don't have liberty and independence? So far, it is an undeniable fact that from the moment we had a state "like all the other nations," we wanted to be gentiles like them. While they in turn are already willing to be a bit more Jewish than they were.

＋⟫━·━⟪＋

Father, where are you? I want to start from the beginning. Differently.

CHAPTER 7

BALANCING HEROISM AND THE SHOAH

THE HIGH POINT OF MY SEVENTH GRADE SCHOOL TRIP WAS the visit to kibbutz Yad Mordechai shortly after the Six-Day War. In Jerusalem, the windows in my neighborhood were still covered with brown adhesive tape that we had affixed during the three tense weeks of waiting, which had unnerved my mother. The tape was supposed to hold the glass together in case a bomb shattered it, so we would not get cut. We did so because "experience teaches." This teacher said that what happened in 1948 would repeat itself. Car headlights were still painted dark blue to dim them at night so as not to be seen by bombers in the sky, just as in Dresden. The sandbags in front of buildings were beginning to crumble, and we, as boys, used them for war games. The Old City had been opened and we searched it for bargain-price switchblade knives imported from China. They had wooden handles, tin patterns, and scary edges, like the curved Arab knives. To us, the war seemed distant already, and the farther the war, the closer we were to Yad Mordechai. There we looked, amazed, at the perforated water tower, a relic of the 1948 War of

Independence, and near it, as if emanating from its top, the monument of Mordechai Anilevich, commander of the Warsaw ghetto uprising. I visited the kibbutz again as trainee during the IDF squad-leader course, then again during the officer's course, yet again during the tour guide course, and during annual trips with my children. The place never changes at all, the hero is still entangled in the siege thicket, and I still learn from this experience. The meaning of the place, however, has become deeper. The heroism of the ghetto rebels, said the guide during my first trip, was the heroic spirit that founded our nation. I bought the Zionist goods without much rummaging and checking. I loved my childhood heroes, leaned on them and trusted them, knowing they would always be available to me. They included the legendary IDF soldier Meir Har-Zion and his comrades, the heroes of Unit 101; and Mordechai Anilevich, of whom I learned from Leon Uris's book *Mila 18*. Other heroes were the Maccabees and the Hasmoneans, the Massada faithful and Bar Kokhva's brave fighters. The historic truth, if history can be regarded as truth, came later, bit by bit; it slowly seeped in, eroding the fanatical Zionist patina. I experienced it, as did my friends.

The influence of heroic legends on everyday life became apparent to me in one occasion when I was serving as chairman of the Jewish Agency and the Zionist Executive. I wanted to cut the budgets of the youth movements, which were also financed by the national institutions. "You can't do this. This is anti-Zionist," the Likud representative objected, shouting. He was serving then as the Betar commissioner, the senior leader of the right-wing youth movement founded by Vladimir Zeev Zhabotinsky.

I told him that I myself was also a graduate of a youth movement, the Zionist religious Bnei Akiva. "Don't I know what Zionism is?" I asked him.

"We have to maintain the youth movement," he hollered. "The youth movements rebelled in the Warsaw ghetto and saved our national honor. The Shoah can happen again. Who will then fight back?"

I was speechless. It couldn't be that in the last few years of the twentieth century one would use such an argument when discussing a budget cut. I asked for time to decide, and then used a tactic borrowed from Levi Eshkol, my favorite prime minister. I compromised and compromised until they accepted my position. I recalled the incident with the Betar representative on another occasion, while I was attending a relative's funeral. She was a Shoah survivor. The funeral took place in a southern kibbutz near Yad

Mordechai. Among the mourners was a teenage boy, who wore a sweatshirt that read "The journey to discover the roots of the Zionist Revolution and the Zionist youth movements' rebellion in Poland."

In the face of such a slogan I could not hold back.

"The roots of the Zionist revolution started hundreds of years, or dozens of years at least, before the Warsaw ghetto uprising," I commented to him at the end of the funeral. "And in any case, the Polish uprising was not only driven by the youth movements."

"Who are you?" he asked.

"My name is Avrum Burg," I answered, using my nickname.

"Oh, you're the famous Burg. Then you're a post-Zionist, maybe even anti-Zionist. I'm not even surprised by your comment," he retorted, ending the discussion about the controversial statement on his chest. Indeed, there are no easy funerals.

There are still people who believe this nonsense. They still live by the myth created by the founders of the state, who take false credit for the desperate uprising, grouping Warsaw with Dgania and Kinneret. They removed the Shoah aspects and dimensions from the rebellion of despair, from its communal aspects and monstrous dimensions, and added it to the portfolio of Israeli legends, making it part of the Zionist ethos. Why did Israel adopt the Warsaw rebels posthumously when the pre-state Israel did so little for them in at the time—if anything could be done—against the forces of death and destruction?

As the great calamity in Europe was unfolding, the leaders of pre-state Israel had two options. One was to resign their public posts forever, as the national leadership had proved itself to be inept. The second was to claim ownership of the little that was done, to magnify it into an ethos of the national Zionist narrative. They chose to use deception and planted two historical misunderstandings in our minds.

One error was that their uprisings and heroism were equivalent in size and intensity to the Shoah and its victims. Shoah Remembrance Day was altered to become a remembrance day for heroes and a day of some contempt, almost official scorn, of the Shoah and its helpless victims. The second error was that the uprising in the ghettos belonged to us, the natives of the Land of Israel. We were programmed to believe that the Shoah belonged to Hitler, the slaughterer, and to the small-town Jews, the sacrificed. Heroism belonged to us, the modern Maccabbees, the Hasmoneans' scions, Bar Kokhva's descendants.

Lieutenant General Ehud Barak, then chief of the IDF staff, paid a visit to the Auschwitz-Birkenau camps about the time of the 1992 Shoah Remembrance Day. He gave one of his most beautiful speeches there, a cynicism-free speech of pure Israeliness. The crooked axioms that fed his mind and ours are glaring. He said: "At the end of March 1942, gas chambers were operated here in full force. And we, the soldiers of the Israeli Defense Forces, arrived here fifty years later, perhaps fifty years too late."[1] These words must be read again and again in order to understand the depth of ignorance that created this text. Barak seemed to suggest that only a delay prevented us from liberating the camps. It was a glitch, no more than tardiness. The fallacy is that at the time, Israel did not have an army or military capability; we were not even a minor player in the world stage. The chief of staff had his times mixed up, and the same happened to all of us. Many of us believe that the state of Israel could have, and should have, saved more of the slaughtered Jews of Europe. Except for one simple fact: the state did not exist then. Furthermore, it is unlikely the state would have been established if not for the heaps of human ash that enabled modern Jewish nationhood. The Shoah's timing was paradoxically advantageous from the Zionist point of view. It propelled Israel into statehood even though the Zionists could not save the Shoah victims. Had full salvation materialized, maybe the state would have not been founded; Israel did rise from the ashes. Barak's beautiful words, later in the speech, are true and accurate:

> Like a flash of lightning, the Shoah illuminated the essence of the Return to Zion as a struggle for our very existence as a people, on the edge of the abyss...the insight that the struggle for the Land is not merely about the space that is between our back and the sea, but about our very right to stand as a people on the "end of line" upon which lies the entire Jewish fate.[2]

Barak's words sounded exciting to me at the time. I liked his message and did not pay attention to the details. Only now, when I look for the distinction between the meaningful and the frivolous, do I discover the Israeli DNA's defects as Barak represented so well. His words that day did not evaporate in the frosty Polish winter like the breaths of the prisoners and the dead; they moved with the speed of sound and a decade later, they were re-expressed in an extravagant way when the Israeli Air Force jets buzzed over the cursed place, the ashen planet of Auschwitz-Birkenau.

An impressive ceremony by the former Allied powers took place on the sixtieth anniversary of the liberation of the death camps. On the ground, Israel's Air Chief Brigadier General Ido Nehushtan placed a wreath on the ovens in memory of more than a million Jews who had walked here on their last path. At the same time, three IAF F-15 fighter jets flew above the barracks, the bunk beds, the marching grounds, and the ashes. The planes saluted their commander on the ground and the dead under his feet. Colonel Shai Gilad, native of Kibbutz Yifat, flew one of planes. His grandfather and grandmother, whom he had never known, were reportedly among the victims. He carried with him in the cockpit the documents of his lost family, given to him by the Yad Vashem Institute for the memorial flight.

Israeli journalists interviewed the pilots after they returned from their mission. In one interview, a journalist for a periodical of a Kibbutz movement asked the pilot, "Did your flight above Auschwitz-Birkenau take place sixty years too late?"

The pilot, one of the finest native-born Israelis, replied naively, in the spirit of Barak's speech:

> It reminds me of the sentence that Ehud Barak said ten years ago when he, as [IDF] chief of staff, visited the death camps. "We arrived fifty years too late." I assume that it was not easy to bomb a camp like this. Also, a targeted bombing would have not prevented the Shoah, and many innocent victims would have died as a result...This act was meant to unite the heart around the ethos of the memory of the Shoah and it should not be taken any further.[3]

I disagree with him and wish to take this further. The chief of staff and his pilot, together with the Israeli masses, anachronistically identify military uniforms and the Israeli armed forces as an integral part of the Jewish history of the Shoah period. But the Shoah happened before the IDF was formed. We did not just arrive late, as we keep saying, as if it were simply tardiness due to technical difficulties, a scheduling conflict. We did not arrive and could not have arrived. We did not exist and therefore could not aid and rescue. It is nonsense to say otherwise. The intimidating flight mission above the death camps was a show of bravado and arrogance, in the same manner of the supersonic boom-producing flights of folly above the Syrian presidential palace, or the low-altitude sorties that scare shepherds and refugees in southern Lebanon. It is a way of showing off, and it underlines the difference between us and them. It is like saying to the dead, after their unheroic, unimpressive, pathetic deaths, that to us, the Israelis, it would have not have happened. We speak not just to them, but also to ourselves: We are pilots and generals and veterans of war; we are not lambs for slaughter. This artificial, technological sign of respect that we give them is another certificate of shame that they receive against their will. Indeed they did not die as soldiers but as minorities, persecuted for being different.

Does the military ceremony produce identification and empathy for the cause of their deaths? Not at all. The words of the former chief of staff, and the extravagant flyover, express nothing but our own ego, our sheer joy in force, the narcissism of physical heroism. They contain almost nothing that is sincere and compassionate that would connect us to the dead by way of identification, and that would recognize their disaster as our own. Our folly is best expressed in *Air Force Magazine*:

> The idea to execute a flyover above Auschwitz is the fulfillment of a personal dream for Air Chief Brigadier General Amir Eshel. "This is a fifteen-year old dream," says Amir. "This is the most meaningful expression for the revival of this people. As an air force, we are the most tangible expression of strength for the people, and nobody can express this better than us...We tailored a plan, like the Air Force plans a mission...The more you look at the mission's details, the more you see how operationally complex it was. As in every military operation, the first stage is definition of the target. There were two central questions that we dealt with," Eshel explains. "One, how do we execute this from a professional point of view? The second, what national and emotional elements do we want to emphasize? Where do we want to pass? From which direction? How do we produce the best picture? What text accompanies the event? And, of course, who will be flying?"[4]

All we have left to do is to announce over the unit's radio network: "We got Auschwitz-Birkenau."

The founders of the state and many of their sons and daughters had a vital need to own this heroism because it creates the sense that pre-state Israel was fighting for its life alongside the ghetto rebels. An artificial equation was formed, which forged an illusion that what had happened in Europe was half Shoah and half heroism. At the same time, a tacit message was conveyed, according to which the Shoah half belonged to the Jews, the Diasporic Yids, the degenerative, rabbinical types. Opposite this was the heroism half, which belonged to the true Zionists, the ghetto rebels and the disciples of the youth movements. From them it is a short distance to the Palmah, the pre-state Israeli militia, and later on to the IDF Special Forces, the Nahal Pioneering Combat Youth, and rest of the armed forces. The Shoah belongs to the crooked Jews; heroism to the erect Zionists, and this is how we share them equally. In effect, the Zionist's claim a dispro-portionate share of history and created an Israeli version of Holocaust denial. We did not see, most likely did not want to see, the other Jews, the masses, the overwhelming majority, who did not rebel and fight back. They were just ordinary people, like us, that the Germans and their collabora-tors humiliated and drove to a terrifyingly wretched fate, piled in pits and stacked in mass graves. Those who survived did so in ways that defy the laws of nature. We did not know how the other Jews lived, but glorified endlessly the few who took up arms. Our boast of relatively minor hero-ism silenced all the other voices for shame. This silence is like denial: that which is not spoken does not exist. Without words we effectively erased the experience and sacrifice of the millions of Europe's Jews who are no more. We did not acknowledge them in their life and we became, in effect, their deniers after their death.

We have not yet been cured of this disease of denial. Indeed schools teach of the days of darkness and fear, but these are lessons about life out-side life. This is reminiscent of the current denial of Diaspora Jews. Who among us really knows about the Jews outside Israel, who are the majority of our people? What do we Israelis know of the lives, dreams and fears of American Jews? What did we learn of the North African Jews who emi-grated to France, or the Latin American Jews? Not a clue, and worse—we simply do not care. "They should either come and live here," the late President Ezer Weizman once told me angrily, "or they should go to hell." This was the thinking when he grew up in the British Mandate Palestine-Land of Israel, thus they were ignored during the Shoah, and this is still the sentiment today. If they are well, they do not interest us at all; if their condition worsens, it only justifies our choices.

This is catastrophic Zionism at its worst: what is bad for the Jews is better for Zionism. In this sense, I am not just a post-Zionist, but an anti, anti-catastrophist Zionist. I believe wholeheartedly that if we do not establish modern Israeli identity on foundations of optimism, faith in humans and full trust in the family of nations, we have no chance of existing and surviving in the long run—not as a society in a state, not as a state in the world, and not as a nation in the future. The era of fearful Judaism and paranoid Zionism is over. The time for integration in a free, positive world has come. The faith of the Jewish people in the world and in humanity must be rehabilitated.

Our obsessive need for heroism is caused by a great weakness and a lack of confidence. We no longer rely on unequivocal inner strength. Military heroism, like many physical manifestations of force, has become part of the nation's obsession with its appearance. The hero develops his muscles, admires his reflection in the pond, the house mirrors, and other shiny surfaces. Israeli belligerent heroism, and the unnecessary brutality that comes with it, are integral parts of a narcissistic nation that adores itself. Isn't narcissism caused by lack of self-confidence? After too many years of the world's indifference, the heroism of the rebels and the fighters created a pleasant illusion of normalcy, of historical continuity and a heritage of battle, struggle and heroism, like all the other nations whose family we wished to join. The French had Joan of Arc, and we have Hannah Czenes. The English had Robin Hood in the Sherwood Forest and we have Yitzhak Sade in the Carmel and Menashe forests. The Swiss have Wilhelm Tell, who shot the apple and never missed, and we have one-eyed Moshe Dayan, who lost the eye to a sniper's bullet "when in Syria the Palmah marched," as the song goes.

The missing link between Bar Kokhva (A.D. 135), the last physical hero of the ancient Jewish history, and the heroes of 1948 and the later struggles is found in the ghetto rebels. As a military event, the Warsaw ghetto uprising was not as important compared the multitude of battles in World War II. When, several years ago, an IDF commander said that in order to enter and control a refugee camp we needed to study and learn the doctrine used by the Germans to gain control and occupy the Warsaw ghetto, he caused a great, hypocritical protest. Saying this, he revealed some very precise axioms. The first is the overt and covert association between what happened there and what happens here: moral deterioration and its extensions. As I have written many times about our actions in the territories, this is not the Holocaust! It is not all good, either. The commander's technical truth was no less important than the ethics of it: the Warsaw ghetto was in essence no more than one big refugee camp. This is not an extraordinary military story or operation. Nothing that the few brave rebels did could have shortened the colossal war or brought down the evil Nazi dictatorship. Not one Jewish life was saved. The rebels rebelled, the Germans suppressed, and at the same time other Jews were methodically and mercilessly exterminated. A group of Jewish youth in Warsaw rose to fight for their lives. Against all odds, they acquired weapons and for an entire month in the spring of 1943 held back the German military and even inflicted losses on their enemy. But the end of the month also meant the end of the ghetto and its heroes. The densely populated ghetto was ravaged, burned, and ground to oblivion. The fighters met their deaths in every possible way: on barricades, in close combat, in the last battle at the command bunker on 18 Mila Street, and there were those who shot themselves dead lest they become prisoners of the Nazis. Others suffocated from the gas that the Germans poured into the trenches, and only a few escaped and fled to Warsaw's Aryan quarters and zigzagged their way through Europe.

As modest as the victories were, the ghetto rebellion became the symbol of light that defeats darkness. We did not understand the Shoah then like we do today, but we understood heroism right away. The rebels have names and faces. It is not an anonymous industry of genocide, a concept beyond human comprehension with inconceivable numbers. It is a contained, human, and heroic battle. The Warsaw ghetto uprising caught the Jewish and the world's imagination and at once became an equal component of the Shoah-and-heroism equation, half and half. The heroism is ours, of the Israelis, and the Shoah is theirs, of the Diasporic Jews. They are from Auschwitz, and we are from Warsaw.

Following the Shoah, Zionism became the movement of the winning majority. All the other Jewish ideological movements were destroyed by the Nazis or silenced forever behind the walls of the Soviet bloc. Only the Zionist movement remained free, outside in the West. By then it had the tools of a state-in-waiting. All its resources and skills were harnessed to erect and build the foundations of the state. And not least of all: It invented and aggrandized myths and legends and misrepresented them. Shamelessly. The end was holy and the means justified. As Woody Allen once said: "If the end doesn't justify the means, what does?"

Thus the rebels who did not fit the Zionist stereotype were deleted from the private and collective memory. We were not taught, for example, that the uprising was overseen by an umbrella organization that included everyone who was in the ghetto, all the Jewish political parties, many of whom were socialist Bundists and anti-Zionist Communists. They hid from us that the uprising would not have been possible without the support of the community's institutions, leaders, the non-Zionist Jewish Joint Relief organization and even the non-Jewish Polish Underground. The roles of these organizations were concealed and silenced. Literature by the non-Zionist Jewish partners in the rebellion was not translated into Hebrew. Polish writer Hannah Krall wrote a book, *To Steal a March on God*,[5] which tells the story of Marek Edelman, a Polish Jew, who was a socialist and non-Zionist and served as a deputy to the adored Mordechai Anilevich—a fact that has not been widely publicized. He loved life and was very much non-Zionist; he was a Jewish humanitarian who later became a physician. Marek Edelman represented the Bund, an anti-Zionist Jewish Socialist movement, in the rebellion leadership. As the uprising was suppressed, Edelman managed to flee the ghetto through the sewage system with some of the surviving fighters, and later participated in the Warsaw Uprising of 1944. After the war he remained in Poland, studied medicine and practiced cardiology in Lodz. He became a member of the Solidarity movement and voiced his opinions on issues of human rights. In 1988 he received the highest Polish decoration, the White Eagle Order, from Polish president Aleksander Kwaśniewski. He is still alive.

Immediately after the war, Edelman wrote his story,[6] a very different interpretation of what took place during Passover 1943 in Warsaw, Poland. The book was not translated into Hebrew; the Zionist censorship kept the book outside the national consciousness. He was not a Zionist! Poland was his motherland and he fulfilled his role as second-in-command on behalf of the non-Zionist Bund.

Edelman told Krall that he thought suicide should not have been committed in the 18 Mila Street bunker. "It should have not been done, even though it was a very powerful symbol. Life should not be sacrificed for symbols," he said. He was critical of Jewish combat abilities and claimed that the uprising could have been more effective, killing more Germans and saving more rebels. He acknowledged the strength of German soldiers as a fact. These are dissonant notes in the concert of heroism.

Because no one was willing to hear from him the naked truth:

> Could this really be called an uprising?...It was, after all, a question of not letting them slaughter you when your turn came. It was merely choosing how to die...Humanity agreed that to die with a weapon in hand is more beautiful than without a weapon, so we conceded.[7]

The monument to Anilevich at Yad Mordechai depicts an athletic man holding a hand grenade. Natan Rapoport, the sculptor, created the hero's image as a conclusion, memorial, and monument to all that embodies our attitude toward the Shoah. Anilevich the rebel is the symbol of those days. Larger than life, a giant cast in bronze, he is all energy and might, power, heroism, and hope. The image of Anilevich in 1943 shadows the perforated water tower in 1948, leaving the visitor with a distorted sense of concepts and dimensions. How could it be that the Shoah looks so good, while the Israeli resurrection looks like a tower full of holes that will never hold water?

Edelman did not buy into the Zionist ownership of the uprising and its conversion in the myth sequence that may have or may have not happened, from Yosef Trumpledor and Tel Hai to the Warsaw ghetto. For him, the uprising was not Zionist, but universal, part of the universal plight of humanity against satanic men:

> The uprising was the logical consequence of four years of resistance by a population that was confined in inhuman conditions, humiliated, despised, that was treated...like a population of subhumans. In spite of the conditions...the ghetto residents organized their lives, as much as they could, according to the highest European values. At the time when the criminal occupying government prevented from them the right to education, culture, knowledge, life, a respectable death, they built underground universities, schools, aid institutions and press. These actions, that caused resistance against anything that threatened the right to an honorable life, resulted in the uprising. The uprising was the ultimate means

to refuse inhuman life and death conditions; the ultimate way of struggle against barbarity and for the maintenance of human dignity.[8]

Edelman's book was not translated into Hebrew until 2001, and Krall's book didn't find an Israeli publisher, even though it was published in many languages throughout the world. Zionist Israel did not tolerate divergence from its canon. In the last part of the twentieth century Edelman and his memoirs became a litmus test for the Zionist and post-Zionist attitude toward the Shoah. I doubt that this was Edelman's intention. He lived by his Bundist faith, the heritage of his mother, who sent him to the Bund's youth movement. He did not compromise his faith under the Nazi boot nor under the Soviet hammer and sickle. Daniel Blatman, his Hebrew editor, aptly described Edelman's place in history:

> Edelman did not become the ultimate hero of the Warsaw ghetto after the war. But then, as today, he is the hero and the voice of the hundreds of thousands quiet, unknown heroes who were not commemorated in studies or in memorials.[9]

We did not listen to the poet of the period, our own Natan Alterman, who wrote the poem "Memorial Day and the Rebels," published in *Davar,* his daily, on Shoah Remembrance Day, 1954. The poem created a great controversy. On one side were those who wanted the uprising to become the temple of Zionist heroism, and on the other, Alterman spoke for those who understood the much greater complexity of the matter. Alterman reinforced his arguments in prose:

> One foundation of that picture which the rebellion created...is presented by us...as the sole response...so natural and righteous that all other forces and instincts are rejected by us from it and are intertwined in the same veil of blindness and error or of treason and crime.[10]

A few years ago, Ehud Barak, then still a promising prime ministerial candidate, aroused passions when he said that if he were a Palestinian teenager, he would have joined a terrorist organization for his land's independence.

Such a remark is natural to a native who grew up in Israel and knows only weapons and insurgency as the sole instruments of national expression. As for myself, if I lived in a ghetto today, I am not certain that I would resort to arms. I would ask myself until my last moment on earth whether rebelling is like lighting a flame to the gods of war; once lit, the flames might go out of control and destroy everybody. I would have pondered day and night the same question that must have tormented the people in the ghettos from day one of the siege to the end: "Can we take responsibility for all Jews, risking their lives, and effectively aid the destruction process if we fail?" It seems more likely to me that I would have survived or died by my faith against armed resistance. I can imagine standing beside Mordechai Tenenboim, the young commander of Ghetto Bialystock, who said with supreme restraint during a meeting with the Ghetto chiefs:

> "I tell the assembly that if an *Akzion* (deportation) takes place ... we will not respond. We will sacrifice the six thousand three hundred Jews to save the remaining thirty-five thousand." In another instance he testified: "We knew that the fate of the Bialystock Jews was annihilation, to the last. We sacrificed the first thousand to lengthen the lives [not to save the lives, as this was impossible] of one tenth of Poland's Jewry for another month or two. Each day, in the current situation in the front and in the country, may bring salvation. We said 'no.' We are responsible. Had we not, not a single Jew would have remained here."[11]

If I was a Palestinian today, I would put down my weapon and hug Israel in the only embrace from which it cannot free itself: the embrace of peace. If I were a young Jew in the Shoah, I would have probably been torn between the seductive hand grenade of Anilevich and my own inner conscience, and finally chosen Mahatma Gandhi's spiritual resources and tried to ferment nonviolent civil disobedience throughout Europe. This is how I think and this is how I educate my children.

This is not what I thought when I grew up and joined the IDF's paratrooper brigade, proud of my officer rank, paratrooper wings, and the red beret. In those days I felt that I was continuing the path of Anilevich, Abba Kovner, Antek Zuckerman, and Hannah Czenes. Today I look back differently. If I had had to fight for my life—fall on my sword, throw a grenade, or draw a gun—I would not have wanted to be part of Israeli defiance. I would have rebelled as a European Jew, a child of the Diaspora, and then sought, in Alterman's words, "to return and mix in the dark with the history of the masses of the people of Israel"—to become a universal Jew, not an arrogant Israeli separatist.

Why was it wrong to accept the Jews of Europe? Why did we, the Israelis, refuse them as they were? They were ordinary Jews who were not born to become fighters or symbols, heroes or myths. They were simple people, grocers, small-time merchants, leather workers, scholars, employees, parents, and children, talented and average. Nothing in their personal background and nothing in the collective Jewish history trained them to withstand Hitler's mania and his collaborators' obsessions. They were just like any other people under occupation. The countries of the world refused to open their gates to the Jewish refugees, including neutral Switzerland, Britain, and even the United States of America, Canada, and Australia. We received the emasculated, displaced survivors, but locked our hearts to them. We judged them harshly, too harshly. We maintained the ideological, mental and spiritual disconnect that the Zionist pre-state Israel imposed on its Diaspora origins. We forced ourselves not to understand their experience and its context. We adopted the phrase that Abba Kovner, a leader in the Vilnius ghetto uprising, coined, "like lambs to slaughter," to describe the slaughter of one thousand years of Jewishdom in Europe. We found fault in their passivity, which was no different from the historical passivity of Jews since ancient times. Zionism became the active; Diasporic Jewry the passive. We elevated our status at their expense. From the outset it is simple, but in fact it is damaging—another mysterious complexity in the maze of Jewish history. The refugees who came here were called "human dust." Each one became a living testimony to early Zionism's failure and its inherent contradictions. As we know, when arguments are weak, the volume is raised. The dismal near past was now present, and the new Israeli future was tattooed in blue numbers on the arms of the newcomers. The arrogant, boastful sons of the land could not withstand the Arab invasion to ensure the security of the just-proclaimed. We needed the human remnants as cannon fodder, lest we too be ejected and displaced. The refugees, who came here by no choice of their own and ours, became the cold water that washed the young smooth face of the newborn state.

Both the graduate of the Shoah and the alumni of heroism logically concluded that the entire world was against them. This was another point in the historical mental sequence of the Jewish people, who viewed themselves in a constant conflict with the world, from our first instant to this very moment. Our language, Hebrew, is Ivrit, after Abraham the Ivri. *Ivri* is derived from *ever,* meaning the other side. Abraham the Ivri means that he was born across the river, the Euphrates, and therefore belongs to the Western Semitic family of tribes. This is what it says in the text, although it is interpreted differently in the later Jewish studies. The Midrash explains, "Rabbi Yehuda says the whole world is one passage across and Abraham is one passage across."[12] It was so from ancient times on, that the world was on one side and the Hebrews on another, and Hitler reiterated this existential point, which is now a well-seeded post-Shoah belief. One of the greatest hits by an Israeli band, Lahakat Pikud Dizengof, named after Tel Aviv's most Parisian street, is called "The Entire World Is against Us." It is self-evident, is it not?

Thus it came to pass that Israel is the Shoah's only legitimate daughter. One part of the argument is directed at us: Nothing serves better as a common denominator to unite the people than an external enemy. And because one of the Shoah's legacies is the vow *"Never Again,"* "No more Auschwitz," as Barak concluded his speech at the death camp, we could always be recruited to fight any enemy, real or imagined. Always, to the end of time, as enemies do not end, they only alternate. The other part of the argument that Israel is the daughter of the Shoah is directed outward, both to the Jews of the Diaspora and the non-Jews in the world. Its essence is an endless extortion by emotional manipulation that is self-replenishing.

The Israelis repeatedly elect generals and security officials to lead us. Is this meant to deter the Arab enemy or to pacify ourselves? Clearly it is to allay our built-in fears and cover for our weaknesses. The leadership of generals serves today as the best response against the Jewish weakness during the European destruction and throughout Jewish history. My late father once described his boss, Yitzhak Rabin, general, ambassador, minister, and prime minister, as a "retroactive activist." So indeed we all are. We choose retroactive leadership, as most of our lives and energy are derived from a past which we haunt again and again. We do not see a future, hence we have no need for a leadership for the future.

Unfortunately, the few times we chose civilian leaders, they were assimilated into the patterns of the past and did not succeed in changing them. The late Levi Eshkol led Israel in the Six-Day War, simultaneously the most successful and most damaging war in our history. Ehud Olmert and Amir Peretz, as prime minister and defense minister respectively, acted early in their terms as phobia-ridden arch-generals, sending the IDF to fight the second Lebanon War, and did not act like reasonable civilians, as they should have. Perhaps one day we will rid ourselves of the constant paranoia and the troops will return to their barracks, as Herzl envisioned, and the generals will not fill the halls of power. When this happens, civil leadership will look to the future, not to past traumas and threats, and we will be rid of anti-pogrom and anti-Shoah walls and minefields.

The same tantalizing emotions were repeated in the 1990s. I was then deeply involved in the struggle to repatriate Jewish property and the dormant Jewish accounts in Swiss banks held since the Shoah. As chairman of the Jewish Agency and member of the myriad committees and organizations, I received periodic reports on the media coverage of the issues. The world media never stopped discussing these issues. Everything was covered from all possible angles: Switzerland and Germany, the Jews and money, banks and the war industry, the property and funds of Eastern European Jews, the Shoah economy, and so on endlessly. In contrast, the Israeli media was almost silent, which is a paradox considering the recent over-reporting of the Shoah in our lives. More than one senior journalists told us: drop the subject. I remember a bold headline in a major daily: "Burg—Leave the Swiss Alone." Even when the negotiations with the Swiss banks concluded, the Israeli press coverage remained thin, and much of it expressed hostility to the givers and the receiving survivors. Looking back now, the Israeli media treated the subject by looking at it from behind, from the past. There was a feeling that the negotiations on Jewish property were revealing something of the ordinary life of the European Jews, the human, natural and normal. The Jews saved kopecks and crowns, marks and zlotys and deposited them for a rainy day. Not the heroic, pioneering Jews, but the simple folk. Restitution negotiations involved an examination of the life of the prosperous and wonderful Jewry until the days of its eradication; a glance back at Jewish normalcy that was not explicitly Zionist, and even anti-Zionist, opposing the gathering of the Jews into one place. The Israeli press coverage of the 1990s was consistent with that of embryonic Israel during the Shoah: it continued to show judgmental skepticism of everything that was from the Shoah. Because the money and the property belonged to the Shoah and its Jews, not to Israel and the ghetto rebels, recipients were treated as if they were looting German army soldiers and SS officers that we had just defeated in battle. The small details of money and property did not align with the myths of weapons, struggle, uprising and heroism. An Israeli officer would not loot, would he?

In time, reality overcame the Israeli public's aversion. Retrospectively we can clearly see that the 1990s were a decade of transition from the mythology of the early state to the obsessive journeys to the scenes of crime. It was a more universal Jewish decade, and much less so Israeli or Zionist.

The two emotions wrestle inside us, and we are confused. Heroes or persecuted? Resistance fighters or perished victims? Slaughtering shepherds or bound lambs? Disoriented and lost. Every hiker knows the basic rule of navigation: If you lose your way, do not persist in your error. Go back to the last point of certainty and restart your course. Somewhere between the over-heroism of then and the over-Shoahism of now we got lost. We need to return to a point of certainty in the past, know where we turned the wrong way and try to get on another course, a better one. To understand the wrong turn we took, we need to go back to the 1960s, the Eichmann trial, the Six-Day War, and all that lies in between.

My mother told us about Hebron where our grandfather rented an apartment from his Arab neighbor. In his old age the Arab bought a young Turkish wife. The Turk had two sons with her, Yasser and Shaqer. One day, one of the boys fell ill and needed penicillin or some other special medicine to recover. That night the doctors said that his soul would leave his body and return to its Creator. My grandfather sat next to his bed, prayed and read Psalms. And "obviously" in the morning the boy's temperature had dropped, and he recovered. In the summer of 1929, my grandfather's old Arab neighbor was in the vineyards, picking the lovely Hebron grapes. As was the custom of farmers back then, he spent the night in the field, like Boaz in the Book of Ruth, in order to till the land until dark and wake before first light to return to his toil.

When the mobs began rioting, his wife sent her son to call him back from the field. When he returned, she ordered him to stand at the gate and defend his Jewish tenants. He was wounded by the rioters' daggers and sharp blades but did not budge from the gate. Half my mother's family was at the synagogue and were butchered cruelly at the Sabbath's high noon (save two, my uncle Hanaya and my cousin Shlomo, who were hidden under the corpses and were saved). The other half of my mother's family, including her, found refuge in my grandfather's house, believing that the Creator would defend the rabbi's house. Everyone who had sought refuge in my grandfather's house were saved by the Arab landlord and his Turkish wife--we owe them our lives. This is how the story was told and retold. At home, in memorial ceremonies, in the media, while entertaining guests-- fascinating, surprising, painful, but devoid of almost any emotion.

I recently watched a television program produced by my daughter, where my mother told the story of her life in Jerusalem. The interviewer, a young religious woman with rightist views, asked my mother why she didn't return to live in Hebron. My mother interrupted her. "Hebron is trauma, Jerusalem is where my childhood began. . . " and that's when I knew what my mother had felt all those years. Hebron is trauma, and my father and the rest of us are the recovery.

After many years, the Arab landlord's Turkish wife, who was an old woman by then, came to visit us. There, in my parents' living room, sat a character from the fairytales. The Turkish woman who had sent for her husband who then suffered wounds at the rioters' hands. The woman who had saved my mother, and thanks to whom I exist. What an incredible woman. No wonder she was the only person in the world my mother allowed to sit crossed-legged and place her bare feet on the large sofa in the living room. She deserved it, because of all the thanks we owe her. As she sat cross-legged in our German-Israeli living room, East and West merged. In a certain sense, that old Turkish woman is like my mother's second mother. The first gave birth to her and died, and no memory of her remains, while the second, who saved her life, was there in our house. Father met her. I saw her, and mother waived all house rules in her honor. Yes, for a moment then I had a grandmother. For a moment I had a Turkish, Arab grandmother. All my friends, Israelis of different origins and hues, true yekkes and the rest, never had such a grandmother, not even for a moment.

CHAPTER 8

THE EICHMANN TRIAL

BECAUSE OF ADOLF EICHMANN, I CAN'T STAND VINEGAR OR anything associated with it. Eichmann was the reason that I spent hours arguing with my father, and also the reason I rediscovered my father years after his death. Because of Eichmann I will love my father forever. It turns out that Eichmann is much more present in my life than I knew before I embarked on this strange search for both my inner and my collective identity.

When Mossad agents abducted Eichmann in Argentina in 1960, I was learning how to read and write in the first grade. When Eichmann was caught, I was readying myself for a future free of worries. I was not told that Eichmann was brought to Israel. Then, as now, I hardly read newspapers; then because I barely knew how to read—and now because I do. Yet I knew that something was happening. Workers placed a huge container for trash halfway between my school and my home. I had never seen such an enormous container before. Galvanized metal garbage cans lined the sidewalks, and the emptying of these cans in the early mornings, with the workers shouting "stop" and "go," was an urban symphony. Suddenly, a frog-like green monster appeared, massive and intimidating, in the yard beside the neighborhood's auditorium—the People's House. They were building a courthouse for Eichmann, we whispered to each other. We still did not know who this Eichmann was, much less what a trial or a court was. The People's House itself seemed grand and mysterious. So I assumed that Eichmann was probably a very important person if a massive garbage-eating frog was placed there in his honor.

The school was in the vicinity of the market. In my memory, "the market" is the open-air produce market of Mahane Yehuda, a magical place of vivid colors, strong scents, loud shouts, and all the flavors of little Jerusalem. Half my schoolmates came from the market neighborhoods, Sephardic children of Middle Eastern origins. They pronounced consonants differently, in a guttural manner, and their prayers were different. It was said that they were poor, but we did not see their poverty. At the time, everybody bought their clothes in the Labor Federation's Ata stores, everyone wore the same Hamegaper shoes, ate black bread with margarine and olives, and prayed for better days. The rest of the schoolchildren were Ashkenazis. We lived in Rehavia, which is considered an upscale neighborhood today. In school however, there were no such boundaries. I loved Avram ben Zekharia, who was a tall and talented athlete. I adored Shimon Cohen, who was stronger than all of us. I envied Matzliyah Cohen, who always had cash "from his father's can in the souk." I wanted to be as strong as Shlomo Vaaknin, who we left behind in the second grade, though not before we had a fight. Rafi Refaeli's father was a Kabbalah scholar and a cadaver washer in Hevra Kadisha, the society that buries the dead. Shlomo's father was an insurance agent. Most mothers did not work outside their homes then. Yossi's mother was a great cook. The other Yossi's mother worked with his father in a Hungarian tailor's shop. Avram ben Zekharia's father owned a concession stand at the Cinema Orion.

This is how we were, very similar yet different. One toiled all day in the sun, another owned an electric fan; each of us had his own accent, his own origins, his own neighborhood. When school was over, we went home, Ashkenazim here and Sephardim there. The space between the market and Rehavia became the ethnic divide. I would walk with the two Yossis, whose parents were Shoah survivors, and with Shlomo and

Friedman, who prayed by the Ashkenaz Siddur and later became rabbis. The other children returned to the market and its neighborhoods.

Then that big green container suddenly appeared. One day, as four or five of us were returning home from school, we adventurously decided to deviate from the shortest path, which my mom preferred. We were tired from school but excited by the prospect of mischief. There stood the green monster and we were thrilled by the new technology, trying to figure out how to operate the green trash machine. But the discussion about garbage technology was cut short when a small girl's head peeped out like a turtle from the container. She looked scared and poor, probably a girl from the new immigrants' transition camps. We knew nothing of hunger and could not imagine anyone looking for food in the trash. We thought that a kid in a garbage container was funny, an opportunity for a prank. We surrounded the container, laughing and teasing, being as nasty as only young boys can. She was terrified, like a wild animal in mortal danger. Suddenly she disappeared into the container and reappeared with a bottle in her hand. She threw it forcefully at the wall beside me, breaking it into pieces and splashing me with its contents: vinegar. Sour vinegar for sour play. Since then, all cruelty tastes like vinegar in my mouth. This includes the evil Eichmann, the reason the container had appeared, and the evil prank that we played. Disparity, boorishness, poverty, and insensitivity—all taste like vinegar, like Eichmann. The ban on vinegar is my first vow. I have never broken it.

We all grew up and went our separate ways. The transition camps were dismantled; childhood bands disbanded. The "good" kids went to yeshivas and elite institutions; the "other" kids to professional schools or to work, helping their families. Once in a while we said hello in the street. Jerusalem was small then and its residents were few. Later, we would hear faint echoes about some childhood friends. Avram joined the Chief Rabbinate and became active with Chabad's mitzvah tank. Yaakov became city and country champion in all types of athletic specialties and had a girlfriend before any of us. He married the daughter of a conservative rabbi and became head of transportation to Uman, Ukraine, for the Breslav Hasidic movement. Rafi Refaeli grew a long beard and became a Kabbalist like his father. Avraham Betish served many years in the IDF. Gershon, who drew airplanes in art classes, became a senior army officer. Yigal Amadi, a leader in the Kurdish community of Jerusalem, almost became mayor. I went on to become a paratrooper, and for the first time in my life, I had the opportunity to be myself, so I ran as fast as I could. No one could have said that I was the fastest runner in class or in the platoon because my father was a minister; or that I was a good marksman because of my dad; or that I had a red beret because my father had an important yarmulke. I tried to be the best for me.

Then I crossed paths with Eichmann again in the parachuting course, the ultimate test of fearlessness. The red beret was a legend since the British Mandate. Hannah Czenes and the other World War II paratroopers, the heroes who liberated Jerusalem and the Western Wall in the Six-Day War, all wore a red beret. They were the models of heroism, attracting us like moths to a flame. Every child dreamt of a red beret folded under the shoulder strap, paratrooper wings on the chest, and red boots. Being a paratrooper was pure Israeli-ness at its best, and I wanted to be one. I wanted to run fast, strike, sneak around, and fight. I wanted to be an Israeli hero, different from my father, the Jew in exile. He walked and I ran; he escaped and I jumped from the sky.

Before I could jump I had to train on the ground at the school for paratroopers. To this day the school grounds include all the classic torture installations: dive boards, huge swings, sandboxes, and the worst of all: the Eichmann. The Eichmann is a high tower from which you jump, harnessed to a wire. Here we met again; here again was the taste of vinegar. I climbed the tower reluctantly with leaden feet, weak knees, and racing heart. I climbed the Eichmann as the son of a Jewish refugee from Germany, jumped and landed as an Israeli that even Eichmann could not scare any more. Never again, Herr Eichmann.

I had a wonderful childhood. Like everybody else, we were not wealthy but we were not wanting. Our margarine sandwiches with olive kummel bread were much better than today's fancy bakery baguettes and exotic cheeses. But, in retrospect, the 1960s were also my saddest years. When the West launched forward into the future with the Beatles, Woodstock, and Twiggy in a miniskirt, Israel sank back into the dark, primeval, and fanatic past without boundaries. The 1950s were still connected to World War II and the past; on the other side of the watershed years of the 1960s, the 1970s were already part of the future, of the twenty-first century. The 1960s

transitioned us from the past to the present. We moved from women wearing girdles and men wearing hats to the freedom of blue jeans and brand
names. Before the 1960s we listened to the radio, rode buses, and went to
cinemas. Homosexuals were deep in the closet and sex was matrimonial,
at least officially. Then television came along, as well as the Walkman, the
private car, the Pill, and free love.

It was the decade of metamorphosis, of opportunity and change—
from the caterpillar to the butterfly. Many times I think of the distance
that separated me from my father and measure it by the scale of the
1960s, which created an unbridgeable gap between my father's world
and mine and my children's. My father was forty-seven when I was born,
undoubtedly older than usual but not rare. But his biological age was
less significant than the cultural, mental, intangible divide between our
worlds. Nowadays, youth can last forever. We can carry on wearing blue
jeans, sneakers, and listening to rock music, stretching our teenage years
well into middle age. On the other side, maturity begins much younger,
with earlier puberty and sexual behavior, with earlier consumption and
materialism; children in their early teenage years do things that no one
imagined just a few years ago. In our times, the intergenerational gap
between me and my father would not be daunting. But at the time it was
an unfathomable difference because Dad was born three world orders
before me. He was born in the first decade of the twentieth century and,
as a child, lived in a world based on the structures, traditions, and orders
of the nineteenth century. That century really lasted until 1914, when my
father was just a first-grader. Between the end of the Great War and the
start of World War II, he was a teenager and a young man, the son of a
well-to-do Jewish family in the Weimar Republic until it crumbled with
Hitler's rise to power in 1933. My father stayed in Germany until the last
possible moment, emigrating to Israel at the very last second. He watched
with his own eyes, helplessly, the destruction of his beloved Europe, his
Jewish Europe in particular. He witnessed the Return to Zion when he
was one of the 120 elected representatives of the First Knesset, the Israeli
parliament. He died just a few years before the third millennium. He
could be described as a man who was born into a world that followed the
laws of the nineteenth century; he lived through the two world orders
of the twentieth century, the one before the Nazis and the one of their
aftermath—three world orders all together.

By contrast, I was born after the state of Israel was founded. My coming of age occurred between two wars—the Six-Day War and the Yom Kippur War—and most of my life has been and still is lived in the nightmarish present of an imperial Israel, the Israel of the seventh day.

In the legendary decade of the 1960s, many genies were let out of their bottles, and it is still unclear if they can be returned. In those years cracks formed that became chasms between us and our parents, between us and ourselves and between us and many of our peers in the world. In the sixties, Israel started to sever itself from the legacy of its founders, the old-time members of Mapai, the Israeli Laborers' Party. A new cadre of professionals and politicians began their ascent to power and influence in that decade.

In the 1960s, superpowers engaged in war games, including Vietnam and the cold war. Politicians and statesmen tried to stabilize regions of influence according to their ideologies. The rules of the game, as well as manners and conduct, also changed in the West. Anything went in the 1960s, a complete inversion was suddenly possible. These were the years in which students turned the academic establishment upside down and in which human rights, women's rights, and other rights were finally recognized. Race barriers were removed, and American Jews achieved full equal status, sidestepping overt and covert forms of discrimination, and became the most influential minority in the nation. The world, it seemed, understood and applied the lessons of the Shoah and negotiated its way to the opposite pole, the pole of love.

But in these turbulent years, when the world progressed from rigidity and conservatism to creativity and liberalism, Israel moved in the opposite direction. Israel and significant parts of world Jewry regressed to the fundamentals, which we wished to abandon when we entered the modern age. As the other nations of the world abandoned their dark sides, we confined ourselves in a prison of our own. As they broke their shackles, we locked ourselves behind bars. The West was our main point of reference; we wanted to be part of it, but when it expanded its consciousness, we consolidated our own. Jewishness won over Israeliness, the Jewish paranoia won over the newly acquired Israeli confidence. Severing us from the newly acquired connection to the new era of universalism and love that shone on the horizon. Only time will tell if we missed the opportunity of our life, since the tide has turned since then, and the West, led by the United States, is huddling once again in conservatism and xenophobia, fleeing terror and scaling down rights and liberties.

In the 1960s, Europe came to accept that war was not an option anymore. Nikita Khrushchev was de-Stalinizing the Soviet Union and the European states were pondering the idea of an eventual alliance. Across the Atlantic, Martin Luther King Jr. was fulfilling his dream of equality for all, and mass protests helped bring to an end to the Vietnam War. While all this was happening, Israel was somewhere else. We started the decade with the Eichmann trial, continued with the Six-Day War, and ended it belatedly in the autumn of 1973 with the Yom Kippur War. The Eichmann trial connected the new Israel to the recent past, which for fifteen years had suppressed any mention of that dark time. The Six-Day War connected us to a distant past, the historic Land of Israel, the biblical homeland, and the glory of the independent Jewish Commonwealth, the cradle of our civilization. This complicated, unhealthy connections recreated dreams of bygone grandeur that would in turn unleash the present-day nightmare with no end in sight.

Ruin and resurrection, 1945 and 1948, Shoah and struggle, fear and glory, cleared the stage for young Israel, then reappeared center stage in the 1960s. First it was Eichmann and his trial, then the IDF and its victory. The war created a bridge founded on a military miracle; and Biblical regions were gained as compensation for the European ruin. What Hitler and Eichmann had destroyed, the IDF and our national spirit brought back in one flash war. A victory for an instant, against all our enemies.

Suddenly we weaklings had become saber-rattling, laurel-crowned victors, like Roman emperors. When we were scattered and isolated throughout the world, we were destined to be losers. Once we took our fate in our own hands, everything changed. We weren't just victors, but the most powerful of all victors. Here we stood against three armies—Egypt, Jordan, and Syria—representing a population of one hundred million, and we won in six symbolic days, the six days in which God created the world. It was our own re-creation. It was the sweetest victory, and we humiliated our enemies. No wonder that those six days were followed by six years of national hubris, insensitive and irrational, that ended only with what we perceived as defeat in the killing fields of the 1973 Yom Kippur War.

In 1967 we sang the tearjerker "On the Wailing Wall." We did not know that the song was about us, our own hardening hearts that would turn to stone. We were united miraculously by the miracle of war, lead, and blood with the relic of the temple that was destroyed in blood, fire, and smoke 1,896 years earlier. We were changed beyond recognition. In great haste we bulldozed the western area of the wall to create a plaza, thus destroying the Maghreb neighborhood's homes, expelling the tenants overnight for the sake of our renewed holiness.

Today, I think back to the 1960s to understand what went wrong and what got lost, and what more there is to salvage for a journey leading to a better tomorrow. The years between Eichmann's dramatic capture and the depressing end of the Yom Kippur War became the watershed years.

"I must announce to the Knesset," Prime Minister David Ben-Gurion said one day in May 1960, "that some time ago the Israel Security Services found one of the worst Nazi criminals, Adolf Eichmann, who is responsible with the Nazi heads for what they called 'the Final Solution to the Jewish problem,' namely the annihilation of six million Jews in Europe. Adolf Eichmann is under arrest in Israel and will stand trial in Israel according to the law of trying the Nazis and their collaborators."[1]

I can imagine the tumult in the house assembly, in the hearts of the members, and in the tortured souls of the survivors. The announcement was history in the making. The public was caught by surprise; there had been no leaks. It is unlikely that such a dramatic announcement will ever take place again.

At once the genies were released; matters that had been hidden in people's hearts came out to the open. Israel's personal silence on the Shoah, its terror and dilemmas, erupted privately and collectively. Everyone talked about the Shoah. The tough native Israelis sat quietly in the corner of the hall while the Jews from "over there" took center stage.

Mountains of words have already been written on Eichmann and his trial, including on the staging of the event and Ben-Gurion's role as producer and director, deciding the political aspects of the trial. Attorney General Gideon Hausner played the leading man and used all possible means to transform the hall into his stage. Adolf Eichmann was cast as the most unlikely supporting actor: a gray, boring bureaucrat, perhaps even stupid, and very different from the blond, blue-eyed Aryan stereotype. K. Zetnik and Abba Kovner led the march of witnesses who talked about the Shoah but who were clearly not related to the charges against the defendant. They were cast as representatives of the Israeli and Jewish expressions for the decades to come, as Eichmann and his trial were merely used for the education of that and future generations. Under this heavy Zionist cover and tight political control, the story was told the way they wanted us to hear it. The few other voices, like Hannah Arendt's—a German-born Jewish philosopher who went to Jerusalem to cover the trial for the *New Yorker* magazine—were hushed, silenced and banished from us. She did not hesitate to cut the Ben-Gurion "show" to shreds and as a consequence faced incredible resentment and hostility. The choir had difficulty with the few dissenting voices, which included German-born Israeli philosopher Martin Buber. Their voices sounded out of tune to the national ear, which only wanted to hear a single anti-Eichmann harmony at the right pitch. The forces of Jewishness and Israeliness wanted to feel the state power that they now enjoyed; they did not wish to discuss abstract philosophy or ethical questions that Arendt and others raised. We struggled with her criticism, and therefore her best-selling book on the trial, *Eichmann in Jerusalem,* was not translated into Hebrew for many years.

A debate about Arendt has become public only recently. In her introduction to the book, which summarizes the fifty-year debate, Israeli historian and writer Idit Zertal, who co-edited the book with Moshe Zukerman, writes: "There are many ways to read the history of the twentieth century; but there is no way to read it without reading Hannah Arendt. In this sense, Heinrich Heine's saying on Spinoza—that all our present-day philosophers, possibly without knowing it, look through lenses ground by Baruch Spinoza, can be applied to Arendt as well. Hannah Arendt delivers the lenses and concepts that are necessary to study and understand the century in which human-made progress and grandeur converged with their worst atrocities, and with the extreme, total elimination of man himself, his humanity and his life."[2]

Arendt was not completely right, and Hausner and Ben-Gurion were not completely wrong. As always, the truth is made of layers; some are Arendt's and some belong to the Zionist establishment. Yet then, in the times of Zionist orthodoxy and monolithic thought, it was impossible to switch to another channel or to hear other opinions beside those that crackled from the transistor radios, newspaper headlines, and living-room conversation. Sixty percent of Israelis aged fourteen and over listened to the live radio broadcast of the trial's opening session. Many of them followed the heavy media coverage closely. Israel's population then was just a third of what it is today, but many of those children and teenagers who were listening are today's leaders. So it is impossible to understand contemporary Israel without studying the experiences that shaped the consciousness of the leadership's generation. This generation did not hear the other voices, like Arendt's. At the time, I did not know her work, but today I turn to this honest and courageous woman to find the tools and insight when I try to understand those years.

I increasingly feel that the sixties, beginning with the Eichmann trial, were the real watershed moment after which Israel's political processes and public culture changed unrecognizably. I understand the childish need of a very young country to hang Eichmann. Finally, an authentic Nazi with a known name had fallen into our lap. He survived Germany's defeat, the Nuremberg trials and the little vengeful executions of the survivors. Now we will torment him. Not with torture, but by talking him to death—until his soul leaves his body on the Israeli gallows. Then we will hang him and calm down. Indeed, twenty years later we brought in Ivan Damjanjuk in shackles—identified by Israeli Holocaust survivors as "Ivan the Terrible," a notorious SS guard at the Treblinka extermination camp, and sentenced him to death for war crimes—and later spared his life when his conviction was overturned by Israel's highest court because of reasonable doubt. By that point these trials had become too pathetic for us and the judges. Menachem Begin, a theatrical personality in his own right, wanted to impersonate Ben-Gurion in his search for grandeur, but we declined the invitation.

What happened to us after Eichmann's hanging and the scattering of his ashes at sea? Why is it that after we killed him he still haunts us? Could it be that something in the legal and political process escaped our attention, and now these hidden aspects of the proceedings are coming to light?

Soon after World War II, the Allied powers conducted a speedy legal process against the surviving Nazi leaders. The Nuremberg trials opened a door to a long and complex process of a universal criminal law and a new international language of ethics. Crimes against peace and humanity became part of a constitutional basis for the new world order and for globalization. In the aftermath of the mass killings of the Jews, the Gypsies, the homosexuals, the communists, and the other good people who are no more—victorious humanity decided that enough was enough, and rules should govern what is permissible and prohibited in the practice of death. In a world of open borders, *Pax Europeana,* and increasing democratization, common legal and normative foundations were needed to protect civilians from themselves and others.

Rafael Lemkin, a Polish Jew, coined the term *genocide* in 1944 while attempting to have the assassination of a people defined as an international crime. His goal was fulfilled when the United Nations General Assembly approved the Convention on the Prevention and Punishment of the Crime of Genocide in 1948. The treaty entered effect in January 1951. The Nuremberg trials created the precedence for the trials of Slobodan Milošević in the International Criminal Court in The Hague, and of Saddam Hussein in an Iraqi court. Both men were tried according to international legal principles as criminals against peace, humanity and the world.

Before my generation knew it, a great feeling of redemption had, in fact, come to pass. In stark contrast to the Nazi practice of execution without justice, or warning, the victors at Nuremberg presented, ostensibly at least, justice before death. Yet today, in retrospect, some basic facts can be questioned. Was the hasty legal process of the Allied powers genuine, or was it biased and contrived? My sense is that the Americans had some very good reasons to execute prominent Nazis, like sacrificial lambs on the altar of the goddess of justice, and then quickly announce, "Game over." They needed to remove the noose from around Germany's neck quickly, so that the major European powers would side with them in the new cold war against Joseph Stalin, World War II's primary victor. The German rank and file was not really de-Nazified. Many who were released from prison returned to their old jobs as if nothing had happened. Even in 2004, fifty years after the war, the German foreign minister, Joschka Fischer, felt compelled to apologize that Nazi officials had gone on serving in his ministry after the end of the war. The American space program relied on Nazi scientists, research and know-how that were once used in the *Blitzkrieg* against Britain. Who knows how many contemporary medicines and scientific breakthroughs originated in the studies that Nazi researchers did on our brethren, twins, dysfunctional people, mental patients, Gypsies, communists, homosexuals, and the Poles who were helpless in their hands.

Did someone instruct the victorious judges to accuse and convict the Nazi celebrities—members of the Gestapo, the SS, and the Nazi party—but spare the Third Reich's government, the general staff, and the commanders of the German army, who were also tried but not executed? Did the Allies want to create the false impression that the perverse depravity of the Nazis had nothing to do with the German state, its institutions, and systems? Is death the appropriate punishment for flesh-and-blood angels of death, or did these men die just so the victors could convey the message that the previous chapter was closed even when it hadn't really ended?

I confess that I am prejudiced. I am uncompromisingly against capital punishment anywhere. This is because I believe that as a mortal, I cannot play God Almighty. The God of the Universe and its Creator—whoever he or she is—is endowed with two mighty powers: creating life and ending life. The Sublime's ability to create life and instill a soul in his creations and his ability to slay and destroy are the secrets of his power. We were created in his image and likeness, but are nothing more than his shadow.

If we cannot give life, we must avoid taking life at all cost. However, even for those who believe in the expediency and morality of death as a legitimate human verdict, it is unlikely that killing the most prominent Nazis was a wise decision. Would it have not been better to leave them in prison until their death, thus serving as living examples of the consequences of their deeds? Indeed, the moment their souls left their bodies, the process of amnesia began. But why did we have to accelerate it? Is it surprising that the young Prince Harry, who may become king of Great Britain one day, wore an SS uniform to a costume party because he did not know that "the Nazis killed like Hitler"? They died long ago and the past belongs to old people; the future, and the world, belongs to the young.

We, too, tried and killed Adolf Eichmann in great haste—so quickly that even academics and researchers had no time to interview and study the last available senior Nazi. They lost the opportunity to shed some light on the incomprehensible inhumanity of those days.

The Israeli media were outraged by the publication of a British survey, according to which only some forty percent of the British public knew about Auschwitz. I looked at the data and wondered—not about the sixty percent who did not know the history of Europe, of their own people and mine, but about the others, who did know. It is probably thanks to the British media that consistently report and debate the subject. So much so that Joschka Fischer was quoted once referring to the wonderful British TV satire *Fawlty Towers* in which comedian John Cleese mimicked the Nazi goose step. Fischer said that in order to learn the goose step you had to watch British television because none of the new generations in Germany, not even his own, knew how to do it. The mass media, as superficial and problematic as it may be, preserves modern memory. Television is today's tribal fire, where we sit together, watch the same show, and exchange ideas. News anchors and the hosts of TV shows are the modern-day storytellers, and this is the new face of historical awareness and consciousness. The absence of the criminal Nazi faces from the screens is fatal to the memory and facilitates amnesia and denial. Eventually they would have died a natural death, but in the meantime, the generation that came after them would have been molded differently. As always, revenge and rage are bad strategic advisers.

Eichmann was a major criminal who contributed to the destruction of one-third of the Jewish people and many others. Yet we hurried to prosecute, sentence, and hang him. He was a different type of criminal: a desk villain, a destruction bureaucrat of the highest order. Without people like him the Shoah would not have happened, not with such efficiency and scale. When Eichmann said that his hands had not shed that blood, from his narrow, verbal, and legalistic point of view, he spoke the truth. But this is almost impossible for us to accept. Who then shed that blood?

Eichmann's interrogation was conducted by a special Israel Police unit, Bureau 06, which yielded material to indict him on fifteen counts, including crimes against the Jewish people, crimes against humanity, war crimes, and membership in the SS, the SD, and other organizations that had been declared hostile in the Nuremberg trials. The indictment also included crimes against other people, such as mass deportations of Poles and Slovenes, the murder of tens of thousands Gypsies, and more. He was convicted on most counts, but on one count, the murder of a Jewish child by his own hands—the so-called Cherry-Garden Murder—he was acquitted. The prosecution insisted on that charge. Avraham Gordon, a witness, testified to the investigators that he had been present and seen Eichmann personally kill a boy who stole cherries from his garden. The investigators did not believe him, but the prosecution wanted real, red, Jewish blood on Eichmann's hands and summoned him to testify. Of all the witnesses, this one's credibility was questioned by the judges. Eichmann was acquitted of conventional murder. He was hanged, "until his soul left his body," in the words of the sentence, even though he likely did not see one drop of blood of the millions of victims he so efficiently and industriously murdered while devotedly following his orders in the spirit of Nazi Germany.

Today, my sense is that the prosecution, like the rest of us, did not understand the criminal and the essence of his crime. The rhetoric employed by Hausner, the prosecutor, accused Eichmann of crimes in the framework that was known to us then. The prosecution assumed that it faced a despicable murderer whose victims constituted a simple multiplication of the classic murder as we knew it from when Cain murdered Abel. It was hard for them to understand when the Shoah was still an open wound that Eichmann aided and abetted a crime against creation. He and his friends sought to take God's work from his hands into theirs. They wanted to administer nature differently, according to the laws of annihilation, whose purpose is a world that belongs to the cruel, the victorious and the evil. The whole essence of human culture was—and I hope still is—to remove man from the laws of animals and a Darwinian way of life. All my life I have supported a culture that maintains the narrative of "A man hath preeminence over a beast," in moral responsibility and sensitivity, and thanks to the tools of speech, thought, memory, and skill. Unlike us, the Nazis wanted to return to the law of the jungle, with one species of man who is the son of the gods, and views the other as if they were disease-carrying rats. This was their culture of crime, and Eichmann was one of its best technicians. Because of the short lapse in time, the depth of Eichmann's depravity escaped the prosecutors, judges, witnesses, listeners, politicians, and executioners. He was an effective murderer even though no corpse was available to which the prosecution could indicate and say, he killed this man. This was a murder case without the *habeas corpus* that is essential to ordinary criminal procedures. When Eichmann said again and again, "I never killed a Jew, and for this purpose a non-Jew... I never gave the order to kill a Jew and no order to kill a non-Jew," he meant it. Neither the prosecution nor he himself understood his innovation. In his eyes, he was just a bureaucrat, a bolt in a machine. It is unlikely that he understood that the machine was a Golem, a Frankenstein who assaulted the entire human creation. Reading the trial's minutes, it appears that Eichmann was quite limited mentally and could not conceptualize and grasp the essence of the crime that he had committed. His belief that he was only responsible for the transportation of the victims but not for their deaths sent him to his death feeling that a great injustice was done to him. But in those days, the jury did not make the distinction between a murderer with blood on his hands and a murderer whose forms, regulations and clerks sent the Gypsies, Slovenes, and Jews to the slaughterhouses of his Aryan brethren.

When I read the minutes and the exchanges in the court hall, I remembered my father's story, told again and again by him and by us after his death, how on one night the Nazis knocked on the door of the apartment that he shared.

"What should I tell them?" the German landlady asked.

"Tell them I'm not here," my father said, begging for his life.

"But I cannot lie," said the lady, shocked. Her honesty would not stop at the gas chambers.

"Then I'll leave the room so you can say that I'm not in the room," my father whispered with his classic Talmudic sophistry.

"All right then," the landlady said, "but please leave the room."

Thus his life was saved, and our own.

My father's landlady and Eichmann came from the same place. Until the moment that his soul left his body he was convinced that he was paying for others' crimes. The landlady did not lie, and nevertheless my father was not murdered. Eichmann and the landlady had both sinned in the crime of German obedience, like many others who could not lie, only obey. The Eichmann trial presented two fundamental problems: capital punishment on one hand, and the limits of obedience on the other.

I wonder what could have been done differently. I pray that the Israeli criminal code regarding the Nazis and their collaborators will remain a legal monument and not be used again. Despite the forty-plus years that have passed, the trial still makes me restless. I feel it was a turning point both personally and collectively; I can still feel the aftershocks. On the one hand, the trial undoubtedly had a major part in forming my personality as a first-grader, and as a man today. It assured me in my self-confident Israeli-ness. He was confined in a glass booth and I was roaming free, walking past the People's House—now the Gerard Bachar Center—on to school and back home. Sometimes I walked alone by the People's House, looked around and then spat toward the detainee behind the bulletproof glass, just to prove (almost) to him and to myself that I was not afraid. I liked my streets and trusted that the soldiers would guard the beast well and not let it roam the jungle and hunt me and my dear ones. I had a father from Germany, a mother from Hebron, and two sisters, all of us named after dead people whom we had not known. Today, I cannot escape the feeling that the glass cage has expanded so much that it confines us and disconnects us from the world, from the universalism and humanism that I wish to be part of. In the wake of the Eichmann trial, everything that was buried with great emotional toil during the years from Hitler's rise to power in 1933 to Ben-Gurion's announcement in 1960 resurfaced. The trial was like the cork capping a fermented drink in a bottle. Almost thirty years of upheaval turned into an endless flow of talk that wished to express all: pain and trauma, rage and frustration, vengefulness and feelings of guilt.

In those days political correctness did not exist, and no one paid attention to the hidden meanings of the drama. In any case, no one asked. Could a nation that claimed to be the victims' heirs and their embodiment appoint itself judge to try its murderers? What about impartiality and the presumption of innocence? But from the moment that Eichmann landed in Israel, the whole country—newspapers, crowds, politicians—proclaimed his guilt. Everyone said he must die. For one rare moment the entire Jewish state was united, and the whole nation could participate daily through live radio broadcasts of the proceedings.

The Eichmann trial was an initiation ritual in which Israel reasserted itself as victim. As years passed, the melody remained the same. The victims are still dead, Eichmann's remains are still in the Mediterranean Sea, and I believe Hausner is in heaven, as are many of the witnesses, judges, and attorneys. Yet Israeli victimology prospers. We hanged little Adolf and still refuse to divorce the big Adolf, Hitler, who committed suicide in his Berlin bunker but remains for us as mythical as Haman the Wicked. Haman was hanged in Shushan, the capital of Persia, many years ago, yet he is remembered every Purim holiday to give us the sweet taste of revenge. He is revived to provide an explanation and justification to many of our deeds and omissions. We must always feel like perpetual victims and must always sacrifice to avoid responsibility for the reality that we face. No wonder then that every incidental enemy becomes Hitler in our eyes and is inducted into the Israeli hall of shame.

One of my children returned one day from kindergarten having learned about the festive holiday of Shavuot. Since he had already been taught about Haman for Purim, the Pharaoh for Passover, Hitler for Shoah Day, the Arabs for Memorial Day, and the Romans for Lag Ba'Omer, he innocently asked, "And who is the villain of Shavuot?" This is how we are educated: from one villain to another, from one memorial to the next. We are still obliged to wipe out the memory of Amalek, the grandson of Esau, for how he persecuted us in biblical times. There are no more wicked villains like him, but we are still their victims.

Eichmann was undoubtedly among the important villains of the Shoah period. When we tried him for genocide, we meant only genocide against ourselves. The prosecution, judges and all but one of the witnesses were all Israeli. The others had their trials in Nuremberg, the Soviet Union, and perhaps a few more venues, but this was all our own. Emotions were so high, we did not pay attention to the voices among us who offered alternatives, such as an international tribunal in Israel or abroad, and a judiciary that would represent humanity and not just us. The legal gladiators had already entered the arena, and the spectators had already filled the stands in the People's House and demanded to see blood. But what would have happened if the world was granted access? The educational message to the children of the 1960s would have been that the good world is with us, and not, as always, against us. Had non-Jewish witnesses joined the more than one hundred witnesses, of whom only one was a non-Jew, a great deal of trust would have been added to our relations with Europe.

Another point about the trial is that it would have been better if the charges and the public debate had focused not only on atrocities but also the inner meaning of criminal Nazism: the attempt to annihilate Jewish culture and sterilize world culture from its Jewish influence. Perhaps even more: the presumptuousness to cleanse the Jewish relative, undoubtedly an important member, from the family of nations, and the attempt to force Darwinian behavior on humanity.

When Israel decided to turn the Eichmann trial into a founding experience, it should not have been limited to the few years of the Shoah and annihilation. If it were to become a historical trial, then witnesses should have been called to testify on the relations between Europe and the Jewish people during the Jewish Millennium. True, this was also a millennium of hatred, pogroms, and crusades, but not only enmity existed. During these centuries the scattered Jews fertilized Europe with their philosophy, trade, poetry, debates. Without us, the Jews, the European history of humanism, liberty, philosophy, and other accomplishments cannot be fully understood.

It is common knowledge that a common denominator unites all the players in the courtroom: prosecutors and prosecuted, witnesses and spectators, anyone who is thrown into the emotionally charged spiral of events has no choice in the matter. The judges who presided over the trial were partners to both us and Eichmann. The trial was the climax of a series of trials on Shoah affairs, in which Kapos and other Nazi collaborators were prosecuted. Israeli society aspired to cleanse itself, through the justice system, of the ungodliness that had infected us, the citizens of the ashen Jewish planet. About forty trials took place under the *Law of Punishment of the Nazis and Their Collaborators*. Three of the defendants were non-Jews, of them one, Damjanjuk, was acquitted; all the other defendants were Jews—Nazi collaborators who had betrayed their own people and worked for the Germans. From a society that aspired to realize the dreams of its founders to a persecuted and sanctimonious nation that is easily frightened, vengeful and coercive. The self-confident founding generation succumbed to the survivors. But the process had started several years earlier, during the Kastner trial.

Rudolf Israel Kastner was born in 1906 in Klozh, Transylvania, and was an active, political Zionist all his life. In 1943 he was appointed chairman of the Aid and Rescue Committee of the Hungarian Jewish community. When the German army invaded Hungary, the country's Jews were in jeopardy. The committee members contacted Eichmann, who had arrived in the country to organize the annihilation of its Jews, and Kurt Becher, head of the economic division of the SS. Eichmann and his staff proposed to transfer the Hungarian Jews outside the Nazi occupied territories, sparing their lives, in return for ten thousand trucks and other goods, in a program later called "Goods for Blood." As a minor consequence of these negotiations, a train with 1,684 Jews, chosen by Kastner, left the country for a safe haven. Although the passengers represented diverse Jews, including several Hassidic leaders (albeit without their Hassidim), the rumor was that many of the passengers were members of the Zionist movement and of the Kastner family, as well as the community's wealthy members, who had financed the deal. Kastner naively believed that this was the first train of many to come. It was the only train to leave Hungary.

At the same time, the murder of Hungary's Jews was happening at full speed. In a few months, half a million Jews were shipped to Auschwitz in trains. The rescue train, it was later claimed, was an alibi for senior Nazis, headed by Becher, who were expecting defeat, trials, and executions. In his defense, Kastner once claimed that he saved a hundred Hungarian Jews, many more than others, who did not try to save any.

Kastner immigrated to Israel in 1947 and was Mapai's candidate to the second Knesset. In 1953, a leaflet was circulated in Jerusalem that accused Kastner of the worst. The author was one Malkiel Grunwald, an older, bereaved Jerusalemite, who was also a grumpy religious extremist. It was his habit to circulate leaflets that presented extreme opinions, dirty laundry, and juicy gossip. In this leaflet he accused Kastner of collaborating with the Nazis in the annihilation of Hungary's Jews and the ransacking of their property. "My friends and comrades," wrote Grunwald, "the stench of a carcass is bothering my nostrils. This will be the best of the best of funerals. Dr. Rudolf Kastner must be eliminated."

Kastner's political employers forced him to file a complaint with the police against Grunwald, who was charged with libel. But something went wrong, as the defendant was elevated, and the politician was debased. During the trial, Kastner became the de facto defendant, and Grunwald the accuser of much wider charges.

The Grunwald trial had become the Kastner trial, in effect the Mapai—the labor party—establishment trial, and became a precedent for the Eichmann trial. Between the two legal events, Mapai, Ben-Gurion's party, the major force in founding the state, began a decline from which it did not recover. That is when the process of distrust between the Israeli constituency and its leaders began. The feeling that leaders take care of their own interests more than ours began to germinate. With this sentiment came rage, cynicism, and distrust.

The trial became an extensive examination of the Hungarian Jewry's holocaust and was the model of clarifying the issue of issues: Could the pre-state Israel do more for the victims and the communities that had perished forever? Shmuel Tamir, a former member of the militant Zionist group Irgun, represented Grunwald. In overturning the libel charges against his client, he created a political trial against his accusers. Talented and articulate, Tamir used the opportunity to express his right-wing Revisionist opinions. He sharply accused the socialist establishment, the Jewish Agency, and Mapai of backing Kastner and deliberately silencing the news from the Shoah in accordance with British directives, thus evading their duty to rescue Jews, especially those who did not share their political views. The longer the trial dragged on, the more attention it received. The public was impressed with Tamir's brilliance, and Uri Avnery's encouraging articles in *Ha'Olam Ha'Zeh,* the sensationalist, anti-establishment weekly magazine, added fuel to the fire. Avnery's opinion was that the trial proved that the government was run by corrupt Mapai cronies, rather than by those who deserved to lead it, namely, the 1948 generation, who shed their blood in the War of Independence. The now-defunct magazine became Tamir's platform. He and Avnery were New Israelis who held views different from Ben-Gurion, Israel's sole leader at that time, and they opposed him vehemently.

On June 22, 1955, Judge Binyamin Halevi read his verdict and sent shock waves throughout Israel. "Kastner sold his soul to Satan," he decided, acquitting Grunwald. He ruled that Kastner collaborated with the Nazis in the annihilation of Hungary's Jews and spared war criminal Becher's neck from the noose. In his 270-page decision the judge determined that Kastner had divided the masses from the select few, his relatives, friends, and other favored people.

The legal proceedings continued for years. On January 20, 1957, an appeal session took place at the Supreme Court before five justices, headed by Chief Justice Yitzhak Olshan. While the appeal was in process, Kastner was murdered. Three young men lay in wait near his Tel Aviv home for him to return from work at the Hungarian-Language daily *Uy Kelt.* When he left the car, a few minutes past midnight, an assassin approached him, asked if he was indeed Dr. Kastner, and shot a bullet to his head. This was the first political murder in Israel, and since then, weapons have become a normal aspect of the country's political life.

On January 17, 1958, the Supreme Court overturned Halevi's verdict and criticized it sharply. The decision cleared Kastner posthumously of the main charge of collaboration with the Nazis and facilitating the annihilation of Hungary's Jews. It was too late for Kastner and for many others.

The first to accuse the pre-state Israel's leaders of inaction during the Shoah, Tamir continued fishing in muddy waters. It is unlikely that more people could have been rescued: the state did not exist, nor any political capabilities. Ben-Gurion invested the little resources available in building the state-to-be. He assumed that it was impossible to both rescue the dead and build the future, and therefore preferred setting up an infrastructure for those who were to come to wasting resources on an impossible task. But Tamir was rich with words, and there was a wealth of victims, survivors, and their family members who heard for the first time that there had been a "Zionist selection" in the rescue effort, and found an easy scapegoat.

Israel's public opinion, not the general but the private, was prone to shifts in those days. Just as the state's early years were euphoric and joyous for the long-awaited redemption, they were also days of suppressed pain caused by the great losses of World War II and the War of Independence, and the frequent skirmishes on the borders. In those days the people embraced Ben-Gurion, the father of the nation, his vision, manner, and acts. When Israelis needed a strong, determined leader, he was a ram before the herd, no one questioned his judgment. Only with the passage of time, with the realization that Israel, a fantasy just a few years earlier, now existed, did people start opening their eyes and relating differently to Ben-Gurion and his colleagues. Tamir blinded those wide-opened eyes with his searchlight of demagoguery. He turned it around and illuminated dark, unsettled corners. When he did his trick over Kastner's soul, he caused not just Kastner's murder, but conjured sandstorms and chaos for the future.

After the Kastner trial and Tamir's heyday, Mapai's rule started to crumble. The trio of Tamir, Avnery, and Grunwald was a coalition of the spurned right, the extreme Canaanite left, and the yearling of religious fanaticism. They opened Pandora's box. They spoke over the head of the court and behind the back of the tightly organized political establishment. They spoke directly to the people and opened the worst festering wound in Israel's young body. They manipulated the survivors' feeling of guilt.

In her book *Trauma and Recovery,* author Judith Loyis Herman explains that the phenomenon of survivor's guilt is common among survivors of war, natural disasters, and nuclear holocausts. Guilt is especially hard for survivors who witnessed the suffering and deaths of others. Survivors who endured war and disaster are haunted by images of the dying. They feel that they did not do enough in order to save others. Traumatic events undermine the bond between individuals and their communities and generate a crisis of trust. As long as the trauma of the Shoah was expressed collectively, Israeli society provided a positive alternative and hope. The cracks that Tamir and Avnery made in the new fragile Israeli ethos facilitated the breakup of solidarity, and consequently guilt surfaced among the masses of Shoah survivors. The dam broke and it was impossible to stop the deluge of mistrust in the community and the perceived false world. The community was Mapai and its chapters; the world was Mapai and its government. In the Kastner trial, the falsity claim was argued forcibly, and everything seemed to disintegrate.

I imagine that few at the time were aware of the criticism that is expressed today, retroactively, against the Zionist leadership of those times. True, Ben-Gurion focused his efforts in setting the foundations and the scaffolding for the construction of the state at the first available geopolitical moment. He turned his attention away from everything else and did not misspeak once, testifying much more to his Zionist devotion than to his opinion of the annihilated Jews. Had he given it a second thought, I believe he would have spoken differently. Yet one issue is agreed: the Zionist movement took advantage of all opportunities to reinforce the small but growing pre-state of Israel. The leaders did Zionist selections, favoring the young and healthy. "Every lad good for arms, every lad on guard," says the Palmah Anthem. Not only did they select in Europe the fittest to pull the plough of the Zionist Revolution, they also did not welcome the Jewish masses from the *shtetls* or from the *luft-gescheften* (literally, air businesses, meaning nonproductive wheeling and dealing) of Eastern Europe. They despised them, as they themselves had come from there and knew precisely what they did not want. Individuals, whether survivors or otherwise, cannot always grasp the big picture of national planners and strategists. Individuals have their own problems to worry about beside nation building and history.

When Tamir called up his witnesses and aired his arguments, he turned his attention to the masses. "They did not want you!" he cried, and people heard and listened. Survivors who were physically and mentally impaired, immigrants from Muslim countries, and other refugees who had arrived here for lack of other places started feeling that there could be an alternative to the Israeli-ness that was embodied by Ben-Gurion and the ruling native-born elite. The path to the New Israel started at the Kastner Terminal. It took them few more years to assemble the coalition of the spurned and to bring it to power in 1977.

It is hard to believe that Ben-Gurion, ever alert and suspicious, had misread the process. He knew and lived history and read it daily. He knew what Tamir was doing, saw the cracks, and did everything to put the house in order. Today I have no doubt that Ben-Gurion searched and found a powerful way to offset the damage from the Kastner trial. He did have sincere reasons for bringing Eichmann here and trying him publicly and extravagantly; one of them was the battle for history and his reply to his anti-Mapai detractors. The Eichmann trial was the most aggressive defense that Ben-Gurion presented before the court of Israeli history. Eichmann thus extended his presence from the glass cage to the internal politics of the state. The trial delayed for a few years the erosion process that began with the Kastner trial.

Ben-Gurion captured Eichmann and fulfilled his wish. The leader seized his prey and did not let go until the Nazi died. He succeeded, for an historic moment, to create the impression that he was the one who retro-actively won against both Adolfs, Eichmann and Hitler. Against the line of witnesses who turned the Grunwald libel trial to the trial of Kastner, his party and the Zionist establishment, Ben-Gurion and Hausner summoned a line of witnesses who testified on the Shoah and heroism, whether they had anything to do with the Nazi bureaucrat or not. Dozens of witnesses described in gory detail their personal and communal atrocities. The destruction of European Jewry was laid extensively, with the amplified ghetto uprisings and heroism receiving ample time. The trial was a turning point from national rhetoric to personal histories, then back to a very different national level.

The Eichmann trial was meant to hit several targets in one go, just as the Nuremberg trials were meant to cleanse Germany and legitimize it as a "kosher" partner of the West against the Soviets and Stalin. Our goal was to punish the villain, to shape a new Israeli generation that had begun to forget the Shoah, to raise the world's conscience, to save Mapai, and, first and foremost, to cleanse the ground for the secret relations that Israel was already having with West Germany. Executing Eichmann was like executing old Germany; now we had the time, energy, and legitimacy to build the relations between the other Israel and the other Germany. This is why Ben-Gurion demanded that Hausner change the wording of his opening statement from "Germany" to "Nazi Germany." The message was that we know that there is another Germany, just as there is an

Israel that is other from the one that perished. Eichmann's death was to symbolize the end of the Shoah and the beginning of the post-Shoah period. In reality, the opposite happened. If Kastner's trial was an indictment against Ben-Gurion, Eichmann's was the defense sheet that formed the official history of the Shoah from the Israeli establishment's point of view. Between the former and the latter an upheaval took place. Until Eichmann, the Shoah was part of official rhetoric, justifying Israel's establishment and its claims, but the trial "personalized" the rhetoric. It was no longer the State of Israel vs. Adolf Eichmann, but the people of Israel vs. the Nazis. The Shoah discourse had begun. The young could listen, and the adults could speak freely for the first time what they only dreamt of in their nightmares.

For years I was angry with my father for having no opinions. Yeshayahu Leibowitz was an Israeli philosopher and scientist noted for his outspoken and often controversial opinions on Jewish ethics, religion and politics. He was my mentor and one of the most influential people in my life. He once told me with considerable subtlety, "A scholar without an opinion is worse than a carcass." Then he stopped for a moment and said, "I don't know what your father's opinion is on the matter." I had not known at the time that they had an axe to grind. I knew nothing of their differences and conflicts. I knew that both prayed at the Yeshurun Synagogue, and that both were infinitely important to me. I did the accounting for myself; I was hurt by the philosopher's harsh criticism of the statesman, my father. I could not reply that my father was better than a carcass and better than a scholar for he had wisdom and opinions because even I did not know his opinions. Among the major criticism I had always had of my father was my feeling that his consistent position was to have no position. "But I am centrist," he once told me. "How do you determine center?" I shot back. "In the center," he said. I replied "With you, the extremes move and so does the center." "Others determine your position. If you want to be center, become an anchor, dig into the ground, stand fast, be a man. Don't move. Force the extremes to reposition based on your position." It went on like this for years: him in the center and me firmly at the pole. He was obdurate and moderating; I'm absolutist and frenetic.

How should I have understood European finesse? Where could I learn understatement? How can an Israeli from a yeshiva, barracks, and the corridors of political power understand existential humor that is not obscenity, male sexism or anti-Arab racism? I was not taught. I grew up deaf, not listening. I was blind, not discerning. I rebelled against my father and his origins and lost his wisdom and heritage. My father had opinions; hidden, shy, sad ones. They were buried under the deluge of Israeli extremism. Our *Sabra* thorns protected the fruit from the pickers, and the thorns stabbed him, the fruit itself.

My father connected, built bridges. Without such people, life is impossible. In order to keep the whole, he compromised, doing away with the noise of opinion. Leibowitz thought that he had no opinions; I took it upon myself to search for my father and I discovered him to be the hero of my youth.

For days I rummaged through Knesset protocols. I went to the state and government archives. I read years of deliberations for hours in a quiet library. Then, suddenly, in all this reading I saw my father. Here he was, a giant, greater than anything I have known—"made of the stuff of legends," as his grandson Hillel, my beloved nephew, said.

On the day Eichmann was captured, they held a meeting, and the following was said, according to the minutes.

Ben-Gurion: *Our security services searched for Adolf Eichmann for a long time, now they found him. He is in Israel and will stand trial here.*
Yitzhak Ben Aharon: *How? What? Where?*

He is so shocked he continues in Yiddish, "*Wie macht men das?*" How does one do that? Then the personal confessions begin, and my father joins the discussion with his typical rationalism.

Yosef Burg: *Is there a danger or a fear, I don't know how to put it, that in the trial . . . he would use expressions that are dishonorable?*

Pinhas Rosen, then justice minister, also German-born, seems a bit restless. But my father, Yossel Burg from the Dresden yeshiva elementary school, continues apologetically in his manner of the exile, because he is an *Ostjude,* not a *Yekke* like Pinhas Rosen, aka Felix Rosenblitt.

Yosef Burg: *I am asking because of the general impression in the world.*

A few more days passed and the cabinet again discussed the matter, and my father thinks historically, in an orderly and clean fashion, as befits a graduate of a classical Saxon Gymnasium and of someone with a master's and doctorate of philosophy from Berlin University.

Yosef Burg: A. If we want the press to report on the issue daily, then we should save some material for the trial. If we want great drama in court, then I don't know if, after heavy reporting in the newspapers for months before the trial, anything interesting will remain to attract attention. B. Will our consulates abroad be guided on how to present the issue from our point of view? C. Finally, I am absolutely of the opinion that the documentary evidence should be brought first to the knowledge of the Jewish public and then to the world. There are documents that were used at the Nuremberg trials. Is it possible to bring in photographs of the evidence in Nuremberg? . . . I will say one thing: It is known that there are minutes of the SS meeting regarding the Final Solution to the Jewish problem. According to the minutes, Eichmann was there; it is written in the minutes that all the Jews must be destroyed. Is it possible to make a copy of this document?

The State of Israel was acting vengefully and as the world's educator. Now that the educational role was over, it was time for Jewish accounting.

Yitzhak Ben Aharon: If Eichmann tries to defend himself, he has some line of defense. Until 1939, and also during the war, for many deals that [the Jews] wanted to make—he was the address, including [the lives] that we saved.

Here it begins. Ben Aharon throws a bomb: Jews made deals with Eichmann, and this will be his line of defense.

Weeks before the trial, the Eichmann question repeatedly engaged the Israeli cabinet from several aspects. My father was almost always involved. He opined, proposed, compromised, and stressed the historic aspect again and again. The question was whether a German defense attorney should be allowed to represent Eichmann.

Yosef Burg: In my opinion, considering our public's sensitivity, a German attorney in a public trial will upset the public. No one can be responsible for what may be done by someone to such a person.

Ben-Gurion: What is this? Anarchy? Shall we be afraid of hooligans?

Yosef Burg: Here, in our land, he can consult whomever he wishes, but in the public trial: no German, no Swiss, and no Austrian. (Almost begging) Please! The attorney will express his arguments in this language, and if you add on to this a German national—I do not know if this is desirable.

When the pandemonium ended, the trial began and Hausner walked to the stage, pointed his accusing finger at the glass enclosure and said: *"Ani Maashim!"* ("I accuse!") He then continued his opening prosecution speech for three more days. Holocaust writer Yehiel Dinur, also known as K. Zetnik, fainted. Baruch, my father's driver, listened to all the sessions on the kitchen radio, and many people started rolling up their sleeves, revealing for the first time the numbers tattooed on their arms. The verdict was read, the sentence spelled out: Death sentence to the *tzorer,* the bitter enemy of the Jews, Adolf Eichmann. All said in unison: May his name and memory be erased, and we say Amen. The cabinet met again and the minutes speak for themselves.

Ben-Gurion: I talked with Martin Buber; it was a long conversation. I will tell you in brief what he said. A. He thinks that executing Eichmann will create a new legend of the anti-Jesus type. Maybe not this year and not in two years, but the legend will be created and the Jewish people will have trouble. B. I received many letters, and will report on one. An important man, a Princeton professor, a Jew of German descent, Walter Kaufman … He thinks that it would be honorable for Israel if an announcement were made that we brought [Eichmann] to fair trial, denounced his deeds and the Nazis'. We are not bloodthirsty, and by setting him free we will demonstrate the Jewish genius in Israel.

The minutes shook in my hands. It was worth building this country and having a twisted trial just for this cabinet session alone. Light to the Jews, light to the nations, light to humanity. But they continued to debate whether to recommend to the president to grant clemency, to pardon Eichmann and publicize the reasons.

Levi Eshkol: Is it possible to reduce his sentence with an announcement stating why?
Ben-Gurion: It is possible.
Eshkol: I would tend to this option.

I always knew that Eshkol was the best prime minister Israel had ever had. Here was the proof. He was a giant, a hero, brave and humane.

Ben-Gurion: Does anyone else agree with Eshkol's opinion?
Dov Yosef: I want to speak against it.

Forty-five years have passed since that cabinet session, and yet the anxiety and distress can be felt in the old typewritten pages.

Minister Haim Moshe Shapira, who met Eichmann in Vienna, pleads.

Shapira: Can we break the meeting to think?

The train has left the station. It is not possible to hold back the urge to continue to the end.

Yosef Almogi: I have no doubt that even those who support execution do not discount the important arguments that we heard… I praise Eshkol's courage, but I should say a few things. I became a Zionist at age ten for one reason. In my town, a sheigetz, a non-Jew, came and killed a young Jewish man for no reason. The Polish court did not sentence him to death. Not even to fifteen years' imprisonment. In another instance, a murderer was sentenced to death. Since then it became clear to me that Jewish blood is unworthy… We are facing a symbol. True, the punishment is not enough, but there is not a more severe punishment.
Eshkol: He should die—in prison.
Almogi: In prison he will be more comfortable than in Argentina. We are facing a symbol… We have no choice.
Bar Yehuda: Eshkol, I disagree. Even though, in some way I would have understood if you said release him. No form of punishment is enough. But if you say, keep him in prison, how is it possible?
Shapira: (pleading) I ask that we adjourn the session…

The train was speeding to the gallows.

Golda Meir: Commuting the sentence will demonstrate not superiority of the Jewish people but inferiority of the Jewish people. No other people in the world would have shown such concern [forgiveness]. Such [forgiveness] is only demanded from the Jewish people. Jews and non-Jews make this demand… No one told them that they should demonstrate a deeper sentiment. They demand this only from us, because the world has not yet become accustomed to view Israel as [one of] the other nations. I am not ready to go with the philosophers. We are not bloodthirsty. I only feel sad about one thing: that a Jewish boy will have to do this, but it will be to his honor. I am against any thought of…

My father has not spoken yet. Why are you silent? Talk to me from history.

Ben-Gurion continues. The ministers discuss killing a gentile. What to do with the body, and the ashes? And the burial? Who will witness the hanging?

My father was still silent.

Then my father, my biggest hero, appeared. He is a hero because, with restraint and self-discipline, he made a moral and political proposal of stunning dimensions, as it is stated in the minutes of the cabinet meeting of May 29, 1961.

Yosef Burg: I understand that this is not a matter of formal vote. We are sitting and observing tendencies. These are also moments when a man faces his own conscience, history, and should say his word. I want to say: I reflected a great deal on this matter, although this does not guarantee that I thought correctly... My opinion: The State of Israel has said what it had to say in the trial. It can afford to let the murderer die anew every day. I cannot raise the subject of official pardon in this context. If this should be formally called amnesty...

Ben-Gurion: Amnesty or commutation of sentence?

Burg: ... but not commutation either. [My father is looking for a third way. Not an execution and not a commutation. And therefore he rejects Ben Gurion's words.] *But there is a possibility for a suspension. That the sentence be suspended daily, and not just to evade a decision... I asked people every once in a while for their opinions. Opinions are divided. It can be said that the more Diasporic a person is, the greater his fear. When a person who left the Diaspora and settles in Israel, his fear decreases... I want to say my opinion. If he can be left in this state, that any day his sentence may be executed, this is what I want, although it is cruel...*

Almogi: And what if not...

Burg: Will there be a vote here? I don't know if the cabinet should do it.

Ben Gurion: The cabinet must do it. The president will ask for the opinion of the cabinet. It cannot be avoided.

Eshkol: For me the question is not of conscience, not of misgivings... From the first moment of his capture, I said to myself: If it is possible that after the trial he will walk in the world with Cain's mark and be treated accordingly—it is much more than the five minutes of an execution. I tried to talk with some people. I know it is not likely. Probably the matter will be over in the five minutes of the execution.

Ben-Gurion: *We should also decide on the official pardon. If it reaches the president, the president will ask the cabinet for its opinion. Burg's proposal, according to the attorney general, is against the law.*

Burg: *I propose we make an experimental vote on Eshkol's proposal, and after the experimental vote, a final one.*

They vote. The whole cabinet is against Eshkol and my father. The minutes state: "Eshkol's proposals get two votes."

Ben-Gurion: *After the experimental vote—the final vote.*

Decision: *(unanimously) Not to recommend to the president to commute the sentence of Adolf Eichmann.*

My father and Eshkol lost that battle. But the days did come, the days of my father, when his astonishing Jewishness, morality, and wisdom will go hand in hand and will be the column of fire that leads Israeli decision makers. Eichmann was hanged and burned, my father is dead. As time passes I discover him more and miss him even much more. I have no words; I do not know how I would have voted then and there. Thanks are due to Eichmann, under whose dark light I found my lost father. All I have left is to ask forgiveness for the many years of criticism. Forgive me, father. You towered over me.

The chapter of Adolf Eichmann's personal life ended, but only then did the Shoah chapter in Israeli identity begin. The Eichmann trial took place during the Bar Mitzvah year of the state, in which the state's parents would have proclaimed publicly, "Blessed He that exempted me of this one's punishment," according to Jewish custom. We are free of Eichmann, but not at all resolved by his punishment: the Shoah and its interpretations.

Compared to that year, my Bar Mitzvah was in the year of the Six-Day War. Victory was magnified, even beyond its natural dimensions, because of the depth of the fears and worries in the three weeks of build-up to the war. Three weeks is a symbolic period. It took the Romans three weeks, from Tamuz 17 when they breached Jerusalem's walls, to Av 9, when they ransacked the temple, burned it, and destroyed Jerusalem, in the year A.D. 70, the year of the Ruin. It is the ultimate Jewish expression of awaiting the inevitable annihilation.

Governments do not fall at once, and movements do not end in one fell swoop. Processes and trends take time to ripen and form, and public opinion needs patience to translate feelings into political acts. The dying Mapai government was given another shot of life with the Six-Day War, which coincided with the tumultuous years of the stormy 1960s. The war captured the imagination of the enthusiastic Israelis for another moment in history. In the eyes of many, the war was the last battle fought in the War of Independence. It was a miraculous war that brought to the surface great patriotism and renewed trust in the leadership. It was followed six years later by the "Third Temple Ruin" war of Yom Kippur. The images of defeat were shocking compared with the bravado born in 1967. When Israeli TV broadcast reels of humiliated Israeli soldiers holding their hands up, they looked like the child wearing a cap and holding up his hands in the burning Warsaw ghetto. It shattered the image of the undefeated native Israeli, the *Sabra,* a member of the Labor Movement by birth. History is not just extraordinary events; it is also the consistent, ordinary flow of everyday life. The next historic coalition was already flowing in mental currents, flushing all until it crowned Mr. Shoah himself, Menahem Begin, the first prime minister who came from "there," from over the river, from the right and the Shoah.

We pruned and cut out our horrific holocaustic experience to fit into some of the traditional Jewish pattern. We added symbolism of our own. We called it Shoah, not Ruin, as is the custom. We designated a special day of remembrance, wrote special prayers, and created a new ritual and ways of worship. We made it into an event more Israeli than Jewish. Yet we fell back into past patterns, underlining the message that "the entire world is against us." We revalidated the existential Yiddish equation: Is it good for the Jews or bad for the Jews? And we took the Shoah to be exclusively our own. Thus we missed the option of turning its horrors into a much more meaningful, universal event. It is not something between us and the world, but between all the good in the world against all the bad. In short, we nationalized the Shoah, monopolized it and internalized it, and we do not let anyone get closer.

It is not too late. It is still possible to redefine the relationship between the world and the Jews. We can turn the word *Jew* into a concept that is much wider than mere nationality, religion, genetics, and traditions. A Jew in its new definition is the answer to the Nazi in its old definition. Wherever the Nazi turns off the light, the Jew comes to turn it back on. Just as our call "Let my people go" is echoed beyond history whenever and wherever people demand their liberties all over the world to this day, the term *Jew* can identify anyone who refuses to bend in the face of discrimination, evil, and persecution. It will mean a free person, and *Judaism* will be a synonym for equality, freedom, and fraternity. Modern Israel is a tremendous treasure of unfulfilled potential. We have much of the positive, except in one aspect. I want to believe that one day we will be part of a worldwide cultural process of universalism and a force in bridging the gap between nations and cultures.

At a time when the world progresses toward being more "Jewish" in adopting our traditional morality, we Israelis become more localized and provincial. We have not joined the post–World War II world revolution that is directed at forming a fraternity of nations against the Hitlers of the world. We were there; we started on that path in the first years of our independence. Many in the world looked up to us in admiration. Here was a persecuted nation that converted the energies of wrath, frustration, and revenge into energies of building, creation, and absorption. We inspired emerging African nations and others who followed in our footsteps. Not all was perfect, but the direction was correct, until the metamorphosis of the 1960s and the Eichmann trial that opened that decade. I know it is small wisdom indeed to analyze retroactively, but we must examine the past so that we can make a change in our current direction. I want to believe that the Israeli state is not just the incarnation of the Shoah victims and the other Jewish victims of hate throughout history, but that Israel can be a light unto the nations, a light of universal humanity. Israel should take the responsibility to become a stop sign against tyranny and should strive to change world morality. In this sense, the Shoah is not only ours, but the legacy of the entire world. Every global citizen has a part in this; it is much too big to be carried and remembered only by the Jews. Shoah that belongs to all will create powerful coalitions that will be obliged to prevent atrocities everywhere. Rwanda is ours, as is Cambodia; they belong to us and to our brethren from Warsaw and Bialystock. There is no difference between a Jew and an African or an Asian; the persecuted and the "other" are the same for us; they are all part of our responsibility for a better and repaired world. Wherever a crime against a people, helpless innocents, humanity, and humanism is committed—we will be there in any possible way, in protest, action, assistance, and even in defense and rescue. For this to have happened, the Eichmann trial should have taken place in Jerusalem, as it did, but the tribunal should have been inclusive. I hope that Israel will establish an international court of justice with judges from all nations and creeds, including good, decent Germans, of whom there are plenty. This is the court that could have turned Eichmann into the Jewish people's "gift" to the world. It would have been an opening trial and not a trial of self-confinement. It is highly likely that walking this path would have prevented several human calamities. It would also have prevented Shoahs that are not our own.

CHAPTER 9

OWNING THE HOLOCAUST

"**W**HO REMEMBERS THE ARMENIAN HOLOCAUST today?" Hitler is said to have asked. One cannot but be impressed by Hitler's intuition and his ability to manipulate his country's policy and actions according to the human failings of his rivals. He apparently had a canine-like nose that could sense fear and weakness. As much as he was deaf and blind to his own weaknesses, he was alert to those of others.

Indeed, in the 1930s, few people in Germany and in the rest of the world remembered the Turkish massacre of the Armenians. In 1915 and 1916, hundreds of thousands (some say the number is as high as a million and a half) Armenian people were slaughtered by Turkish troops and agents. More than a decade later, the Jewish poet Franz Werfel, native of Prague, set out on an excursion to the east. In the spring of 1929 he arrived in Damascus and met for the first time Armenian refugees, invalids, orphans, and other victims who had found refuge in the city. For the next four years he wrote an epic novel, *The Forty Days of Mussa Dagh*. This was the story of the Armenian Masada and the tragic end of the violent struggle against their Turkish oppressors.

The book was published in Germany in 1933. Perhaps the book describing the cruelty of the massacre relates to what Hitler allegedly said. Werfel provided the memory; Hitler did everything he could to deny, forget and to make others forget.

With his book, Werfel reminded the Germans of an historical event that was quick to pass from memory. Gabriel Bagdarian, the book's hero, prepares for the last night of his life, having lost all his family and friends. "Why not look for shelter? Such a question did not arise." No mortal could have lived after such darkness fell. Indeed, pitch-darkness fell after the Armenian genocide, yet no one paid real attention. No such question arose, not in Germany and not in the rest of the enlightened world. The Turks vehemently denied the genocide and presented a totally different picture. Hitler, who counted on a world that does not ask questions, understood the power of denial and took it all the way to the Final Solution. No excuses and denials, he lay it all openly on the table. You can destroy, and no one will inquire. Hitler was a denier of previous holocausts and based his annihilation of the Jews on the forgotten and denied Armenian Massacre. He hid the destruction of the Jews in the open public arena. No one protested.

Werfel's book brought the horrors to light. Henry Morgenthau Sr., the American ambassador to Turkey, said: "I am convinced that in the entire history of the human race no such horrible event occurred, the biggest crime of modern history...of all modern history's dark pages, this is the darkest."[1]

Hitler probably figured that if the massacres on Europe's doorstep just twenty years earlier were forgotten, who would remember his own at the dawn of "the Thousand-Year Reich"? If the world did not act for the Christian Armenians who had hurt no one, why would it mind if he rids it of the hated Jews? Hitler thought associatively and was impulsive. He had the combination of a devout believer, fully committed to his opinions, and a gambler's extremism of all or nothing. This is how Ian Kershaw, the most recent Hitler biographer, describes him in his book *Hitler 1889–1939: Hubris*:

There is no need to underestimate the contribution of Hitler's personality to the way he seized power and exploited it.

Single-mindedness, inflexibility, cruel removal of all inhibitions, cynical operative talent and a gambler's instinct to throw all in the balance...

We must never paint Hitler in inhuman colors and thus exempt ourselves from dealing with the human aspects of his personality. For us and for the world he was total evil, but he was also:

...an ideologue with firm beliefs, the most radical of all radicals, representing a worldview with inner integrity (as much as it is abhorrent to us). The driving force of this worldview was derived from a few basic ideas united in the perception that world history is the story of interracial struggle.[2]

People often react to natural disasters quickly, as in the case of the 2005 tsunami in Southeast Asia. It was one of the world community's finest hours. But when compared to the world's response to man-made disasters and atrocities, as in the case of the Armenian Holocaust, it is cause for shame and sadness. Yair Oron, of Israel's Open University, has dedicated much of his life to the study of the Armenian Holocaust, paying a personal and professional price. He believes that as a Jew who lost members of his family in the Shoah, it is his duty to remember and understand any holocaust, massacre, or genocide: "This is the major moral insight we must draw from the Shoah and other genocides. Humans did it to other humans, and therefore they can repeat it anywhere... We must ask ourselves what can we can do to prevent such a threat."

The issue here is: Why does the world mobilize with all its might when dealing with natural disasters, but remains on the sidelines, reserved and distant, in the face of man-made disasters? The sad answer is the same one that served Hitler: indifference. Perhaps even more sinister: no moral, ethical, or political position should be held when confronting the wrath of nature; not so in the face of human wrath. The political scientist R. G. Rummel estimated that between 1900 and 1987, the unimaginable number of 169,198,000 people perished in genocides, including the ones perpetrated by Stalin and by the Chinese on their own people.[3] The figure does not include the deaths that occurred after 1987, in Rwanda, Yugoslavia, East Timor, and elsewhere.

What did we do in order to stop, prevent, alert, or resist these killings? Nothing. Sometimes we paid tickets to watch movies of superior white people slaughtering Native Americans. Our childhood movie-heroes of the Westerns are the arrogant icons of the white genocide of the Native Americans. Thus, through the movies we became, in retrospect, participants in the genocide of America's indigenous peoples. We are still in the dark about the genocide of the Australian aborigines, and we are still blind and deaf to other acts of sadistic brutality that are committed in these very days even within the field of view of our media's cameras.

In 1994 a million Tutsi died at the hands of the Hutu militia, armed with machetes and light arms, during just one hundred days. It was the fastest genocide ever. Then, again in Yugoslavia, East Timor, and Darfur. In none of these places was the world quick to react. Why did the 1995 tsunami stir worldwide empathy, but outright murder inevitably meets inaction?

When it comes to humans killing humans, people—namely you and I—must take a stand beside one of the parties. Who is right? Who is our ally? Who is the enemy? Very often people do not have a clear position on their immediate reality, so how can humans be expected to form an opinion regarding the reality of other people so distant from their hearts and minds? When we must take a position in other people's politics, we must also be introspective, look honestly at ourselves and take the same moral stand regarding the evil among us. This proves to be too much. Our evil, it turns out, is at the very base of our convenient lives. It has taken years for us to reach this state of comfort and we are not going to give it up just like that. Thus our indifference becomes our complacency: Let's not take sides and let them die. We cannot hear their sobbing and crying where we are, anyway—whether we're in Manhattan's high-rises, London's subways, or Tel Aviv's shopping malls. The millions of people who were slaughtered in the twentieth century are victims of those who stood and watched or looked the other way. And we are at the top of the list of guilty ones. Yes, we the Jews are again to be blamed. How is this possible?

We have taken the Shoah from its position of sanctity and turned it into an instrument of common and even trite politics. We turned the Shoah into a tool at the service of the Jewish people. A weapon, indeed; mightier than the Israeli Defense Force itself. The Shoah has become our exclusive property. We also expend enormous amounts of energy to make sure that no one else enters "our" holiest sites. The Jewish state stood time after time beside the Turkish government in denying the Armenian Holocaust. Except for a few politicians like Yossi Beilin and Yossi Sarid, all Israeli officials adhered to the Turkish propaganda lines. It seems that the reason was strategic: to maintain good relations with Israel's only Islamic ally in the region. But everyone close enough to the Israeli psyche knows that we deny the Armenian Holocaust to ensure that the Jewish Holocaust stays our own. We have taken the oath that there will be no more Shoah. Never again is our mantra, and never again is our obsession. "The Eskimo and the Armenians do not interest us, only the Jews do," the Prime Minister's Office chief of staff once said.[4]

Today we are armed to the teeth, better equipped than any other generation in Jewish history. We have a tremendous army, an obsession with security, and the safety net of the United States, the world's greatest superpower. Anti-Semitism seems ridiculous, even innocuous compared with the strength of the Jewish people of today. Therefore the oath "never again" takes on new dimensions and nuance.

Never again? We have made "Never again" possible for ourselves. What about never again for others? Never again? On the contrary, it happens again and again, because of indifference. This apathy to their fate was made possible primarily by the operating system that was installed in me at birth: The Holocaust is ours, and all other killings in the world are common evils, not holocausts. Well, if it is not a holocaust, it's none of my business. Therefore I am not responsible. Therefore I do not have to cry out in protest. The lives of many thousands, perhaps millions, could be saved if the State of Israel and the Jewish people, myself included, had stood at the head of the international struggle against hatred and the annihilation of any people anywhere, regardless of color, gender, creed, origins, or residence. We did not stand at the head of this struggle. And the swords are still drawn.

For us, the Shoah is unique in the history of the world. It is the logical climactic outcome of anti-Semitism. We have never sought to view our Shoah as an event in the historical continuum of others. We do not know the universal context of the Shoah and therefore do not realize the consequences of our absence from protesting, alerting, and struggling against other people's holocausts. My favorite bookshops in Jerusalem, like in New York, organize their bookshelves so that Shoah literature is on one shelf and World War II on another. I read somewhere that in Germany, a mirror image of the German bookshelf exists: an artificial separation between Nazism and Shoah. There is an artificial, even political, wall in the realm of consciousness. "The division between the meaning of persecution for the persecuted and Nazi policy...blocks the ability to understand causative contexts of historical events," Yifat Weiss of Haifa University writes. "In addition to the direct damage that this division causes, more problems rise. The place of Nazism on the German history bookshelf and the place of the Shoah on the Judaism bookshelf differentiates the various aspects of a common historical event and attribute them to separate histories...disconnected historiography traditions, German or Jewish."[5]

If we broaden our discussion we cannot escape the conclusion that the teaching of Jewish history as unique and separate from general history is much in line with other stories of the Chosen People, the people with a history of its own.

For many, the Shoah is the deep abyss between the magnificent Jewish past and the wretched world that we saw when the gates of Auschwitz were forced open. "The Shoah is a different planet," K. Zetnik testified at the Eichmann trial. "We chanted the Yizcor prayer," wrote a young Israeli girl in a diary on her visit to Poland and the extermination camps, "I was crying, and I saw a group of youngsters from abroad. They didn't look Jewish to me. What were they doing here? Why are they desecrating the holy?...In the evening, when we sat and summed up the day's events, I did not ask anymore. I said they should have no part in our Auschwitz...Everyone agreed."

For the non-Jew, the Shoah is a chapter among chapters, a trauma among the other European traumas. It resides in history alongside Napoleon, Versailles, Lenin, Spain, World War I and the divided Germany after World War II. Historians attempt to join the past's fractures into a logical sequence, to connect the Jew to the German, the European, and the universal. But the Jewish narrative collects testimonies and memories, painstakingly adding details. Our facts. Life in the shadow of trauma does not allow room for a bigger picture to emerge—that of the universal context of hatred and its origins, of dictatorship and tyranny, of the history of genocide, not just the Jewish genocide. "Two people emerged from Auschwitz," wrote Professor Yehuda Elkana, a wise man, a Shoah survivor, and an early mentor to me, "a minority that claims 'this will never happen again,' and a frightened majority that claims: 'this will never happen to us again.'"[6]

Although the Shoah was, and still is, an opportunity to join the Jewish people with the other peoples, we have not yet honored the invitation—on the contrary. Whatever the reason, we joined ranks with the indifferent nations that stand by. How different are we now from the other nations who stood by while we were being slaughtered?

Late in the 1980s, the Israeli writer Boaz Evron wrote the following sobering opinion:

> I am willing to bet that if we had a border with Nazi Germany, and Germany turned against a minority within it, and we had good trade relations with it, we would have acted as the worst among them. We would have collaborated in the hunt of minorities such as the Poles and Romanians. We would have shut our border like the Swiss. If we act with such cynicism with a country such as Turkey, which is not that important to us, what would have we done with Germany...Perhaps there is another reason: we who speak Shoah all day, we do not allow anyone else any part of our Shoah. This is our main asset nowadays. This is the only thing by which we try to unify the Jews. This is the only way to scare Israelis into not emigrating. This is the only thing by which they try to silence the gentiles.[7]

We are certainly not as bad as the murderers and exterminators but we are as bad as the apathetic bystanders, if not worse. Have we not sworn "never again"? Then why do we not engage when there is more of the same evil perpetrated against others and we do not engage? Did the million innocent Rwandans walk to their slaughter saying, "Never mind, our holocaust is not as important as the Jewish Holocaust"? More likely they wondered why the world was silent as machetes cut their throats.

The indifferent bystander who does not prevent a crime is also a criminal; at least a minor one, an accomplice. An apathetic Israel and a passive Jewish people are more responsible than the other perpetrators of inaction. We have been there; we know what it is like. Well-filmed rescue missions, field hospitals, and air force transports are no more than public relations stunts. They do not substitute a national moral stand and diplomacy in the face of human distress. I assume that other post-traumatic peoples insist that their own genocide is the ultimate one and other massacres are just a horrible crime, a tragedy but not more. But we should have known that. The Shoah can remain locked in a gated Jewish ghetto, but it can also be a world heritage. We who rose from the ashes should be the best friends of the persecuted everywhere.

How can this be translated into practice? We can start with the law. Early in the 1950s the Knesset passed the *Law for Trying Nazis and Their Collaborators*. This was the law used to convict Adolf Eichmann. He was charged with crimes against the Jewish people, crimes against humanity and war crimes. The Knesset should strike down the exclusive clause of "crimes against the Jewish people." There are no more real Nazis. Our people should return to be part of the family of nations. We have a section on crimes against humanity, and it should suffice. Are the Jewish people not a part of humanity?

After deleting this section we should consider a fundamental change in foreign policy. The government of Israel should declare publicly that it will not cooperate with immoral regimes, and that it will disallow commerce with states and governments that do not observe human liberties and rights. Thank goodness we are no longer a "small country surrounded by a sea of enemies." The paranoia that is responsible for the above statement is no longer true. Even Iran's stated position against Israel and Judaism does not scare me. They are not only our problem: they threaten and challenge the entire Western word, and most of the Arab and Muslim world as well. We should not take the lead on Iran; let others also worry. Much has changed since Auschwitz. We can now safely stop dealing as merchants of death with those who do not share our view of war ethics.

A moral foreign policy is not only possible but also feasible. Early in my term as Knesset speaker, I was asked to host the Dalai Lama, the exiled spiritual and political leader of the Tibetan people and a true man of peace, whose teachings and actions I had admired for many years. I approved the request without hesitation and my staff started to prepare for the visit with phone calls, letters, faxes, and schedules.

Then very quickly other forces mobilized. Without realizing it, by approving the visit I had apparently pushed some very sensitive buttons. Within hours of my decision I received an urgent call from a senior foreign ministry official: he must see me at once. The meeting turned out to be one of the most embarrassing in my life. The diplomat, a very senior one, stood before me and pointedly demanded that I not receive the Tibetan.

"Why can't I receive the Dalai Lama?" I asked.

"You just can't," the diplomat replied.

"Why?"

"It's against Israeli foreign policy."

"Why?" I insisted.

"Because one week after the Dalai Lama, the Chinese president is coming for an official visit," the diplomat explained.

I still did not understand. "So what?"

"The Chinese president is threatening to cancel his trip to Israel if you, the Knesset speaker, receive the Tibetan."

It turned out that the Dalai Lama, whose people were slaughtered and exiled by China's communist regime, was traveling the world hoping to arrive ahead of the Chinese president, or any representative Chinese official, wherever they planned to appear. He was trying to generate positive public opinion and stir nonviolent action against the injustices done to his people and his homeland. Likewise, China's diplomats threatened and pressured host countries not to provide a venue for Tibet's high priest. The Israeli parliament seemed to them too prominent, its clout extending from Jerusalem to Washington.

"You must cancel the invitation," the senior diplomat demanded, but I was enraged. I took a deep breath, counted to ten, and replied as softly as I could: "The visit will proceed. I'll try to publicize it as much as I can in Israel and in the world. If Israeli foreign policy is based on arms-dealing interests with the murderers of Tiananmen Square, I want no part of it. Although it wasn't my intention, I'll be the happiest man alive if the Dalai Lama's visit to the Knesset will open your minds a bit."

The quarrelling volleys of letters carried on until the last minute. In the end, life was mightier than all the bickering. The Dalai Lama honored the Knesset with his soft, peace-loving presence. The international press coverage was extraordinary. One week later, as planned, the Chinese president arrived at the Knesset and a gale of worldwide protest flooded the foreign office. Israel's official response was surprising. Diplomats abroad were directed to reply to the protestors who condemned Israel for hosting the Chinese dictator that just a week earlier, the Dalai Lama had received the same honor: a visit to the Knesset.

Hypocrisy is often the essence of the diplomatic profession, yet I learned my lesson. Israel's foreign policy must conform to the values that we call our own. We may have great interests with Turkey, yet we must not deny the Armenian Holocaust, and this will eventually help Turkey as well. Israel's arms industry may be important, but under no circumstances should Israeli arms be part of the Rwandan genocide. Between Tibet and China, we choose Tibet. We must not be indifferent to Kosovo, Yugoslavia, Indonesia, or East Timor, nor to civil injustice in neighboring Palestine, or to the undemocratic U.S. actions in Iraq, Afghanistan, or Guantánamo Bay. A moral, committed Israel with a binding, ethical foreign policy is what a democratic state of the Jews is all about. Thus it should have been inconceivable for Israel's late president Haim Herzog—who publicly tore to shreds the United Nations resolution that equated Zionism with racism—to visit China so soon after the People's Army slaughtered peace and freedom activists in Beijing's central square. It should have caused an earthquake in Israel. Shamefully, it did not.

We must turn the poles upside down. Instead of acting like a major power when we attack, then like a small vulnerable country when we are assaulted or criticized, we must act as a superpower at all times. Konrad Adenauer, Germany's first post-war chancellor, once said, "World Jewry is a superpower." He was right, though he did not define the character that this superpower should assume. There are all kinds of powers, money-based and demographics-based. There are powers of the past and of the present, based on force and militarism. What about us, then? Shall we always be a superpower of memorial politics? Or maybe it is time to become a super-power of moral statesmanship?

We, the Jewish Israelis, are the core of the world's Jewish superpower, and must act toward our enemies as a moral superpower: forcefully, uncompromisingly, and fearlessly. We should not evade the ethical challenges that face a Jewish foreign policy. We can declare a moral war against China, fight Indonesia on the basis of ethics regarding East Timor, and even argue with the United States in the same manner that Abraham argued with God on Sodom: "Far be it for you, will the judge of all the land not do justice?"[8] As a bonus, moral-based policy will give us as the opportunity to change Israeli domestic policy, a chance to mount a no-holds-barred struggle for justice that will rid Israel of sick and malignant policies vis-à-vis our minorities and occupied neighbors. Indeed, the world is full of preachers who fight to the death about other people's consciences when their own remains spotless for lack of use. The time is ripe for a different morality, not the kind that defeats its own conscience daily, but the kind whose conscience wins all. I do not want a preaching, sanctimonious, and hypocritical Israel. I want an Israel that fights for its inherent convictions in the world arena, whether it rallies supporters or not. It is time for one state to call out "Follow me!" and hope that others will join in. But even if they do not join, we should carry out our moral charge and not relent.

Until then, we remain veiled by the Shoah blindfold, which causes us time and again to side with the worst evildoers of recent history. Take Yugoslavia, for instance. In the early 1990s the communist Yugoslav federation disintegrated into its ethnic and tribal components. This was a multinational state that functioned well for decades, but was suddenly torn by a civil war. The basis for the violence and atrocities, the worst in postwar Europe, was a decades-old conflict that remained unsolved. During World War II, an estimated half a million Serbs, Gypsies, and Jews perished in Croatia. With the fall of the Berlin Wall, as the Soviet Empire was gasping its last breath, the unsettled accounts came to close, and the ancient enmities erupted like lava from a volcano. Serbs, Croats, and Muslims slaughtered each other. While the Serbs fought the Croats and the Bosnians in the early 1990s, a regional peace agreement was signed in Dayton, Ohio with the purpose of resolving the irresolvable. It was a regional peace agreement. The press covered the event, but people like me lost count in the deluge of names, positions, and nations: Bosnians, Croatians, Albanians, Christians, Muslims…Then, less than four years after the signing of the Dayton Accord, Slobodan Milošević, Serbia's ruler, sent his armed force—army, security forces, and paramilitary mob—to remove the Muslim Albanian component from Kosovo. The international community failed to stop the massacres. Although humanitarian aid and medical convoys arrived at the province, the mad dogs did not relent. The massacres and atrocities continued unabated. Consequently almost the whole world opposed Milošević and his henchmen. Political and economic sanctions were imposed on the Serbian Republic and on him personally, but to no avail. Jewish organizations in the world took a clear stand and argued that we cannot stand idly by while words such as "ethnic cleansing," "cattle cars," "selections" and "concentration camps" hang in the air. Jewish and non-Jewish opinion-makers denounced the ethnic cleansing without reservations. The whole world took a stand that had its roots in the Jewish Holocaust.

Whose voice was not heard? Israel's, and this is not surprising. When the whole world tried to stop this outrage, Israel sided with the Serbs. The international community did all it could, albeit poorly, to end the round-the-clock killings while Israel the moralist stood by. Furthermore, Israel provided the Serbs more than once with moral and political support. Some even say that Israel supplied them with arms and ammunitions from the Israeli Defence Forces emergency stores. Shimon Peres, then foreign minister, exercised his verbal acrobatics in the Knesset as only he knows how. He denounced "strongly and in no uncertain terms the concentration camps, the murders, the shocking harm done against innocent women and children." But in the same breath he evaded, in double talk, answering the simplest of questions: what are the relations between Israel and Serbia? He gave Knesset members Rafi Elul, Dedi Zucker, Ran Cohen, Yossi Sarid, and speaker Shevah Weiss many empty words, hot parliamentary air, under which Israel continued with its policy toward Serbia. Knesset members repeatedly attempted to raise the subject, and the government repeatedly evaded it. The government was "shocked" to the depth of its soul, not acknowledging that the murderous Serbs were Israel's partners. Alain Finkielkraut, the prominent Jewish French philosopher and intellectual and an expert on anti-Semitism, racism, and Judeophobia, stated that the Serbs had launched the first race war since Hitler. Why, then, did Israel did not take a public stand against them on every possible stage? Yair Oron provides an explanation by Professor Igor Primorek of the Hebrew University. He argues that the long war in Yugoslavia was perceived in Israel as a direct extension of World War II, when the Croatians and Muslims supported the Nazis, aiding and abetting them in exterminating the Jews. The Serbs, on the other hand, fought the Nazis, aided the Jews, and protected them. According to this rationale, "Jews are historically obliged to understand and support the Serbian interest..."

This is horrifying and disgusting. When the world opened its eyes and took on the fight for a better future, we were stuck deep in the depths of the Shoah and we were unwilling to acknowledge that our allies of the past had become actively Nazi-like in the present. We were (and still are) willing to look the other way as long as they passed the test of the Israeli ethic: Were they on our side during the Holocaust?

This test is wrong. It may suit someone who thinks that the Shoah is all there is and nothing else is like it. It manifests the failure of a state that expropriated the Shoah, including the right and duty to speak for the victims and the survivors, "our" victims and survivors. None of the other victims are our business. Our Serb partners or Rwandan clients may slaughter them. Had we broadened the jurisdiction of Israeli law, Israeli collaborators, elected and appointed officials who supported Milošević's regime and assisted in doing unto others as they would not have others do unto them, would not have stood alongside him. Milošević died during his trial at the International Criminal Court in the Hague, which Israel, naturally, opposed.

Can our looking the other way in the face of ethnic cleansing in Serbia explain Europe's disregard of the Armenian Holocaust? Hitler's words regarding the Armenian Holocaust are more easily understood in the context of the German experiment farm in Namibia. Imperial Germany could not stay behind when France, Belgium, and Britain seized territories far from their borders. German colonial energy, late to emerge, was directed at the very few territories that remained free, one of which was the spacious land in south west Africa that would be known as Namibia. An empire without colonies launched a drive to settle an empty, uninhabited territory—not that it was without humans, but "humans" at the time meant white people, especially German. The Herero, the largest African tribe in the region, were no obstacle in the Germans' view. But the "non-human" natives rebelled ferociously against the German occupation and the result was expulsions, settlements, confiscations, abuse, and humiliation. They did not heed General Lothar von Trotha's clear message, "Get lost or die," but defended their homeland. The cost was sixty-five thousand Herero dead. All German methods were implemented: bullets, mass graves, water poisoning, expulsion to the desert, death by hunger and thirst. This tragedy happened just a short time ago, at the dawn of the twentieth century.

German colonialism's high degree of evil efficiency bested other colonialists, including the settlers of North America just twenty years earlier. The colonial process is inseparable from comprehending the Shoah. The Final Solution was launched somewhere in the new world, decades before Auschwitz. Extermination took place in the New World of North America, and four decades before the Holocaust in Europe, Germany perfected the model in Africa. Namibia was the introduction to the Shoah; the Herero were Africa's "Jews." Although "only" sixty-five thousand (some estimate eighty thousand) Herero were murdered in Namibia, a fraction of all victims of colonial Europe, their annihilation was the first genocide to be carried out by an explicit official order. Lieutenant-General von Trotha signed the order, with the full backing of the political system and the press of the German Empire. Von Trotha arrived in Namibia after the rebellion had erupted in order to crush it, and later became Namibia's governor. As a good, organized German general, he left his hot-blooded enthusiasm at home. Everything was done in cold blood, with detailed planning and murderous efficiency. His predecessor, Major Theodor Leutwein, opposed the annihilation of the Herero for economic reasons, because "it is not easy to kill sixty or seventy thousand people." Von Trotha had no such worries or compunctions. He had brought with him the proper imperial spirit. "I will wipe out rebellious tribes with rivers of blood and rivers of money. Only following this cleansing can something new emerge," he wrote in his diary, reported in the German press in 2004, on the hundredth anniversary of the Herero Holocaust. This spirit was delegated to his subordinates and reported up to his superiors in Berlin: to destroy, slay and exterminate, per Haman's words in the Book of Esther.

The Reichstag debated the issue several times. Their view was totally different than the Herero's. "They are beasts...they slaughter innocent white settlers," explained Graf Ludwig Rowenthlow, according to *Haaretz*, a hundred years later. "Africans tear out women's intestines while they are still alive and hang them on trees." This was propaganda, typical of any evil colony anywhere in the world. The same historical report in *Haaretz* quotes the officer August Bosehart: "The negro is a wild beast...It can be taught to be respectful only under the gaze of the tamer and his whip."[9]

Anyone who reads the testimonies that were collected by the survivors cannot help but be reminded of the Jews. Replace the African names with Jewish ones: Mendel, Yankel, Antek, and Abba, and here is a stunning introduction to the Shoah. The Germans, for example, surrounded about thirty thousand Herero—men, women and children—together with their cattle, in a place called Watterberg, shelling and shooting them for hours. The only escape was to the arid Kalahari Desert. The German forces then surrounded the desert, erected watchtowers, and poisoned wells inside and around it. Then, as if that was not enough, von Trotha issued the following order: "Any Herero found within German borders, with or without a gun, with or without cattle, will be shot. I will receive no women and children. They will be expelled back to their people or shot. This is my word to the Herero people, signed the Grand General of the Powerful Emperor." According to the report in *Haaretz:* "The Grand General ordered his soldiers to shoot above the heads of women and children to force them to flee. This was obviously cynical, as he allowed them to escape only to die in the desert. Anyone who tried to flee the desert was murdered."[10] It was an African Babi Yar.

Much time passed between the day that Berlin issued an amnesty order sparing the remaining Herero and the day it finally arrived by a slow ship; there were no faxes and e-mail, no airplanes or text messages. The lucky survivors were sent on death marches to concentration camps. One third of them died on the way, and half would eventually die of typhus, smallpox, pneumonia, exhaustion, and other diseases—exactly like my grandmother, who also "died naturally of typhus" in Teresienstadt. Those who survived the marches worked in forced labor, including railway construction and quarry work. They were whipped and beaten endlessly. The German settlers waited for the Herero slave laborers, just as German industrialists did forty years later, profiting billions of Reich marks. The killings of war-capable men continued. Women were raped and forced into sex slavery to satisfy their German masters.

So familiar and yet so far removed from us, from the historical humanistic values of the Jewish people. The history of the Herero is not part of the mandatory curricula of Israeli high schools. The Herero are not a subject for discussion in the Shoah trips to Poland, and not mentioned at the fast-growing Shoah museums. The hair-raising similarity between the two holocausts does not end with torture and death. The humiliating laws governing both the Jews and their brethren in southwest Africa were similar: banned ownership of firearms, land, and cattle. All adult Herero, from fourteen years of age, were forced to wear a metal plate bearing a serial number. Inside the camps, the German carried out medical and "racial" experiments. Corpses, skeletons, and skulls were scrubbed clean by forced Herero women and sent to "racial anatomical" research labs and museums in Germany. The geneticist Dr. Eugen Fischer, who "investigated" local Herero children, concluded that they were of "inferior racial quality" and that "interracial breeding" degenerates the "superior race." Sounds like an introduction to the Nuremberg laws, does it not?

What was the political, cultural, scientific, and intellectual backdrop in Europe that allowed this to happen? What are the sinister forces in the European first world that burst in such a force against the black third world?

The superiority that healthy and well-to-do individuals felt over the less lucky others translated into the feeling of collective German national superiority. It was possible then, explains Kershaw, that:

> More than anything, the national resolve grew out of the feeling of grandeur that was attained through occupations and was based on cultural superiority—the feeling that Germany was a great and expanding power, and a great power needed and deserved an empire...ideas of territorial expansion to the East at the expense of the subhuman, the Slavic *Untermensch*.[11]

Thus an amalgam of race theories were created based on arrogance, political and territorial aspirations, illusions of worldwide grandeur and blatant disregard for the life of others. Africa was the distant test ground. Eastern Europe was the coveted prize close to home. A line of destruction and killing was drawn from the African Herero to the unwanted Germans who were handicapped or mentally ill to the "inferior" Slavs to the Jews. The latter were at the top of all these theories and the ultimate victims of the extensive German know-how that had been acquired forty years earlier.

In 1918, Germany was a defeated nation. World War I ended, and so did colonization overseas. Humiliated, Germany yearned for glory. The Right-wing propaganda machine took advantage of this yearning and spoke out against the unfavorable terms of surrender at the end of World War I, which had provided the fertile ground on which the extreme right, including the National Socialists, soon flourished.

In 2004, on the hundredth anniversary of the Herero Holocaust, the twentieth century's first mass killing, Germany sent an emissary to Namibia, Heidemarie Vitchurk-Zoil, minister of development aid. "We, the Germans, admit our historical and moral responsibility," she said, in the first public and official admission by Germany.

"An apology, where is their apology?" The Herero descendants demanded from the crowd.

"All I gave was an apology for crimes that were committed in the period of German colonialism," the German minister replied.

Unlike the German press, the Israeli press coverage of the event was minor. This was in stark contrast to the very detailed coverage of "our" Shoah, which is mentioned daily in newspapers in various, sometimes strange, contexts. It seems that only *Haaretz* was interested in the subject. Aviva Aviram wrote about it extensively:

> The German historian Jürgen Zimmermann is right to view the annihilation of the Herero as "the writing on the wall" and "Nazism's prehistory." Naturally there are vast differences between Wilhelmian Germany and Nazi Germany. But Nazism was fed also by colonialism, and much more than others are ready to admit. The annihilation of the Herero was another red line that was cut through colonialism's parameters. Many Europeans and North Americans believed then in social Darwinism, according to which "inferior races" should be extinct. Yet many others who did hold these views believed that Blacks are not exactly human beings, and that crimes against them are not really the same as crimes against humans in every sense.[12]

The circle that opened in distant Africa came to a close inside Europe and its extermination camps. Few know that Dr. Heinrich Göring, Herman Göring's father, was the first governor of southwest Africa. The same was true of other veterans of the colonial experiment who held positions in Nazi Germany. The aforementioned Dr. Fischer, director of the Emperor Wilhelm Institute of Anthropology, Genetics, and Eugenics, was appointed rector of Berlin University in 1933, just as the Nazis rose to power. He was the person who trained a generation of Nazi geneticists, physicians, and anthropologists. His colleague Theodor Molison was Dr. Josef Mengele's teacher.

No politician protested the extermination of the Native Americans; no one knew of the Herero Holocaust; and no one really cared about Franz Werfel and his Armenians. All past holocausts were denied holocausts. At first, whites annihilated blacks far away. Then it was easier to come close, to home, and on the basis of acquired and perfected know-how, slaughter whites from various nations, like us and like the Gypsies, Catholics, Polish intellectuals, communists, Slavs, mental patients, and homosexuals.

It is fair to say that the destruction of the European Jews, our holocaust, was not only a Jewish historical event, or the climax of longstanding hatred of Jews. Perhaps even more, it was a universal, multifaceted event that took place in the historical timelines of the world. The Holocaust is the climax of a process of racial superiority theories of the white races and their contacts with "inferior" races during the eighteenth and nineteenth centuries and half the twentieth century. The Jewish Holocaust was the climax of expanding human evil.

During the past decade, the nations of the world internalized the profound meaning of the European Holocaust. They came to understand what we in Israel have not yet understood: the denier of the other's holocaust will eventually have his own holocaust denied. Lutheran pastor Martin Niemöller, a brave anti-Nazi theologian, wrote a bitter song, often mistakenly attributed to Bertolt Brecht, expressing the idea that if we didn't speak up for others, there would be no one to speak up for us.

The song can be rewritten in many ways: First they took the Native Americans, then the Herero, then the Armenians, then the mentally ill, the Gypsies, the homosexuals, the Slavs, and now they are taking the Jews. But it is too late.

This is not an abstract, theoretical discussion about hatred and death. It is a discussion about the spirit of nations, especially the spirit of the Jewish nation. A Knesset debate on one anniversary of the liberation of Auschwitz will illustrate this. On January 27, 2004, Israel's parliament held a special session on the Israeli struggle against anti-Semitism, obviously an important subject. The anti-Semitic hydra was again raising its heads in many places in the world. The time had come for a special session, attended by the prime minister and visitors filling the galleries to capacity. January 27 is a date that is marked by the West, and later the United Nations, to commemorate the Holocaust, since it marks the day Auschwitz was liberated. All speakers but myself spoke again and again about anti-Semitism, Jew hatred and "the world." One speaker, Naomi Blumenthal, on the verge of tears, even warned of a "second Shoah." Even the usually enlightened justice minister of the time, Yosef Lapid, compared (though shallowly) the horrors of the 1930s and the present time, exposing his innate local bias. He compared European Nazism with extreme Islamism and its suicide bombers. I was the last to speak, before the government representative spoke the final word. I abandoned my prepared speech for the special occasion, and walked to the podium to argue, not orate.

Mr. Chairman, Mr. Prime Minister, Honorable Knesset. I have some reservations on the deliberations and the tone of this session. I do not feel so persecuted. I don't think that the threat of a second Shoah is real in any way...

On the day the world made a historic decision, after so many years, to mark its solidarity against the injustices perpetrated in Europe...at the center of which was the injustice to the Jewish people. At a time when the entire world expresses its solidarity with us it is wrong that from here, the Knesset, a message should emerge that we feel that the whole world is against us. Therefore this day should not mark anti-Semitism, but...should be a day in which the Knesset joins the world in what the world is trying to do regarding the issues of hatred and xenophobia...

The Western World, in which we have lived from the beginning of the twenty-first century, has many more protections for the hated, and especially the hated Jew, than ever before. Strategically, as a nation, we are better off than ever before. Had we had the same friendships we have today sixty years ago, with the greatest superpower, with the three major European powers—Germany, France, and Britain—not to mention other states, the Jewish world would have looked different. We have this friendship unconditionally. The Catholic Church, which used to accuse the Jews for crucifying Jesus, is now a different church...No danger of genocide exists today, certainly not of exterminating the Jewish people...True, there is active anti-Semitism, but today's anti-Semitism is not just the Jew's problem. Today's anti-Semitism, when it exists in a certain society, is the litmus test for the moral quality of that society...Why? Because it is no longer the legitimate legal hatred of the pariahs leprous Jew, but an indicator of the human quality of life of the community in which such things happen. A hateful society, whether anti-Semitic or otherwise, is a flawed society.

Therefore, against the picture of hatreds of the world, including anti-Semitism and Judeophobia, the State of Israel, the Knesset, must ask itself: what should I be doing?...The Knesset and the

State of Israel should extend their hand to the world and say: let us form a united front in the world's struggle against xenophobia, against hatred wherever it is, against hatred against humans, including the Jewish human.

We must not remain in our own shell. We must not repeatedly say that other hatred does not interest us and that we don't care what happens to others; that only the hatred against us is true hatred, and all others are not real. If we are fighting the struggle against world hatred, we shall take what price we paid as victims, and convert it into revenue, as a lesson to the world: we should not be treated this way; no one should be treated this way. When the State of Israel comes with clean hands and Israeli society stands beside those who love and reject hate in the world, we will have to tell ourselves: charity begins at home. Here, too, there is work to be done on the subject of hatred of man.

It is a custom in the Knesset to greet speakers as they walk down from the podium, but this time it did not happen. From the podium I saw people looking at me, some listening, some enraged. The body language at the visitors' balconies, where Shoah survivors and professional Shoah wheelers and dealers sat, was uneasy. I knew I was strumming on raw nerves yet I could not but speak those words. I had decided that I would never again hide the truth. None of the members of my own faction welcomed me as I walked down from the podium, just a few weak handshakes to go through the motions. "Why did you have to say that? It will come back at us like boomerang in election time," a colleague said. Only later was I approached by a group of Arab Knesset members, and one of them said, with tears in his eyes: "Just for this day and for this speech is it worth becoming a Knesset member."

Meanwhile, Minister Natan Sharansky, who at the time was in charge of the government's struggle against anti-Semitism, took the podium. My relationship with Sharansky is impersonal, yet it carries a special meaning for me. On the day he arrived in Israel, shortly after his release from a Soviet prison, an impressive state reception was held at Ben-Gurion International airport in his honor. All the major political figures attended. Every staff member of then Prime Minister Shimon Peres was assigned a task. I was then the prime minister's advisor on Diaspora affairs, and I was charged with chauffeuring Sharansky and his wife, Avital, in the Subaru that I was given for that special evening. First I drove them from the plane to the VIP room, where a press conference was held. Then, after the deluge of interviews and photo ops, I drove them to the home that had been prepared for them in Jerusalem. On our way we stopped at Mount Scopus and the Mount of Olives to "kneel down" to the City of Eternity. I drove, and they were discussing their private affairs and cuddling in the back seat, trying to make up for the years that they were apart and the prison walls between them. From there we drove to the Western Wall, and to their home. I was with them just a few hours, yet Sharansky was etched in my memory not as a *refusenik* (Soviet Jews who were denied permission to emigrate abroad by the authorities of the Soviet Union), but as a courageous activist who struggled shoulder to shoulder with Andrei Sakharov, the greatest freedom fighter of the Soviet Union. Let us be accurate here: it was everyone's struggle before it was the struggle of the Jewish individual. Over the years Sharansky disappointed me again and again.

Sharansky is an impressive, wise, quiet, moral man with extensive personal and public experience. He could have changed Israel's very soul. But he chose to enter a cozy corner, preferring to hide in the Jewish bosom than to play in the open field of universal human rights. He became a *refusenik* even though he had started out as a dissident. He was saved from Soviet prison by the widest coalition of liberty fighters, but he landed in Israel as a limited, localized Jewish immigration activist. Somewhere in the air between Europe and the Middle East he huddled into his own national square and deserted the universal humanistic responsibility that had set him free. Almost always, when he had to decide on matters of Judaism, Israel, and society—which side he was on—he chose exactly the opposite pole from where my Jewish values were. Sharansky had become a typical faithful speaker for nationalist, chauvinist Israel, denying in his decisions his past as remembered by freedom lovers in the West.

On the Knesset podium that day, Sharansky was consistent with his isolationist views:

> Mr. Chairman, Mr. Prime Minister, ministers, members of the Knesset. I will modify my speech a little following the speech of Knesset member Avraham Burg. Twenty-five years ago I was an *Aliyah* activist and human rights activist in Russia, formerly

the Soviet Union...And I was sure, just as Avraham Burg is, that democratic Europe is our ally, and that after the Holocaust, it was impossible that there could be anti-Semitism in the democratic free world...[Today] my position and my concern are exactly the opposite of those of Burg. I think that on the day when they teach in Europe about the Holocaust, on that day, indeed, they ask if it can happen again...Then what should we be afraid of?...One must not forget that it did not happen in one day. Before they collected Jews to the trains, before they brought them to the extermination camps, before they burned them, they had to persuade tens of thousands, maybe millions. They had to convince that a Jew was less than a human, that it was subhuman, that to kill a Jew is not to violate "Thou shalt not kill," but it is almost a mitzvah. If there are no people who think so, who feel so, you cannot motivate a people, all the people, to Holocaust.

So, whether to talk about this? Yes. The preparation has already begun. Demonization of the Jews is happening...the new anti-Semitism is a real danger to the continued existence of the State of Israel. The Palestinian terrorists can kill people, and they can complicate our lives. They cannot endanger our existence. But the propaganda that delegitimizes our right to exist, the propaganda with the goal of isolating us—this is the true danger. Against this we have to fight.[13]

Sharansky, who then read verbatim from his prepared speech, claimed that Israel was facing a threat of the same level as sixty years earlier. To him, Europe is the same Europe, and the world the same world, just as for me he is not the same Sharansky. Without blinking, the Israeli minister in charge added the Palestinians to the Shoah equation.

This official position is the Israeli ghetto at its worst. Without being able to identify and understand the world's dynamics, we are digging in our identity foxholes. Apparently old habits die hard in the face of new realities. Perhaps it is a survival instinct that the Jewish people learned to distrust. Could it be that what we viewed as blessing is now a curse? According to the Bible, King Balak hired the Mesopotamian prophet Balaam to curse us. But instead Balaam managed only to bless and praise us. Balaam was an observer, and he notes: "Lo, the people shall dwell alone, and shall not be reckoned among the nations." In our generation, it seems that our seclusion—and insensitivity to the sacrifice of other nation—is perhaps the core of Balaam's long-term curse. The spiritual isolationism is the national curse of our generation.

Once we decided to accept K. Zetnik's testimony in the Eichmann trial verbatim, without questioning, we exiled ourselves to "another planet" on the Shoah platform, and our lives are a journey between dark planets. As far we are concerned, we live on the Auschwitz planet. All is Shoah and everything is weighed on its scales. The rays of light that reach Israel break as they pass through the prism of crematoria. When it happens to others, we move to the next planet, where there is no room for the other's suffering, no genocides, no atrocities, and no holocausts that are not ours.

We are on the side the Turks in their denial of the Armenian Holocaust, and we are beside the U.S. right-wingers, not knowing anything about America's original nations. We supplied arms to those who perpetuated the massacres in Rwanda and our denial reaches inside the Balkans. Soon after the Eichmann trial concluded, the Israeli government, and society in large, denied Hannah Arendt's argument that the Shoah was a human crime, committed by human beings, made possible by a new type of a murderer, the bureaucrat. The rejection of Arendt's *Eichmann Trial* was brief and fatal. No, protested the Shoah establishment. The Shoah is unique. It happened only to us; do not contaminate our Shoah with other people's troubles. In this manner Israel isolated itself from profound world processes and became a denier of other peoples' holocausts. In a world in which Israel evades, and the Jewish people keep mum, all others can afford to be indifferent. Thus the fate of millions is determined. Our monopoly of a suffering keeps competitors outside the game.

This is how a reporter for the Israeli daily *Yediot Aharonot* quoted a major Jewish leader in the United States: "A day commemorating the Armenians will lead to other memorial days, to the Native Americans, Vietnamese, Irish, or any other people. It will damage the importance of Shoah Day." Israeli veteran politician Shimon Peres, an artist in proving one thing and its opposite in one sentence, said on the eve of his visit to Turkey some time ago: "We reject attempts to equate the Shoah with the Armenian claims. Nothing like the Shoah had ever happened before. The Armenians suffered a tragedy, not a genocide." On the contrary, what is genocide is to be decided by the people who suffered it, according to the definition in international law, not by the supervisors of world holocausts, not by the Jews. Genocide is a long way from tragedy. The term *tragedy* belongs to the personal realm, for cases such as the sudden death of a close friend or the victims of a car crash. A *disaster* is an enhanced tragedy. A *massacre* is what Dr. Baruch Goldstein did in the Cave of the Patriarchs in the city of Hebron, where 29 Muslims at prayer in the Ibrahimi Mosque were murdered and another 150 were wounded. An *act of terror* is the mass killing of innocents in the Manhattan business district. A million and a half Armenians; a million Rwandans—both are genocide. It is genocide by international law, and a holocaust for the survivors and their relatives. What France, Sweden, Belgium, and other nations duly recognized as genocide can be respected and duly recognized as such by Israel as well. Furthermore, Israel ought to be the first to specify standards on issues of commemoration of other genocides.

We must not regret the denial of the past. My question still stands: Are we present-day deniers? Have we learned our lesson? Israel and the Jewish people, by expropriating and monopolizing the Shoah, deny all the other mass killings. It is a denial by means of miniaturizing, dwarfing, and disregarding. The result of this is a world that is saturated with small and big holocausts. A world that does not see Rwandans and Cambodians, Darfuris, and Kurds is a world that is up to the taking; in the end they will come to take me, us, but it would be too late as I/we do not care. How should the alternative Shoah narrative sound?

Israel must leave Auschwitz because Auschwitz is a mental prison. Life inside the camp is survival laced with guilt and victimology; life outside the camp is of constant alarm. Auschwitz and its chimneys are lighthouses to guide us toward a better moral and humanistic life, not a point into which all our life's ships sail and crash. I believe with all my heart that when Israel frees itself from its obsession with the Shoah and its exclusivity, the world also will be much freer. Israel's role will be to watch and sound the alarm and to stand beside the persecuted where they are, without regard to friend or foe. The Jewish people will recognize the persecuted and will mobilize world opinion and the political powers to prevent any atrocity before it happens. An International Court of Crimes against Humanity will be established in Jerusalem, the City of Peace, and its judges will be of all nations. It will be accessible to all, and on its gates Isaiah's prophecy will be carved:

In the end of days, the mount of the house of God will be established at the top of the mountains high above the hills, and all the nations will flow into it. Many peoples will go, saying, let us go and ascend the mountain of God, the house of the god of Jacob, and he will teach us his ways, and we will follow his path, as from Zion the law will come and the word of God from Jerusalem. And he will judge the nations and rule many peoples, and they will beat their swords into ploughs and their spears into pruning shears; a nation will not lift sword against another, and they will learn no more war.[14]

This will be the Third Temple. King Solomon of the Judea tribe built the First Temple. A generation later, in the days of Rehoboam, David's grandson, it was dedicated to Judeans only. The Second Temple was built in the same place and became the temple for all the citizens of the restored Kingdom of Israel. The Third Temple will be built in Jerusalem as the moral temple for the whole world. It will be a temple without sacrifices; it will have no room for fundamentalists, zealots, and blood-shedders. It will be the place to which human victims will turn to for help, and where they will receive it. The place for the new Israeli-Jewish Temple will be elsewhere, away from the Quarrel Mount in the Old City, to the Peace Mount in the western city.

I dream that in the future the International Court of Crimes Against Humanity will be built on the campus of the national Yad Vashem, changing its character from one end to the other. Yad Vashem today is the greatest monument of national impotence; of the moral dumbness and deafness toward others that have resided in our collective soul in recent decades. Yad Vashem, the Holocaust memorial, is the stake on which we raise our guests and force-feed them our exclusive Shoah values. I do not know who chose the name, which in Hebrew means literally "monument and memorial." Whoever that person was, he did not know his Bible, and psychology apparently was not his forte. Had he known, how could that person ignore the immediate biblical context of the words "monument and memorial":

Thus the alien who is committed to God will not say, God has separated me from his people, and the eunuch will not say, I am but a dry tree. For God said, to the eunuchs who observe my Sabbaths and choose what I desire and keep my covenant, I will give them in my house and in my walls a monument and a memorial better than sons and daughters, a memorial forever I will give him that will not be cut off.[15]

The term *yad vashem* in its regular biblical meaning is a "tombstone," a monument for an infertile man, as a substitute for the children that he will never have. Our Yad Vashem magnified the concept of impotence and infertility, ignoring all the other sons of foreign lands. However, the museum in its future form will be the memorial of all human injustices. It will be a place that will radiate the potency of the struggle against violence, wherever violence is. It will have an Armenian wing; and a Serbian wing, exhibits from Rwanda and Namibia; a presentation honoring the Native Americans that were exterminated by blond, blue-eyed generals. Children will come to Yad Vashem from all over the world to be educated on the principles of nonviolence. Race relations will be taught as a counterweight to race-based discrimination and extermination. Both the court and the museum will be recognized as international institutions; their land will be owned internationally and it will belong to the recognized institutions of the family of nations. They will embody a new concept in world statesmanship: World Sovereignty.

Israel's cabinet will add another ministry, the Ministry of Historical Affairs. The new minister will be in charge of commemoration, remembrance, and the struggle against racism and violence against the persecuted everywhere. Israeli students will study according to new curricula that will place the unique events in our history in the perspective of the history of the world.

It will be a world in which the holocausts which were not ours will become ours as well. In order to start the journey to utopia, we have to look ourselves in the eye, to face and sever the new roots of Jewish racism that are rising in our midst and consuming us from within. This new racism, this malignancy, is alien to all I learned growing up in my family and is also foreign to us as a people.

CHAPTER 10

A NEW
JUDAISM

J UDAISM IS A CIVILIZATION THAT IS THOUSANDS OF YEARS OLD. Naturally, this energetic old mistress encompasses all aspects of life. She includes past wisdoms and present follies. She has absorbed all human evil and given away much humanistic goodness. She has seen everything and everyone and survived it all. Judaism is ancient, but her future—and with it our own—is ahead of her.

Judaism is an astounding culture, complex and full of light, and naturally it also contains some shadows. It often blinds us by its brilliance, experience, and wisdom, so we do not pay attention to its other layers. This happens when you attempt to contain everything; there will be much good and also some bad. The solution is not to be a foolish follower of light, nor to surrender to the intimidating shadows. I will not reject the beliefs, people, or a way of life that I abhor if it is part of Jewish civilization. On the contrary, they are inseparable from Judaism and therefore from me; they are like the dark shadows that a painter adds to the outline of a figure in order to accentuate its luminescent qualities. I will not make my work easier by saying that all circumcised Jewish fundamentalists, or extremist followers of Moses' Torah, or the Sabbath-observing racists are not part of me. They are. They are part of Judaism's flowerbed and against them I direct my first battle on the path to returning my people, who have derailed during the past few years, to the tracks that their predecessors and founders laid for them. My father did not raise me by these beliefs when he taught me God's Torah and the People's Commandments. My mother did not raise us on these values from our infancy until her death. We were raised on a Judaism of love, founded on the verse "Love your fellow person as you love yourself." We were educated to oppose what was hateful to us as individuals and as a people, and vowed irrevocably not to perpetuate those hateful deeds on others, not to individuals and not to a people, whatever the circumstances.

Not all of Judaism and not all its followers are to my liking. Some of them are even my bitter enemies. I dedicate my confrontation with them to my love of the legacy of our heritage's firsts: To our first father Abraham, who did not restrain himself from rebuking God, "Will the judge of all the people not do justice?" To the Jewry of the School of Hillel, and to the students of Rabbi Yohanan Ben Zakai, who during the Great Ruin of A.D. 70 preferred Yavne and its sages, its values and morality to the then-corrupt Second Temple and the political, brutal and extremist Jerusalem. These words are written for Israel's greats, from Maimonides, who believed that the world's redemption would come with the annulment of oppression and occupations, to Martin Buber, Abraham Joshua Heschel, and their colleagues, who believed and swore in the name of the religion of peace for the benefit of the entire world. With their power I seek to uproot the evil growth that climbs like ivy on our tree of life and threatens to asphyxiate it. Although many of those described below currently hold the Jewish microphone, in my view they are the cruel abductors of this wonderful culture. They are not its authentic representatives.

In the past few years, miracles have happened in Israel quite openly, as when the tombs of mythical figures are discovered. It is unlikely that the tombs really contain the remains of those figures, or that they even ever lived. In any case, their tombs become places of worship and pilgrimage. A few years ago, a yeshiva was established at Joseph's Tomb outside Shechem (today Nablus). At the outset, the act expressed devotion and love of the land, but in fact it is paganism and Jewish idolatry, which goes against the original biblical prohibition. Unlike other patriarchs of the Israeli tribes, such as Reuben, Shimon, Judah, and the other founders of the nation, whose place of burial is unknown, Joseph's bones were brought from Egypt and buried in the Land of Israel. Like his mother, Rachel, Joseph was buried outside the Jewish Pantheon, namely in the Cave of the Patriarchs in Hebron. Rachel was buried on the way to Efrath and Joseph not too far from her, somewhere in ancient Shechem. In Jewish history, Shechem was a bad place.

Near the city, outside the historic city walls and gates, which are archeological sites, is a tomb identified as belonging to Joseph, son of Jacob, for hundreds of years. There is no point arguing if the site is indeed what it is alleged to be, as its designation took place thousands of years after Joseph's death. In any case, whether the tomb is indeed Joseph's or belonging to a local man of stature, after 1967 the domed site, in the biblical province of the Ephraim tribe, was granted its "Rabbinical Kosher Certificate" as Joseph's. Until the tomb was transferred to the jurisdiction of the Palestinian Authority after the signing the Oslo Accords of 1993, Rabbi Yitzhak Ginzburg headed a yeshiva there. At the start of the Palestinian uprising in October 2000, the IDF and Border Police troops guarded the site, which was surrounded by a violent Palestinian mob. The violence peaked with the tragic death of Sergeant Madhat Yusuf of the Border Police. He bled for many hours in the tomb, and when a rescue mission reached him at last, he was already dead.

It seems symbolic that the last sacrifice to be slaughtered on Joseph's altar was named Yusuf, an Arab version of the name Joseph. The fact is that a Druze a introduced me to the Jewish race theory, its scholars, and preachers. The following is a true story.

After his death, I drove north to pay condolences at his village in the Galilee. I was received with great respect in the *diwan*, the large reception room. As is the custom, I shook hands with the community's dignitaries, the sheikhs, hugged family members, and even went to the separate female section to speak to the bereaved mother and convey the grief of many Israelis at her loss. After the official part of the visit, I walked to my car to drive home. In the yard I saw some young men who seemed enraged. I approached them and we had the following conversation.

"Are you Burg?"

"Yes."

"You're from the Knesset, aren't you?"

"Yes. I am the speaker of the Knesset."

"Then you're an alien. You have no idea what's happening. You were cheated."

"What do you mean?"

"We were there with Madhat in the battle on the tomb. We know what happened."

"What happened?"

"We, the Border Police, are not Jews, you know. We are Druze. We guarded the tomb and the yeshiva. The students are not religious like you, but like the others, with the big yarmulkes and threads hanging outside their shirts. They were inside and we were outside. All day we heard them studying, and in the evening we escorted them and their rabbi back home to their settlement. We heard them talking. And what did they say? That the blood of the *goyim* is not like the blood of the Jews, and that Arabs are like beasts...Our blood is only good enough to guard them and to die for them. That is, like a watchdog."

It went on and on. They quoted distorted verse fragments from my Jewish origins, texts, and sacred sages, the way they heard and understood them. I spontaneously went back inside the mourners' room and requested the book of condolences. Then for a long time I wrote an apology on behalf of the other Jewish people, who do not share the same religion and faith as those who seized the faith of Joseph's Tomb and their rabbi. For me, that rabbi and his friends are heartless religionists, worshippers of another god, and followers of a racist Jewish creed. In my view they are circumcised Amaleki, which we are commanded to eliminate.

Madhat Yusuf's death changed the nature of the dispute I had with the extreme orthodox Jews. Until his death, I focused my argument on the Jewish struggle against the idolatry of places and the territories. In my view, Jews who worship graves, wood, and stones are pagans, the argument with the place rabbis, students, and believers should be focused on a totally different point, and it is not the pagan nature of their Judaism. The argument concerns their interpretation and understanding of Judaism and the Torah as a race theory and a faith of discrimination and violence.

Rabbi Yitzhak Ginzburg is the contemporary link in a long chain of religious and mystical ideologues that view Jewish supremacy as the center of the Jewish nation's soul. Ginzburg is one of the most influential figures of the new religious and spiritual radicalism in Israel. He is one of the most meaningful rabbis for the scores of the so-called West Bank Hills Youth, their parents, and the rabble of dangerous fanatics of Israel. These are the same people that prime ministers and security chiefs have defined as "clear and present danger to Israel's rule of law." The holders of his dogma are the most dangerously violent, racist, and lawless element that threatens Israel's integrity. They are the day laborers that toil to destroy the current state's structures. Ginzburg is their prophet. He was born in America and studied mathematics and philosophy, then repented and became religious. When he was about twenty years old, in the mid-1960s, he immigrated to Israel and became a follower of Chabbad, the Lubavich faithful. He lives in Kfar Chabad and teaches Hassiduth, Kabala and Messianism to the masses. His name appears in the media occasionally, almost always in political context. He once called for the boycott of Arab goods. He was active in publishing the book on Baruch Goldstein, the Brooklyn-born physician who massacred twenty-nine praying Arabs in the Cave of the Patriarchs in Hebron in 1994, and praised him. His deeds and followers underline a reality happening just under our nose, the dissemination of Israeli Race Theory. While many study this abomination, nobody seems to care. An exception is Dr. Jonathan Garb, a brilliant young intellectual and among the most impressive of Jewish scholars I have ever met. His knowledge encompasses the universe and his understanding is deep and subtle. This is how he recently described Ginzburg and his actions:

> Rabbi Yitzhak Ginzburg's writing and teachings express another transition, from increasing the interest in force...to de facto affiliation with radical circles of religious Zionism...By extensive use of new technologies and Internet sites...Ginzburg greatly expanded his support base. His associates in different periods include writers, artists and radical political activists...from the alternative settlement of Bat Ayin, his followers established in the Gush Etzion region...a squad went out and carried out attacks

against Palestinian civilians. [His positions such as] the distinction between "Jewish blood" and the blood of those who are not Jews, deportation of Palestinians and harsh military actions against them...attracted to him many of the "continuing generation" and Hills Youth in the settlements...and led to his administrative detention, an unusual step against Jews.[1]

Ginzburg's writings, teachings, and beliefs shed light on a great darkness that veils significant parts of religious Judaism in Israel and abroad during these days. Around the hardcore groups led by Ginzburg and others are ripples of faith and support, of ignorance and folly and insensitivity and indifference. Eventually there is hooliganism, violence, and lethal incidents. All these connect to a clear and present threat to the modern Jewish identity of the state and its current form. Ginzburg writes:

The Land of Israel is truly a land of destiny, Israel's land, the land that should be settled by those who chose to become the people of God and observe his Torah. Generally, people today are too shy to say that the people of Israel is a "Light unto the Nations," afraid to say that an Arab professor is less smart than a Jew. It is perceived as racism. In this way they want to blur all that was [apparent] also among the gentiles, that the Jews gave morality and intelligence to all the peoples.[2]

I know many Jews who are perfect idiots. I have Chinese friends who are geniuses. I know very talented Lutheran Germans, non-Jewish intellectuals, and moralists who cast a long shadow on some well-known Jews who apparently suffer from serious moral limitations. Deep inside, many thousands of our fellow Jews believe in Jewish supremacy, in the "Jewish Genius," over the rest of humanity. They believe but do not say, think but do not act—but deep inside the feeling exists, and very much so. They are indifferent, passive racists that provide the compost layer from which grow the wild weeds that continue the Exilic mindset during these days of redemption.

Ginzburg is just one of many. Rabbi Ovadia Yosef shares his same views, though he is perceived as very different. Dubbed the "Generation's Great," he is a Halakha rationalist, or a man of religious law, removed from mysticism. But his preaching exposes a worldview that is similar to the one described above. After Hurricane Katrina demolished New Orleans, leaving many dead and many thousands homeless, grieving, and miserable, the much-admired rabbi told his followers in his populist weekly address,

> There was a tsunami and there are other terrible natural disasters. All this is because of the reduction of the Torah. Wherever there is Torah, it sustains the worlds. Over there, there are Negroes. Do Negroes study the Torah? Let's give them a tsunami, sink them. Hundreds of thousands remain without a roof over their heads. Scores of thousands died. All this is because they do not have God.[3]

His words express no condolences and no empathy, only a distinction between Us and Them, the People of the Torah and the "Negroes" of the world who have no God. This is what happens in the process of restricting human wisdom to Jewish wisdom only: The narrower one's lens, the tighter one's limits. It leads to arrogance and patronization, a short way from racism and discrimination. Rabbi Yosef is proof that a giant of Torah scholarship can be a humanistic dwarf.

The late Menachem Mendel Schneerson, the last Chabad-Lubavich Rebbe—whose Hebrew title, Admor, means our master, our teacher, our rabbi—stretched the limits of his Hasidic sect's dogma beyond legitimate Jewish boundaries. When his followers proclaimed him a Messiah while he was still alive, no one protested. Even when his body was lowered to the grave, some denied his death. "The Rebbe is alive," they declared. A poster proclaiming "Long live our master, our teacher, our rabbi, the Messiah King forever and ever," is still among the most conspicuous memorabilia in Israel and New York. They turned the dead rabbi into the second messiah, who died and was resurrected. The first messiah was also a Jew. His name was Yeshua, or Jesus Christ. On their bodies new religions were born, none of them in the least Jewish. With his death and rebirth, the Rebbe's theory of faith did not die. On the contrary, it is alive and kicking. It is the faith of the extreme Right.

From the first days of our patriarchs, two trends rose in Jewish history: exclusivity and inclusiveness. The exclusivists separated themselves from the world and detested the gentiles' being and inputs; the inclusivists were open to adopt positive spirits and ideas from other cultures. These trends began a long time ago, when Judaism was conceived. The first was Abraham the Hebrew, the *Ivri,* who came from across the river, where we originated. But this geographical expression became psychological, positioning us on one side of the balance and the entire world on the other side.

Throughout Jewish history, our forefathers never succeeded in erasing the significance of the gentiles in our lives. Judah, the patriarch of the House of David, was the first Israelite to have a mixed marriage outside the patriarchal family. He married "a daughter of a Canaanite man, whose name is Shua, and he took her and came to her."[4] Ruth the Moabite slept overnight at the feet of the Israelite farmer Boaz, who later married her according to Jewish custom. The couple created a lineage from which David, the king of Israel, was born, starting a royal dynasty. It is clear that the ban on marrying Moabites was softened, perhaps even abolished. This is the weave that produced us. On the one hand, exclusivity; on the other, universalism. Jews and gentiles created the historical Jewish identity. The following conversation took place among some of our sages from the Second Temple period:

> Rabbi Yehuda and Rabbi Yossei and Rabbi Shimon were sitting together, and with them sat Yehuda, son of Jewish converts. Rabbi Yehuda opened, saying: "How good are the deeds of this nation [the Roman Empire]. They built markets, they built bridges, and they built baths. Rabbi Yossei kept silent. Rabbi Shimon Bar Yohai replied, saying: "All that they built they built for themselves. They built markets, prostitutes to please them; baths, to groom themselves; bridges, to charge tolls."[5]

Rabbi Yehuda acknowledges the aesthetics and the infrastructure of the Roman Empire. Rabbi Shimon Bar Yohai, ever the segregationist, is suspicious. For him, any foreign thing is a threat. One is a universalist; the other a xenophobe, as we have always had an agitating split personality from the beginning.

For me, the Jewish appreciation of aesthetics, grace, and charity must keep its respectable place, even when spiritual thugs attempt to exterminate it and eliminate our spirit. The lines of segregation in the world begin with the believer's personal wake-up prayer, which includes the line, "Blessed are you, our God, king of the universe, for not having made me a gentile." It is brought to light at the end of the Sabbath, as we pray, "Blessed...who differentiate between Holiness and everyday matters, between light and darkness, between Israel and the nations." This is a distinct separation of one group, of everyday affairs, darkness, and nations of the world, from the group of holiness, light, and the people of Israel. These distinctions are made in numerous sources. The idea of the Chosen People can be explained in historical and human contexts. It could be that the oppressed Jews, who experienced ruin and persecutions, found refuge in dreams of grandeur. But now we are neither persecuted nor oppressed. The Land of Israel is rehabilitated and built. Reality has changed, but the spiritual condition of some of us has not. Suddenly, the remedy that was meant to alleviate the pain becomes poisonous.

The biblical dispute between Korah and his faction and Moses and Aaron is the most meaningful clash to take place among the Israelites who left Egypt in the Sinai wilderness. It was a bitter struggle over the character of Israelite leadership. Unlike the national leadership of today, a leadership of mortals, whose source of legitimacy is the constituency of voters, aware Moses' leadership was authorized and inspired by the divine. That generation was of the revelation and omnipresence of God among them. This incorporeal God was their electorate body. Therefore the dispute between Korah and Moses and Aaron was not just about who was leading and who represented the people before God. It was a hot debate on God and his Holiness, the identity of his emissary on Earth, on the people and their essence, the nation and its soul.

Korah assembled a flock of disgruntled leaders and supporters, and confronted Moses and Aaron, arguing: "As all the congregation all are holy, and God is among them, why then do you elevate yourselves over the congregation of God?"[6] He actually renders an alternative theology to Moses. Korah assumed that holiness is automatic for all individuals and to the entire community, and he summed it up with the phrase "all are holy." In effect, he was proposing a religious condition that exempts the believer of any responsibility for existence and reality, as the believer is considered automatically holy, as if holiness was etched into his genetic code. Korah's "all are holy" Judaism implies that even the unqualified, bad, and malicious are holy. For them, God's choice of his people and person is granted, and therefore all of us are elevated above other humans, who are our friends and colleagues in the family of peoples and nations. Korah's holiness is only for the Jewish race.

Moses is shocked. Korah's theology is completely antithetical to him. Moses' reply is given in another place in the Bible, in the Book of Leviticus, 19:1–2, "And the Lord spoke unto Moses, saying: Speak unto all the congregation of the children of Israel, and say unto them: Ye shall be holy; for I the Lord your God am holy." Later the text lists basic commandments, relating to values, which derive from the constitution of the Ten Commandments. These rules are the foundations of the biblical society of justice. They include respecting parents, social conscience, justice, and ethics in human relations and an endless love for the other. They include the very meaningful sequence of equal love to your God, your fellow and the resident alien: "And you love him like yourself." Moses' holiness is a Sisyphean effort to repair the self and improve the world. It is an acquired, not inherited, holiness; it's never granted forever and therefore has to be earned and maintained continuously. Moses' holiness means being constantly self-critical and self-guarded so as not to desecrate the name of God, in whose image you were created. This is totally unlike Korah's concept of holiness, which allows you to do all you wish, as God "is always with you" anyway. I am with Moses. I am a Jew of the Tikkun belief, meaning the belief in repairing the world and oneself in the world. I grew out of the earth and am not willing to be swallowed by it—the fate that met Korah and his faction—for the crimes of some trendy extremists.

I became aware of these differences by accident. On the day my favorite writer, the novelist Saul Bellow, died, I took a trip abroad. On the spur of the moment I decided to take one of his books with me. I pulled a book from the bottom shelf, where the older books are, thinking it was Bellow's, and packed it in my bag. After boarding the plane, I felt like holding a private memorial to the great Jewish writer. But alas, the book I had taken was not Bellow's, but by the novelist Heinrich Böll, the German humanist and Nobel laureate. The book, *A Soldier's Legacy,* had been on the shelf for years and somehow I never read it. It seemed that the book had been waiting its turn, for that opportunity on the plane. It is a short story on a moral German soldier, Lieutenant Schelling, and his relationship with his corrupt superior officer, including their worlds and experiences in Germany during

World War II and its aftermath. Böll and Bellow looked similar enough to confuse me. I was disappointed and looked at the cover without reading. Suddenly I noticed the photograph of a Wehrmacht soldier, wearing a wide leather belt with a metal buckle etched with writing. I asked my neighbor, a nice Shoah survivor from Miami, to lend me the magnifying glass with which she read a newspaper. The buckle read *Gott mit Uns,* God is with us. German soldiers went to battle with God very close to their bellies. The soldiers of the regime of race theory believed that God was always with them. The meaning of the ancient controversy of Moses and Korah suddenly dawned on me. The Nazis, like Korah, claimed automatic holiness. According to both, people without moral judgment can be a chosen people, born to the master race.

The assumption of responsibility-free genetic superiority has probably been a psychological need of individuals, communities, ethnic groups and nations since the dawn of civilization. My Judaism, however, is a constant struggle against racism, religious arrogance and the self-appointed emissaries of God who believe that God is always with them and with them only.

Korah's racism lacks the mechanism of self-criticism and self-accounting. The Mosaic-Jewish faith, in contrast, is the constant struggle to improve the individual, the collective and the world. One is an untamed faith, the other one restrained. From a purely religious point of view, the simplest element of faith is always the belief in God. He is the Supreme, the absolute source of authority and nothing is above him. His existence is not denied, and his commands are absolute. Opposite to God is man, the mortal, with all his limitations. Original Judaism created a separation between the holy domain and the laical space. All that belongs to God is sacred, and all that belongs to humans is earthly, temporary and subject to continuous review. "Do not monitor a heavenly message," says the Talmud.[7] Any attempt to extend God's zone beyond its boundaries, to implement it and force it on a secular institution, such as a state, is contempt for the eternal and is bound to end in a spiritual disaster. A state and human society that do not account for their action, government actions that look like supreme decrees, statesmanship and politics that hide behind the word of religious law and claim to fulfill God's will—all these pose real and present mortal dangers. It has happened with us and with others. Korah is the biblical expression of the unfinished psychological process. And the sons of Korah, as the Bible says, never die.

The conflict between constraining constitutional and legal elements and the sentimental eruptions of exclusivity and uniqueness has characterized Jewish religious writings since their beginning. The desire to break out without restraint is typical at any time, especially in times of crisis and Ruin, and is derived from the chosen person's perceived automatic holiness, his enthusiasm of belief that cannot always be leashed. Between biblical times and contemporary Jewish messianic times, many other structures of Jewish superiority were built, as detailed below.

Rabbi Yehuda Halevi, one of the great medieval philosophers and poets, lived in Spain during the First Crusade and created his works in the shadow of the titanic world conflicts between Christianity and Islam. The struggle between the two religions took place also in Spain, which was conquered by both sides several times. This was the spiritual backdrop for his book *The Kuzari*.[8] For years, Yehuda Halevi labored on this work, which is literary and poetic, philosophical and theological. The plot is deceptively simple, though creative: the Kuzari king's conversion to Judaism. The book is a profound, complex analysis of Judaism. In reality, the Kuzari's spiritual endeavors are Halevi's attempt to break the contemporary formulas of thought and philosophy, and to present a religious alternative with poetic charm and philosophical cohesiveness. The book is a classic Jewish masterpiece.

The alternative that Halevi presents is an enchanting story on conversations between the king of the faraway Kuzaries and his "Jewish friend," who convinces him that the Jewish faith is superior. In fact, the book was written for internal apologists. The epic story was meant to explain to the masses of Israel, who were impoverished and suffered great persecution by the other two sister religions, which were prospering, why we are still the best. Above everything else, we are at the top of the ladder. The inorganic are at the bottom, above them are the flora, then the fauna, then the speaking human, then the Israelite, the Jew.

Five hundred years later, another Jewish great, Rabbi Yehuda Liwa ben Bezalel, known as HaMaharal of Prague, left his mark on the Jewish canon. He was a renaissance man with extensive and extraordinary knowledge of the Talmud, Kabbalah, philosophy, and the sciences. His works and beliefs significantly influenced the Hasidim movement a century after his death. The basis of his views is the early seeds of the national theory and it can be viewed as a preparatory contemplation for the revival of Jewish nationalism.

HaMaharal based his theory on his predecessors, Hazal, one of our sages. One of his basic principles is the Jewish nation's exalted role in human history. Like Halevi before him and others after him, he draws a precise line between a Jew and a non-Jew:

"It is written that this nation is holy, that it tends towards [God], for it is the beginning of all nations." In another place he interprets the universalistic, humanistic phrase, "Favorite is Man for being created in his image," thus: Although it says man, it does not include all the human species, as it has already been said, "You are called man and they are not called man"...Nevertheless there is the form of man in the Nations as well; only that the principal form of man lacks in the nations. The stage of Israel in relation to the nations is as the stage of the nations in relation to the nonspeaking animals.[9]

Innumerable volumes can be filled with words and ideas of this type, just as we can, and should, bring the opposing views, as the works of the antimessianic Maimonides, aka HaRambam. All of them belong to the days in which our lives were the opposite of what they are today. We were lowly and all the others supreme beings, rulers and oppressors. The oppressed always look up and aspire to resemble their oppressors.

However, what is correct in one situation—a harsh, painful exile, alleviated by dreams of grandeur, hope and unending optimism—may be hazardous in another situation, when the servant becomes the master. It is like the battered child that becomes an abusive parent and thus preserves the pathology of his life. In the same way, a humiliated and persecuted people can become similar to the worst of its tormentors. Past oppression does not provide a clean bill of morality to the newly freed people, but rather the opposite.

If we return to the *The Kuzari,* we find in the book a piercing honesty that many of its admirers overlook. The Kuzari king wonders about the Jewish condition "that is inferior in this world." The wise man, the Jew, tries to evade the question and asks him cunningly why he wonders about "our poverty and bad condition," as this is the ideal condition of meek modesty and humility that Jesus and Muhammad, the founders of the other religions, preach. According to our current poverty, says the wise man, we are closer to God than the glorious and great kings who are very far from their religion's models. But the king does not fall into this rhetorical trap, and distinguishes between willful adherence to God and one made by force, as was the case for Halevi's people at the time. Forced exile is not the same as humility by choice, he says. He then adds, "And when your hand can reach, you too shall kill your foe." The Jewish friend replies with admiration: "My king, you have found my painful weak spot."[10]

In today's intense life, can we honestly say that we conduct ourselves according to the ideal that we preached to our tormentors, or have we become as insensitive as they were? Quite a few of us, in government and in the street, do not understand that we no longer have a need to patronize, because the State of Israel is meant to be the cure for all Exilic illnesses. Yet the separatists carry on the past's inferiority complex and convert it into an obsession of actual superiority. Its practical outcome is discrimination in many areas and a hint of racism that taints our government's decisions.

After World War I ended, many believed it was the last war, and an enchanting age of world peace would follow. At that time, Rabbi Avraham Yitzhak HaCohen Kook contemplated a radical idea. It was starkly different from the actions of those who were to become his followers, some of whom today proudly carry the banner of racist nationalism. Kook viewed the Diaspora and the loss of independence not just as a historical disaster, but also as a voluntary decision of the people, made for moral reasons. Kook wrote.

> We abandoned the world politics by coercion, which also had an innate will, until a happy era, in which a commonwealth can be managed without evil and barbarism...That is, our ancestors' voluntary decision to walk down the world stage and to wander throughout the paths of Exile originated in the will to abstain from the crimes and sins of corrupt government. "It is not worthy for Jacob to deal with a commonwealth, when it needs to be bloody, when it demands evil talent."[11]

It would be wrong for us to whitewash the truth and say that we are immune and that it will not happen to us. It happened to the Germany of Schiller, Goethe and Mendelssohn, and also to us. In Israel of Agnon, Oz, and Rabbi Ginzburg bad things happened. The source of some is the trauma, and the source of others is the groundwater of Jewish identity and the segregation-ist, confrontational nature of our national existence for ages. I fear certain rabbis and their overt and covert theories, and I also fear there are some thugs among us. There is a built-in element of discrimination, arrogance, and preference for anything that comes from Jewish genes. It is much more present than deniers wish to see.

Not long ago I had a conversation with an acquaintance of mine, a good-hearted, hard-working blue-collar man. I told him that I met the Arab boyfriend of a woman friend of ours. He sputtered a curse, in Arabic, of course.

"What do you prefer," I asked, "that your daughter would have married someone positive, educated, gentle, and well-to-do like Mahmud, my friend from Nazareth, or the lazy, violent, drunk criminal that she married?"

"I, I don't care," he replied. "He can be the meanest man in the world, as long as he is Jewish," he said, adding, in case I still did not get it, "Pure, like this, you know."

Several days later I spoke at one of Israel's finest universities. The conversation revolved around Jewish identity, assimilation, and human-ism. At the end of the lecture, a professor stood up.

"I agree with you in theory," he said, "but in reality, it would be very difficult. What would I do if my son brings home a gentile woman? I am secular, but it is difficult for me."

I pondered for a moment whether to dodge the subject or inflame the discussion. I decided to inflame it.

"I don't think that our generation's choice is linear and one-dimensional, as was the decision of our parents and elders," I said. "In the past, such a deci-sion was binary, either a goy or a Jew, a *shikse* or a *yiddene*. Your choice today is much more difficult and sophisticated. What do you prefer, that your son marry a gentile woman or a Jewish man?"

It took the professor a long moment to contemplate the alternative, but then he lowered his head and said, "A Jewish homosexual is preferable to a gentile bride."

For me, it is important that the person that my child marries is good, ethical and moral. I don't care whether he or she is a Jew or a gentile, homo-sexual or heterosexual. My standard is goodness and morality, not a per-son's origins or sexual preferences. But many others differ. Their basic instinct was programmed differently. For the blue-collar worker as well as the professor, the hierarchy is obvious: a Jew, whether male or female, straight or gay, is preferable to any gentile whatever he or she is.

Purists will say that racism does not exist among ordinary people. "Am I a racist?" they would demand defensively. "Only yesterday I had hummus in an Arab restaurant in an Arab village." There are many slogans and technical denials of this type. Nevertheless, I believe that racism is rampant. I have many times been party to such conversations, which stressed cooperation between Israelis and Arabs as proof of brotherly love, but reality continues to defy them. True, we are not like Germany at the war's end and at the height of the Final Solution. But we are somewhere very close to the first stages of humanistic and cultural Germany's implosion in the face of Hitler and his henchmen, whose National Socialism shredded everything good and beautiful in what had been Germany. To my great sorrow and pain, I cannot always distinguish between the early Social Nationalism and some national theories of here and now.

Germany's moral immunity has been investigated and described in detail, but very little, too little, was said and written about us. We, like any other nation, are vulnerable to the same danger, changing for the worse, but most of us do not discuss it. The sons of Korah still rule undisputedly in the Jewish and Israeli identity mechanisms. When a Jewish rabbi defeats Israeli sovereignty, the danger is clear. The automatic holiness of the ruling classes establishes here in Israel a state that is run by Korah's modern priests. Such a state is Jewish first, democratic second. It is a state of distorted Torah, especially when based on national superiority, contempt for others and belief in an unrestrained Jewish race theory. When I close my eyes and imagine the future, I see the nightmare of a Halakha state that might, God forbid, work here, if the false messiahs succeed.

Some say that only a Jew is allowed to be anti-Semitic, because he knows why. I am worried, because I know why. I come from there, and my relatives and friends are still there. I listen to their talk, know their ambitions, and feel their heartbeats. I know where they are headed: to the Mount Temple and to conquering the land from inside. In the next few years, we will see them bring more and more messianic redemption promises to the military ranks, junior and senior; to the political system; the economy, the newsrooms and Israeli public opinion. Their representatives already control one-sixth of the Likud constituency. It is beneficial to listen to the wishes of rabbis and soldiers who prophesy this. The mirrors are placed before us.

Who thought Hamas would democratically defeat the Palestinians' historic secular movement? Who thought American Christian fundamentalists would have such a tight grip on the American president and his administration? Everyone who had thought this was impossible is invited to rethink what may happen to us here. The fundamentals are already founded, the preachers already preaching and public opinion is receptive. I have an open war with these people, but I do not have enough partners and allies who would alarmingly understand that Nazi Germany, too, was human. It was indeed evil and malicious, but still within the human realm. They were sons and daughters of Eve and Adam, who perpetrated the deeds of the all-Germanic nation, and yet their explanations, too, are human. From there and then, to here and now: in Germany, slow processes altered the perception of reality to the degree that insanity became the norm, and then we were exterminated. It happened in the land of poets and philosophers. There it was possible, and here too, in the land of the prophets. The establishment of a state run by rabbis and generals is not an impossible nightmare. I know has difficult this comparison is, but please open your ears, eyes, and hearts.

The revolution that did not happen in the modern Israeli Jewish soul with the transition from powerlessness to powerfulness is also reflected in the soul of many Diaspora Jews. Instead of harnessing modern Jewish fortitude to repair the world and oppose its injustices, we find too many Jews that are haunted by past traumas. They cannot change and adapt, in the same way that a ship in the ocean cannot come to a full stop in less than a few miles.

Diaspora Jews, including many of their representatives, choose the side of authority and become partners in the world's injustices and insensitivities. I am trying to understand the U.S. relationship with Israel. Often, when I cannot understand my own country, I look at our big sister, the United States of America, and try to understand it, as if it were our mirror. This is the country, society, and culture that I know best outside of Israel's. There are many things to appreciate and even admire in the *Goldene Medina,* the Golden State, as it was nicknamed by the millions of Jews who chose it over their haven in the Land of Israel over the past two centuries. But the same United States is also a place for great worry on a world scale. By its role as the world's peacekeeper, it rattled sabers too often in recent decades, causing unnecessary wars. In sunny days I see America's positive influence in the areas of women's equality, civil and human rights, and freedom for all. Unfortunately, on cloudy days I see things that I would rather not know about myself. Both Israel and the United States are immigrant societies that are based on biblical visions, two new democracies that emerged from old Europe and became magnets for immigrants from all over the world. But is it really so?

I look again and see the symbiosis between us as a disease. Beyond the lip service that both countries still pay to the utopian visions on which they were founded, the mesh between the conservative American administrations and the right-wing Israeli governments is the most blatant testimony to our mental problems.

Jews hold stunningly powerful positions and clout in the United States. The combination of the American state's power and the Jewish power in the areas of legislation, administration, media, law, business, culture, and entertainment have made the Jews a defining factor of contemporary America. Because Israel is inseparable from the identity of American Jews, Israel is inseparable from the American experience. The original pioneering Israel has metamorphosed in the last four decades of its existence; since 1967 it has changed its character. From a weak, embryonic state, it has become the most powerful Jewish entity ever. At the same time, American Jewry underwent a corresponding change, no less profound and meaningful, beginning with the 1960s human rights revolution and the openness of John Fitzgerald Kennedy to Jews. American Jews today are no longer part of the minority coalition with African Americans and Hispanics and the rest of the domestic coalition in the struggle for American justice and liberties. Too many of my Jewish American brothers and sisters have become the beating heart of neoconservatism. They are part of the white, right-wing, nationalist, and powerful establishment, part of an administration and culture that withdraw from the global responsibility that defined America's spirit during World War II.

Israel's place in the American psyche, at least the political psyche, is still an unresolved mystery. The Israel that resides in the American soul is part of the isolationist withdrawal from responsibility and not part of universalism. There is not much dialogue between the Jews and other minorities. The Jews have abandoned the inner cities for affluent suburbs. The American Jews' new camp is not only geographically removed from the nonwhite communities, but implements the same philosophy in the international arena: white and Christian on "our" side, all others on the opposite. Now the Jews are siding with the administration, and together they stand against Arabs and Muslims everywhere.

The Jews' crossing of the "river of power" has major consequences for our national identity and perhaps even for the Western world's identity. What happened to the Jewish communities of Israel and America also happened to one of the most important French intellectuals living today, Alain Finkielkraut. The status French intellectuals enjoy in their country is an impressive phenomenon that testifies to the French people's respect for thought, expression, and intellectual innovation. Among this generation's French intellectuals, a few Jews are prominent, and one of them is Finkielkraut. For two decades he has been one of the leaders of the New Philosophers, who oppose the "tyranny of thought" and the known, conventional philosophies. He is not confined to the ivory tower, and is active in popular venues, being a much sought-after media personality. He writes prolifically and makes many appearances on radio and television. His positions are hard to tag as left or right. He is original and thinks outside the box and when I read him, I have the feeling that he enjoys controversy and provocation, and like me, he believes in the creative power of potemics. More than once I found myself virtually on his side. We walk together, in a virtual world, he in Paris and I here in the Holy Land, in a protest march, against the deceitful war in Lebanon, for the Geneva Accords, and for and against numerous other issues in between.

When I wrote my previous book, *God Is Back,* I felt that I was losing him. I tried to clarify my position regarding the anti-Semitic wave that swept the world in the early 2000s and the increasing feeling that I had that some of us drew sadomasochistic pleasure from it. During this clarification, I reached for a thirty-page booklet by Finkielkraut, *In the Name of the Other.* Daring and innovative, it was originally published in France as the French, and the Europeans, debated the minority challenge. The essay deals with the attitudes toward Muslims and Jews and makes a distinction between anti-Semitism and criticism of Israel. Finkielkraut also discusses Europe's view of the war in Iraq, Osama bin Laden, radical Islam, terror, and more. One of the most prominent debates at that time was the French government's decision to ban traditional Muslim dress in public schools for girls. A state committee examined ways of preserving the separation between church and state, and was the focus of heated public debates.

This philosopher's diagnosis of Europe and its accounting of its past and ours is often stunning in its innovation. Yet something bothered me very much, until I had to ask, You too, Alain? Even you were infected with this national malaise? You, too, obsessively deal with the gentiles as persecutors? I wondered, also to his ears, if he had started to adopt the insights of the conservative Jewish right, which draws from the well of "The Entire World is Against Us."

In a visit he made to the Knesset, and during a meeting he had with several of its members, he tried to pacify me: "No, there was nothing to worry about, but…" That *but* broke out forcefully in an interview he gave to *Haaretz Magazine*. To understand the meaning of the original interview, it is worth reading first the apology he gave, in French in *Le Monde* after he had almost drowned in denunciations. His critics erased all hues between white and black and placed him to the wall next to Hitler, or at least Jean-Marie Le Pen. It is ridiculous: he is far from this place. Yet, what is troubling in Finkielkraut's following words is not where his arrow hits or the size of its vector, but its direction: from humanism to the right-wing— white, patronizing, and arrogant. He is not Eichmann or Göbbels, neither Jörg Haider of Austria nor Vladimir Zhirinovsky of Russia, and not even a common national religious Israeli member of the Knesset, but what he says is still problematic.

> I don't know the man in the *Le Monde* story, and I don't identify at all with his opinions… I abhor the man from the story; he is even revolting. He is he, and I am I. To my astonishment, since the day the story ran, it has become clear that we have the same name.[12]

No doubt this is an elegant denial. Stylish. It isn't me; it's the bad boy in me, as Israeli poet Leah Goldberg wrote in a children's song. It is a song that tries to build a bridge between two temperaments of a child; I am good but the bad boy inside me took over. It is the scared Jew in me, descendant of Auschwitz survivors. But it was he, expressing in his words what many in France and Israel feel nowadays, illuminating with a spotlight the Jews' changed place in the world, and among themselves. From being the one in the family of displaced persons, migrants, persecuted, and hated—to our elevated new status as speakers of the new white conservatism, alienating those who are stuck in the position that we left just a few decades ago. What motivated Finkielkraut to remember our Auschwitz past was the injury to the Jews—which was part of the injury to the native French—by the immigrant youths from the poor suburbs. Instead of identifying with the troubles of the suburban youth from our own place and experience, to put his immense clout behind them for changing the segregationist, rightist agenda of contemporary France, he only saw us, and embarked on a one-way road of racism. He went as far as self-denial and used verbal acrobatics to the point of virtually erasing his own identity. This is what he told *Haaretz*.

> The problem is that most of the youths are blacks and Arabs who identify with Islam. There are other immigrants who live in difficult conditions in France...but they do not participate in the riots. It is clear then that the rebellion has an ethno-religious character...Their message is not a cry for help or a demand for better schools. It is the will to eliminate all the mediators that stand between them and the objects of their desires: money, brand names, sometimes young women...I think this is a stage in an anti-Republican pogrom. There are people in France who hate France as a republic...Colonial history is taught in school only as negative. We do not teach them that the colonial project also strove to educate, to bring culture to the savages.[13]

Why did Finkielkraut give this revealing interview in Israel, to be published in Hebrew and not in *Le Monde*, in French? His interviewers, Dror Mish'ani and Aurelia Semotraze, commented that "he stressed once and again that what he would tell us he could not say in France anymore. 'You cannot say it in France. It is even dangerous to say there.'" Indeed, as long as the interview and the ideas remained in the Israeli *Haaretz*, readers for the most part were happy. Here is proof from someone who was wholly against the 1982 war in Lebanon, the Israeli policy vis-à-vis Sarajevo, and now by his leftist authority, he provides legitimacy to Israel's current wickedness: "Arabs, all Arabs, are the same, aren't they?" Unfortunately for the philosopher, his interview was translated into French and his true beliefs were exposed.

True, Israel is very different from France, at least the one that still exists in our theory. In France, secular citizenship stands in for state religion; in Israel, the state is the state of the Jewish religion. The first is historically human-based, for here and now. Its source of authority is the people who

compose its society, and they are all equal according to the classic foundations of liberty, equality, and fraternity. Our country, however, is a Jewish
state of Jewish people, whose de facto constitution is one law for Jews and
one for the others who reside among us. Israel appears to be a law-based
state; its Declaration of Independence is supposed to be her constitution.
But it is clear that the source of authority is emotional, emanating from
two origins: God and his rabbis, and the Shoah-hood, traumas, and result-
ing paranoia. Anyone who has not been blessed by God above, or has been
involved in hostility toward a Jew or Judaism, will be cast outside the Israeli
circle of legitimacy—unless it is a German car.

The entire Torah in one verse, Hillel the Elder told us, is not doing
to others what we hated done to us when we were others. In Israel today
there are horrible layers of racism that are not essentially different from
the racism that exterminated many of our ancestors. This racism is sanctimonious and slick, so we do not always notice how dangerous it is. It is
also cunning and marketable; sometimes we are mistaken to think that it is
pure patriotism. It isn't. The conversion of everything into holiness, without leaving room for self-criticism, combined with the sanctity of nationhood and the hostile environment that we try daily to withstand, turns the
monopolists of the Israeli religious spirit to de facto and de jure racists. It
is imperative to declare a war of values with these racists, and to present a
practical alternative of faith to the distortion they call "Judaism" and which
they present as our authentic faith.

Often in the heat of arguments with them I am threatened, "There
will be a war between brothers." They use the Hebrew idiom for civil war.
For years I toned down my positions in an effort to prevent a schism in the
nation. Today I am different. Are these my brethren? I ask. I reply with a
resounding *no.* For me brotherhood and national family life are not maintained by an automatic pilot. I have two biological sisters, the daughters of
my parents. I have spiritual brothers and sisters with whom I share the same
values. If you are a bad person, a whining enemy or a strong-arm occupier,
you are not my brother, even if you are circumcised, observe the Sabbath
and do mitzvahs. If your scarf covers every hair on your head for modesty,
you give alms and do charity, but what is under your scarf is dedicated to the
sanctity of Jewish land, taking precedence over the sanctity of human life,
whosoever life that is, then you are not my sister. You might be my enemy. A
good Arab or a righteous gentile will be a brother or sister to me. A wicked

man, even of Jewish descent, is my adversary, and I would stand on the other side of the barricade and fight him to the end. Automatic Judaism, bereft of self-criticism and moral obligations, is for me an abominable race theory. Since the Shoah took place, there is no genetic Judaism, only ethical, obliging Judaism. Therefore a war between brothers cannot be. If a more violent struggle takes place, it will be called a *civil war*, not a brothers' war. This will be not a war between members of the Jewish people of different shades of beliefs, but an uncompromising struggle between good people and bad people anywhere. All their good ones and ours on one side, and all the bad—and there is no shortage of them—of both parties on the other side.

Hitler created a melting pot in Auschwitz. He wanted to cut us off from the world and to shut us all out, indiscriminately and mercilessly, in one big heap of ash. The winning answer to Hitler is the union of all good people in the world against the coalition of evil, which includes some of my people. Israeli humanism must understand that the answer to the Israeli occupation is not just withdrawal from the occupied territories, but also the creation of a new Jewish identity. With this identity we shall launch a struggle for a better world, repaired and human, that follows the values of Moses, not the racist legacy of Korah. Because of my dissociation with them and their exclusion from my brotherhood circle, I have to redefine my whole Jewish identity and affinities. The time for prayer renewal has come. We need to write a new prayer book, a *Siddur*, in which the arrogant verse "You chose us from among all the nations," will be replaced with "You chose us with all the nations." This should be a prayer book that makes no distinctions between one human and another and between Adam and Eve. There will be no mention of sacrifices, slaughters and a bloody temple, but a temple of life and its pursuit; harmony, vegetarianism, and humanism will be obligations for a better future. It is time for a New Judaism.

CHAPTER 11

MAKE GOD
SMILE AGAIN

WHERE WAS GOD DURING THE SHOAH? THIS IS THE MOST frequent question in discussing the century of Hitler, Cain's century. Atheists will say, "A god that allows one and a quarter million children to die like vermin cannot exist," or "If he does exist, he must not be worshipped." Zvi Yanai argues in his wonderful memoir *Yours Sandro,* "If God is involved in the world, he should be prosecuted at the International Criminal Court in the Hague for crimes against humanity. If he is silent as a wall, I prefer to pray to the wall."[1] On the other hand, believers will point to the "Holocaust miracle." Fact: Half a century after the crematoria, the Jewish people are as strong as ever. Fact: I was saved. Observant Jews have become much more religious because of the Shoah and its consequences. Secular Jews have become even more alienated from God, and they put more trust in our own power and aggressive tactics. Zionist Jews have dug in deeper in the Land of Israel as the ultimate fortified refuge.

Jewish residents throughout the world live by Jacob's wisdom, expressed by his finesse in dealing with sensitive situations, as before his potentially dangerous meeting with Esau. "He said if Esau comes to the first camp and strikes it, the remaining camp will survive."[2] An assimilated Jew who marries a partner outside the faith tries sometimes to escape into a new reality where he is unknown as a Jew, therefore reducing the risk that he will be persecuted and eliminated like his predecessors. Does it really matter who is guilty, God or Man? It certainly does not preoccupy the victims, and it is doubtful if it matters at all to the survivors, both the spectators and the rest of God's children. The old God undoubtedly encountered many problems due to the Shoah and its aftermath, but man too, his creation, does not come out clean from the steppes of Poland and Europe's camps and railway stations. This is now our responsibility, and it matters much more.

From the beginning, many paradoxes lay in the definition and understanding of God. In retrospect, these paradoxes became most acute in the middle of the last century. All hypotheses of man and God were tested in the Third Reich and failed. Believers always presumed the trilogy of omnipotence, benevolence, and comprehensibility of God. It means that God can do everything, is good, merciful and compassionate, and can be understood by us, at least partially. This last concept needs a short explanation. Judaism is a religion of revelation; the meeting that took place between God and the nation on Mount Sinai produced a certain understanding of the divine act, his commandments, and logic. When Moses explained the Torah, he revealed a radical element of Judaism. The Torah is overt, not covert and not hidden in the heavens, and exists in us. "Surely, this commandment that I am commanding you today is not too hard for you, nor is it too far away. It is not in heaven, that you should say, 'Who will go up to heaven for us, and get it for us so that we may hear it and observe it?' Neither is it beyond the sea, that you should say, 'Who will cross to the other side of the sea for us, and get it for us so that we may hear it and observe it?' No, the word is very near to you; it is in your mouth and in your heart for you to observe."[3] Moses' Torah was stretched even beyond that by the sages of the Second Temple, who determined that the "Torah speaks in the language of humans."[4] Namely, God's Torah speaks in the language of humans, and assumes, for working purposes, the comprehensibility of God and his significance in the human environment.

How then are we to understand God's intention when humans in his image wore Nazi uniforms and swastikas and did what they did? Then and there God's comprehensibility ceased, as these were acts that cannot be understood by humans. Also his omnipotence was put to a severe test, and his benevolence was doubted. To define precisely the Shoah's theological dilemma, I need to use the wisdom of Hans Jonas, one of the twentieth century's greatest theologists, who was banned by the Zionist establishment. He was born in Germany in 1903 to an industrialist father; his mother was descended from a rabbinical family. He was a Jewish researcher of religion who, like many of his peers, was educated in a Zionist youth movement and was prepared to emigrate to the Land of Israel.

Like my father and many other German Jews, Jonas arrived here in the early 1930s. He served several years in the British army and fought in Italy as a combat soldier in the Jewish brigade. He joined the IDF at the advanced age of forty-five and served in the artillery corps. He then turned down a position at the Hebrew University, preferring a late academic career in North America. In the spirit of those days, he was targeted for academic boycott, and since then very few in Israel have heard his name. This is how the new Israeli spirit lost one of the unique, important contributions of the man who would become one of the most influential intellectuals for the European environmental movements. His book was published in Hebrew only recently. One of his significant works is his contemplation on the meaning of the post-Shoah God:

> Only an absolutely incomprehensible God can be described as absolutely benevolent, generally…Absolute benevolence, omnipotence and comprehensibility are so related that any combination of two invalidates the third…If God is said to be somehow and somewhat comprehensible—and we must adhere to this—then his benevolence must coexist with evils, and this can be only if he is not omnipotent. Only thus can co-exist his comprehensibility and benevolence, as well as the existence of evils in the world.

With great emotional force, probably caused by his mother's death in Auschwitz and his years in the British army fighting the Nazis, he wrote one of the cornerstones of post-Shoah theology immediately after the Six-Day War. Jonas did not question God's failure in the Shoah. He accepted it as fact and tried to understand the qualities of the God who allowed the Holocaust to take place under his watchful—or closed—eye.

Jonas was among the first to read the new map of faith. He understood that it is the duty of each Jewish believer to abandon his faith in the historical God and adopt new paradigms. Ephraim Meir, in his book *Memory Act, Society Man and God After Auschwitz,* explains Jonas.

> Divine intervention did not come to Auschwitz, only silence. Only humans, righteous gentiles, made miracles. God did not intervene, not because he did not want to intervene, but because he could not...God's relinquishing of his power is what enables humanity to exist in all its forms...The advantage of Jonas' story is that the question "Where was God?" is no longer asked. The issue is displaced to the realms of human responsibility, where man can grow towards God.[5]

In light of Jonas's wisdom, which conveys my own feelings so precisely, I cannot but conclude that God, who was so understood and present to my parents, probably withdrew from the world of my peers. As a result, the constructs of faith must undergo profound changes, and new definitions of human responsibility are called for. The old model of relations between believer and God is like the relation between a witness and the justice system: as people, we were summoned to testify or sit in a jury that decided that God existed and that we should worship him. Faith ruled from the time of the Exodus, proving and preserving history. The quote "The people saw God and believed in God and in Moses his servant"[6] means that God acts in history and his deeds and their consequences are seen and felt. Therefore it is evident that the eyewitness becomes a believer and a living testimony to God's existence and his greatness.

As children we asked, "Can God create a stone that he cannot lift?"—inadvertently questioning one of the fundamentals of faith. I know firsthand, through affectionate or bitter ideological confrontations, how difficult it is for believers, whether devout or casual, to accept the reality of a god that is not benevolent, not omnipotent, and not comprehensible. Observing the commandments of such a god may be futile, if only because he may have planned something else altogether of which we are unaware. The difficulty of connecting the sides of the triangle of faith to an understood form makes it mandatory to build a new bridge between God and man that will enable us to conduct ourselves in the world according to our understanding of the meaning of creation.

Instead of placing the responsibility for Auschwitz, Maidanek, and Dachau on God and his inaction, we need to take the responsibility into our own human hands, and remove God from the business of everyday life. We have no control or jurisdiction over God, and, as we have learned millions of times, He does not really control what happens here. But man and his restraints are mine, here and now; I can speak, agree, accept, reject, fight back, understand, or contradict all our doings. Therefore I seek to build a world that is based on the faith of man and his communities, rather than hearsay evidence of what God allegedly said.

In the faith of responsibility, the believer's status is altered anyway. I am no longer a witness to God's greatness on earth; I am the evidence itself. If my behavior as a human being is proper, good and just, and humanity is proper and improving, I am proof of the state of the world, its creator, and its creations. But if I become insensitive, thieving, and covetous, then I am a bad example. From now on we should say: Man is not a witness to God's greatness, but man's greatness is testimony to the greatness of creation. One could stretch it to say that the good man is evidence for a good God. This is the same embodiment of the invisible in the fundamental tenet of God's image. God is not around; he has gone to other pastures, or maybe has never been here. All that is left of him is memory, a stubborn rumor; fingerprints stamped on each one of us. If our conduct is proper and exalted, then the image that we reflect is exalted as well. If the opposite happens, then the image sinks to the depths and God's image becomes a dark, intimidating shadow. Man gives, man takes; may the name of man be blessed forever and ever.

The foundations for this responsibility were laid by the writers and editors of prayer when they concluded, "Because of our sins we were exiled from our land." But the responsibility for the Ruin of the Second Temple, the harshest event in Jewish history until the past century, does not rest on God and his famous whims, and not even on the Roman executioners. Rather, the responsibility rests on us, for we had sinned. At the moment, it does not matter what the sin was. It could have been brotherly hatred and brotherly wars; or it could have been political folly by people who did not understand the stupidity of a tiny nation rebellion against a superpower.

The most important Jewish legacy is to assume responsibility for repair, redemption, restoration, and reconstruction of the ruins. If society is good, the community appropriate and humanity more humane, then Godliness, which we reflect, is better, and vice versa. A bad world and evil people are bad testimony to the state of the world and to its wanting spirituality.

According to this assumption, it seems that God and the Shoah do not belong together. My question is not where was my God, but where were the humans, my enemy-brethren? My Shoah question is not man's question of God—"Where were you when we needed you?"—but God's question to Adam—"Where are you? Man is like me, and where were you when I needed you?" Or, more precisely, as god asked Cain, "Where is Abel your brother?" Adam's son and the patriarch of all killers. Where were you when you killed your brother? The twentieth century was the most nonreligious century we have ever known, it was man's century. Theories and trends from earlier centuries materialized in it, and they were the backdrop to the European atrocities and the ruin of our people. The century expressed a different kind of spirituality: liberation and secularization, ideologies of power and nationalism, all mixed with global materialism and unrestrained idolization of greed. Who failed in the Shoah was not God, but his creations.

Moving from a faith that is based on God's witnesses to a community of man's testimony requires another passage, from the faith of pessimism to the faith of optimism. Leaning on the belief that one day the Messiah will come and everything will be better, and that redemption will change our condition, should not diminish the widespread pessimism in the Jewish world. We do not trust anyone, not our brethren, not our leaders and certainly not gentiles. For us, every killing is a murder, every murder a pogrom, every terror attack an anti-Semitic act and every new enemy a Hitler. Behind every danger lurks a new holocaust. We, and many of our leaders who incite us, believe that almost everyone wants to destroy us. By feeling so threatened by shadows that will attack us at dawn, we have become a nation of attackers. We feel good in this darkness, as we have become accustomed to it.

I want to transform this mistrust into trust. Faith is difficult to endow, but trust in man and nations can be acquired and established. How is it done? We first identify the symptoms, and then cure it by eradicating its cause.

For many years we have lived comfortably, thanks to a national hypocrisy that tries to contain two conflicting worlds: well-being and complaint, power and victimhood, success and trauma. Our private worlds are defined by physical security, personal comfort and even wealth, both as individuals and as a nation. Our state is well established and powerful, almost without precedence since the destruction of the Second Temple. Yet for some acquired psychological deficiency, we try to hide this splendor by constantly whining—because we had a holocaust. We always want a stronger army because of the Shoah, and more resources from other countries' taxpayers, and an automatic forgiveness for any of our excesses. We want to be above criticism and attention, all these because of Hitler's twelve years, which changed the face of Europe and our face beyond recognition. It cannot go on like this forever. This inherent contradiction will smash its vessel, the state, and the society that contains it.

We are fast approaching an intersection where we need decide who we are and where we are going. Are we going to the past, toward which we always oriented ourselves, or will we choose the future, for the first time in generations? Will we choose a better world that is based on hope and not trauma, on trust in humanity and not suspicious isolationism and paranoia? In this case we will have to leave our pain behind us and look forward, to find out where we can repair ourselves and perhaps even the world. During most of our history, we learned how to survive in a flawed world by outsmarting the system, bypassing the laws of hostile regimes, where we were subjects. But now we are citizens of our own state and we continue to beat the system, our own this time, deliberately or out of a habit, not realizing that we are not fooling anyone but ourselves. We need to declare: Mourning time is over; the seven days of *shiv'ah* are past. We are now living in the seventh decade since the Shoah, and we need to get rid of the sack and ashes and get back to living, to a different life.

The public rising from the sack and ashes of national mourning appears in our sources. David's quick rise from mourning his son, the fruit of his adultery with Bathsheba, is seemingly opposed to human nature. When a dear one is ill and struggles to live, we try to preserve hope, to endow him with our strength and the hope that he overcomes his illness. Yet when evil takes it toll and the ill person dies, all our pain and anguish break out in force. We sit in mourning for seven days, according to our Jewish customs. Kings and kingdoms, on the other hand, conduct themselves differently. With the passing of his child, David stops being a grieving father, haunted by guilt, and returns to be the monarch of a sovereign kingdom. He abandons sorrow and rises to normalcy. It is as if he mourns his son before his death, and when the child is gone, the mourning chapter is closed and a new chapter of life begins. This is how he explains this seemingly unnatural behavior:

> And his servants said to him, "What is this thing that you have done concerning the child? While the child was yet living you fasted and wept, and kept watch; but when the child was dead you rose up and ate bread, and drank." And David said, "While the child yet lived, I fasted and wept; for I said, 'Who knows if the Lord will pity me, and the child should live?' But now the child is dead, why should I fast thus? Shall I be able to bring him back again? I shall go to him, but he shall not return to me."

Then the happy ending:

> And David comforted Bathsheba his wife, and he went in to her, and lay with her; and she conceived and bore a son, and he called his name Solomon, and the Lord loved him.[7]

The Shoah happened. The child is dead. More precisely, many children and many parents and very many traditions, customs, and national insights went up in smoke. They are dead and gone forever, never to return. Individuals will continue to mourn them until their last day, but we, the collective, the commonwealth, and the nation must rise from the floor of mourning and the heaps of ashes and return to life fully, not just partially. It is time to leave Auschwitz behind and to build a healthy Israel. We are no longer there, in the barracks, forests and death marches. We should not continue to be just a mirage of normalcy, an Auschwitz country. It is our duty to rise from the ashes, as our King David, the poet, said: "But now he is dead and what should I fast for? Can I bring him back?" They will never return, and we have to be comforted and bring to the world a new culture, a new nation. Because Hitler took more than our lives; he robbed us of culture, heritage, and faith. We must conceive them again and give birth to them, again. Renaissance means *rebirth,* and this is what we should do. In short, to remember forever, yes; to wear sack and ashes for the rest of our lives, no. It is unbecoming of a state, a commonwealth; it serves no purpose.

The Holocaust is over; it is time for us to rise from its ashes.

The Jewish people will find it difficult to rise from the seven days of mourning the Shoah without resolving their issues with God. Faith and traditions are integral to their action and identity. Our national code requires faith and legacy as part of its operating system. In order to leap forward out of mourning and self-pity, we need to leave behind great portions of our old belief system and lay new foundations for our new faith of revival. The twentieth century and its Shoah must be a lesson to humanity, not to God. It is the lesson of man that failed his mission.

The new legacy must embark on a new path with the belief that there is not a God of minute details, of private guidance and of inventory-like accounting of reward and punishment: I pray and he saves me; I follow the rules and wallow in righteousness and he responds in kind. The new practice of faith must be much more sophisticated: God has given us the Earth, the whole universe ("And the Earth he gave to Mankind").[8] If there is God, then, his unseen being relinquished control and gave Man rule over the world. The meaning of faith is to take responsibility over all that the diminished omnipotence has vacated. This is not secular arrogance or fundamentalist detachment from reality, neither ultra-Orthodox phobia nor rebellion nor blind obedience. This is mere responsibility, the meaning and the understanding that when the Earth is in disorder, it is the failure of man, of my flesh and blood. This is not the failure of God, who, if he exists, is merely delegating his authority from the heavens.

Until the modern age, when the secular alternative entered the minds of individuals and communities, man's spiritual reality was binary: yes or no, believer or nonbeliever, observant or agnostic. All three monotheistic faiths—Judaism, Christianity, and Islam—deliberated whether to enforce beliefs, not just deeds. This is what the infamous Spanish Inquisition attempted to do. This is also the source of bans and excommunications within Jewish communities, as against doubters of Judaism, who include Elisha Ben Avuya (dubbed *Aher,* "Other") of Mishna times and Benedict

Baruch Spinoza. You either believed or were excommunicated, without middle ground. Today you can be more than all or nothing. You can observe the commandments without believing in God; and you can believe in God without observing the commandments. Such disputes, when they occurred among us several generations ago, would end in total splits, schisms, and open wounds. Such were the disputes between the Jews who returned from Babel and the Samaritans who had remained in the land, between the Sadducees and Pharisees, between the Karaites and the Rabbinites, and between the Messianic and the Halakha rationalists. Times have changed, and with them also our capacity to contain others whose beliefs or disbeliefs are contradictory to ours.

Perhaps because of the Shoah, or the liberation of slaves and their equal rights as humans in the modern West, or perhaps because of the mass immigration of ex-colonial natives to Western capitals, the West is committed to accept the other, the alien, and the foreigner. Many today fight against xenophobia and rally for the full acceptance of those who were discriminated against and deemed inferior just recently. Having always been the ultimate other and foreigner, the Jews cannot reject the new openness of the world, which includes us too. If we want to be accepted, we are forced to admit those whom we rejected only yesterday because of their different faith and deeds. Judaism today is religiously pluralistic, de facto, and the time has come for a new spirituality, de jure.

This new spirituality is an attempt to scrape off the calcified layers that we allowed to form on our faith and spirit. It would be the sincere effort to reach the emotional core of meaning and security in creation, humanity, and nature. The time of meaningless commandments, texts, and rituals is past. Too many compulsory commandments are examples of the atherosclerosis that is constricting the ancient Jewish arteries. The obsessive book of specifications as to what is permitted, and especially prohibited, totally blocks the free exchange of ideas of faith. It has converted modern religiosity into an entity of robots who have lost the connection between the inner meaning of their religious identity and the daily practice of their closed lives.

The phrase "And I will dwell among them" should not remain an expression for the confinement of God, "who fills the world," inside a temple or a tent in the wilderness or a Jerusalem shrine. Faith, feelings, experiences, and manners of ritual should be transferred to private hands.

Everyone has a different God inside him, and everyone has the right to experience and express his or her faith in a personal way.

India seems to produce the experiences that join together all contemporary Jewish interpretations. Scores of thousands of backpackers and seekers return from the Far East every year, bringing with them an aspect that has been absent from Judaism and its theory. They bring with them the ability to accept, contain, integrate and absorb into their souls, and consequently our souls, the kind of diversity that has been alien to us. One can be religious and still travel on the Sabbath, be spiritual and also have a career; I have an American iPod and yes, it plays soothing, exotic world music. The former and the latter are words of the living God, even though an ocean of concepts and views separate us from each other.

I look at the photos that my children send me from their travels around the world. I try to perceive the faraway landscapes from their vantage point and to share their experience through the images. I think that they travel not only to distance themselves from the impure experiences of an army, war, occupation, corruption and cynicism, but also in search of other landscapes, more sublime than those of the Land of Israel. Although we grew up on the myth that the Golan Heights are the most beautiful in the world, we have come to know better. San Francisco is no less breathtaking than Jerusalem. The Mala Mala Reserve in Mpumalanga Province, South Africa, is much more impressive than the Hula puddle; and polar birds represent wild natural beauty, ancient and eternal, much more than the birds that nestle in the former garbage dump of Hiria. What do my kids say? They send me images of expansive landscapes, but write me of other, spiritual landscapes. The new spirituality that is revealed to them is contained in their letters home. We miss you, Dad, we long and yearn to be with you, but we find here what we don't have at home. We love and want to love even more. We, the generation of the new age, are open to and enriched by meetings and encounters with whatever is different from us. We are not threatened and do not keep to ourselves; on the contrary. My children, our children, seek an encounter with worlds that have not been tainted with the bloody Shoah. They search for a spirituality that is based on dialogue, not trauma. They seek the calm of Buddhist countries and want to bring it back home with them to put us all on a softer course of life that is accepting and containing, not hostile, suspicious, and sharp-edged, that rejects all. They are children who touch the spiritual even though they are not religious.

⊹⊱⊰⊹

The new paradigms that originated from the Shoah must be sensitive and directed toward the creation of a better human and better humanity, toward people and cultures that will never again produce slaughterers like the Nazis and will not allow victimization. One law will be in the land for the persecuted of the entire world, whatever group: Armenian, Gypsy, Jew, homosexual, migrant, or a refugee from Rwanda, Cambodia, or Palestine. The new theology, especially the Jewish one, must break out of the boundaries of the old faith and make the faith in the human, God's creation, a tenet of its legacy and traditions, as a mandatory basis for a dialogue among the believers of all faiths.

It has been a long time since the world was as divided in its principles as it is today. On the one hand, democracy is in bloom, and liberties, rights, and constitutional defenses of individuals are widespread. On the other hand, fundamentalist, absolutist, and impatient beliefs win over many hearts, and bring with them conflict and wars. Among Jews, many anarchists are pressing for a speedy redemption. Among Christians, especially Evangelicals, many yearn for an actual Armageddon. Among Muslims, we all see the extremists, and some of us even understand them.

When the Berlin Wall fell in 1989, many believed that the chapter of world wars had finally come to a close. But soon it seemed that the chapter was just an introduction to a book of altogether different conflicts. The array of faiths in the world, the balance of religious ecology, and all that was stable and known for generations has been violated and implodes before our eyes, only to be rebuilt differently.

I do not know enough of the others, but what I know about the Jews is sufficient to make me annoyed with my own Judaism and some of its followers, and to make me want to work for our repair. When all the faiths and religions that endanger the world today do their own soul searching on a collective scale, as well as on the personal level, the danger will diminish and even be defeated. I will start with us. Meaningful parts of Orthodox Judaism, especially those intertwined with Israeli nationalism, are part of the danger to world peace. Zealots and zealotry

214

were always part of the Jewish soul, adhering to their beliefs through terrible loss and absolute ruin. We have never been short of them. I am not a Jew just for myself. My Judaism is part of my responsibility for the world, nature, creation and humanity. Yes, I am a utopian Jew and I love the entire creation. When I recognize that parts of my Jewish identity threaten the other parts of me, the human and universal ones, I am spurred to action.

The lesson of centuries of torture and millions of human sacrifices, including of my own people, on the altars of extremists and fanatics is not a lesson for exacting revenge. Rather, in the name of those who went through it all and saw the inferno's flames firsthand, we must prepare the ground for a better world. Judaism can spare itself the middle-age crisis of advancing from the old world to the new by leaping to its natural place as an agent of culture and as a spiritual mediator. If there is one thing that the human community needs nowadays more than anything, it is an enormous process of world arbitration and international dynamics of conciliation. This is not just between nations and peoples or organizations and companies, but between the diverse human spirits who can now communicate freely, thanks to technological innovations. The erasing of boundaries, the availability of flights anywhere and anytime, and the Internet, which reaches the remotest human dwellings, have all positioned us at once opposite one another, unfiltered and unprotected. Thus we gain maximum exposure to places and to the richness of people and cultures that until a few years ago were distant from the eye and mind. Hence we can face and authenticate the elements of life known to us against those known to others. Who said that the god of Australian aborigines is less important than the god of the Saudis in Mecca, or the god of Jews in Brooklyn?

So how do we build this new bridge? What are the tools for a better understanding, dialogue and acceptance of those who are so different from us, so that they really shake the foundations of our ingrained truths? The question really is how to extract the good from the bad, or the honey from the dead lion, as in Samson's fable. The twentieth century was the battleground of all man-made faiths: Communism against capitalism and both against Nazism, Fascists and Nazis against Western democracy. We had hot wars and cold wars, local and global, with outcomes still unknown. All these led to mass killings and the eradication of great human cultures, with extensive destruction and ruin. Only toward the century's end did the world begin to stabilize. Where man-made super-theories crumble, individuals take their place with human rights and liberties. Democracy and its liberties are much more commonplace today than ever before. The waste and racism of the second Great War, the race supremacy theories and the obliteration of the human image created fertile ground for democracy to sprout everywhere. Despite the belligerence of religious villains of all faiths, this world is still better than all the past worlds. In every cultural domain where the torch of liberty shines breaks a titanic struggle; the new guard fights the old and innovators and reformers battle conservatives who wish to preserve the old order. This is happening in Christianity, Judaism, and throughout the Islamic world. Today's bursts of political violence often originate in the tension that exists between the old religious elements and the new democratic ones. It is all for the better, as in our age freedom is stronger than oppression. This is also a consequence of World War II and the Holocaust. There are more democracies, more liberties and many more freedoms, rights, and a wealth of good ideas. True, we also have forces of darkness, perceived by us as satanic, strong and getting stronger. But they are not strong enough to really undermine world stability and peace. If anything, the retreat of democracy and liberties in the traditionally free major powers, such as the United States and France, worries me much more than the slowly eroding Chinese tyranny.

The sum total points to an impressive, significant progress of democracy in places where it was meager just one political generation ago. This reality defies our own tendency to paint the world in somber tones, feeling it is sliding downhill and history is in retreat. We point out laboriously how the income gaps between the rich and poor widen in our midst and among nations throughout the globalizing world. We turn on the TV in the evening news and hear the usual fare of murder, rape, pedophilia, disasters, and conflicts. Nevertheless this is a good world. Emmanuel Todd, a French demographist, economist and anthropologist, argues in his book *After the Empire:*

> World history is much more encouraging than what television news broadcasts…Humanity is in the process of liberation from backwardness…illiteracy, high birth rate and high mortality…If we keep remembering this, we will be more optimistic and could

even be impressed with man's ascension to a decisive stage in his development.[9]

For many years we were vagabonds, migrants, living here and there, but at the same time really nowhere, disconnected and lacking feelings of loyalty and stability. We were the usual suspects, cosmopolitans sentenced to exile, while others dwelled confidently in their lands and experienced the eternal stability that is based on their place in the world, where they and their parents before them were born and established their commonwealths. Nomads always posed threats on the land and its residents. Abel, the shepherd, threatened his brother Cain, the farmer, and was slain. The Egyptians distrusted the Hebrew tribes that migrated to their land during famines and feared, "lest they will increase and if a war breaks out, they will join our enemies and will fight us and will ascend from the land"[10] The nomadic Bedouins were always expelled by the farming *fallah*. The Native Americans seemed intimidating to the white settlers in the forts, and the fate of the Gypsies in Europe is known. Jews, like Gypsies, were always perceived as distant, dark, and threatening. These days, however, all this is changing. The world has gone global. Everyone can move freely, change residences, switch careers. Everyone can travel and watch geography, travel, and discovery channels on television. Suddenly the whole world is mobile, foreigners are everywhere, and they are all somewhat Jewish, restless wanderers. Many have multiple passports. The Jews no longer pose a threat. Only those who have not become wanderers still feel threatened by us. The political outcome is that many Western countries attract immigrants who come from economically or constitutionally weaker countries

Israel is the country that leads the world in the ratio of newcomers to its native population; the United States is second. Therefore, a visitor to Israel would not know how to define it. Is it Western, as a quick look at the Tel Aviv skyline may hint, or is it a living museum restoration of the Eastern European Jewry of Poland, Galicia, and the other communities during the nineteenth century and the early twentieth century, as reflected in the streets of the ultra-Orthodox communities in Bnei Brak, Jerusalem, Immanuel, Elad, and some neighborhoods in Ashdod and Arad?

Israel could also be a remote branch of contemporary Iran, as it seems when you listen to some former chief rabbis talk. Or is it a cowboy country, reminiscent of the Western United States during the Gold Rush, judging by the look of plaid-clad, gun-slinging, bearded pioneers walking the streets of its towns? It could also be Brazil, if you jog on Tel Aviv's lovely beaches. Or it could be an economic powerhouse, number three in Nasdaq-listed securities. Looking deeper, Israel could also be a voodoo society, judging by the prevalence of curses and amulets, holy water, bans, and excommunications.

In short, Israel is one big culturally and spiritually chaotic place, second to none in the world. It is home to at least four peoples: Jews, Palestinians, non-Jewish Soviet immigrants and hundreds of thousands of Asian migrant workers, "the Labor movement." This human mix can be a good basis for bridges of dialogue to serve as models for the rest of the world. The decision whether to be torn apart and sink into ourselves like a black hole, or to recognize the diversity, be inspired by it, and become a beacon to the new humanity, a light to many immigrant societies, is in our hands. These inner qualities have always been with us, but never before were we as organized as we are now.

Judaism has always lived an unresolved tension between absolute universalism and high-walled isolationism. The will and the natural tendency to dwell in isolation were undermined through history by individuals who broke out and changed the world—Karl Marx, Leon Trotsky, Sigmund Freud, Heinrich Heine, Moses Mendelssohn, Baruch Spinoza, Abraham Joshua Heschel, and members of the civil rights movement in the United States. This is just a short and very partial list. Can the state of Israel best herself to the level of these individuals and serve the world as a collective of universalistic Jews, entirely diverse but mutually inspiring? Can Israel help the world free itself from its hostility block and blaze new trails to the venue of peacemaking, reconciliation and acceptance?

During the twentieth century, the world tried twice to establish international organizations to deal with global problems, with the League of Nations and later the United Nations. These organizations were founded to unite a world that was alienated along state and ethnic lines and to contain national conflicts in an age that was characterized by such conflicts. These conflicts are not what typify the world today. The fault lines today are along identity and religious beliefs, and therefore it is time to establish a World Religion Organization. It sounds oxymoronic, especially considering today's escalation of inter-religious hostilities. It is also almost impossible, considering the union of the world's religions in their opposition to gay parades, freedom of speech, family planning and the acceptance of beliefs and traditions of others.

Nevertheless it is essential, as the alternative is widening world conflicts. Similar tendencies occur in all the world markets. In the food market, the assumption is that everybody eats, and therefore various manufacturers offer a variety of products to meet the preferences of various consumers. The marketplace of beliefs is one of the last markets where each faith product has its own corner of sellers and buyers, and where no open exchange between the various consumers takes place. It is time to establish the free market of ideas, where everyone can express his or her opinion and everyone can choose according to their own preferences and faith. The example should come not just from believers in the street, the family, or the workplace, but also, and especially, from religious leaders of all persuasions. The World Religion Organization can be established in Israel on an international sovereign land to express its own nature and authority. It will belong to the world, and will admit only those believers, sects, rituals, and beliefs that will be willing to take upon themselves a morality of a certain kind. This morality will be based on shared concern for charity and welfare to the needy wherever they are; acceptance of the other, who may believe and worship differently; and the ceaseless effort to widen the boundaries of world peace and advance the elements of liberty and human rights everywhere.

I have no doubt that such an undertaking will be very difficult. Believers are not the conceding types. Compromise is common in politics and in life in general, but not in religion. Religious beliefs are supposed to be total, God given, and how can the word of God be subject to compromise? Beyond believers, there is the world of preachers, whose livelihood depends on obduracy. Rabbis, clergy, imams, and ayatollahs will lose all the absolutism available to them and thus the control of their flocks, the mindless robots that fear God rather than love him, because of their preachers. If they were to be exposed to other faiths, customs, traditions, and interpretations with much greater relevance to their believers, preachers will be out of business.

Such a project will require an almost impossible stretching of interpretive capacity, and will exhaust religious regulatory entrepreneurship. It will be interpretation for change, not preservation. As with judiciary activism, which has typified constitutional breakthroughs in Israel and other countries in the last few decades, what is needed is religious renewal activism in the interpretation of religious law of the Jewish, Christian, and Islamic faiths. The process will eventually produce a world in which there will be many more options to choose from in matters of religion and faith. In the spiritual marketplace of ideas there will be fewer communities of blind obedience, and many more individuals and communities of meaning and significance.

The building of world institutions for interfaith dialogue as the world's super-policy should lead to the purifying of traditional texts so that they are free of hostility, arrogance, separatism, incitement, and racism. The texts should be open to all, and include more than one truth; they should be alternatives to the orthodox monopoly on body and soul. I do not mean by this that texts should be cleansed, like the totalitarian regimes did. We do not burn books in Judaism—on the contrary, we collect and preserve them. The purification should lead to elucidation and learning, and through them to alteration, adaptation, or shelving for all practical purposes.

I do not know if such tools exist in other religions, but I know where they are hidden in Judaism. The Jewish world always had colossal disputes between colossal figures: Moses and Korah in the Sinai wilderness, Saul and David in the early kingdom, Rehoboam and Jeroboam at the time of the kingdom's split, as well as Sadducees and Pharisees, Rabbinites and Karaites, ultra-Orthodox and Reform, and many others. One of the most important disputes was between the School of Hillel and the School of Shammai. At the outset, it seemed like an expected disagreement on the interpretation of religious law, but in reality it was a dispute on ways, views, and outlooks. It was not just a difference of opinion on text interpretation, but a political argument between the Shammai zealots and isolationists and the Hillel moderates and pragmatists. This is how the dispute is described:

> Rabbi Abba said that Shmuel said: for three years the house of Shammai and the House of Hillel were divided. These were saying the law is according to us and those were saying the law is according to us. A divine voice came out and said: Both these and those are living words of God and the law is according to Hillel. If both

were living words of God, why did the House of Hillel deserve that law be according to them? Because they were agreeable and meek, and they studied their words together with the words of Shammai. And not just that, they cited the words of the House of Shammai prior to their own words.[11]

The dispute between the two schools was so bitter it caused bloodshed between their followers. There followed three years of total disagreement that tore apart Israeli society. The religious dispute is understood, at least on its face: God said his word, and the scholars of the two schools of thought argued as to the meaning of the "one and only," as God is one and his truth is one with no alternatives. At the end of three years, a "divine voice" decided: "Both these and the others are living words of God and the law is according to Hillel." It is not clear what that "divine voice" was. It could be an echo of the public sentiment that became the divine voice, *vox populi vox dei*. It may be what we call today public opinion, yet the voice altered the debate culture in Israel unrecognizably.

If the only God said his word, how could such fundamentally different interpretations exist and still be described as "living words of God"? It is either one that is God's word, or the other, but both? What kind of monotheism allows multiplicity of opinions and truths? It turns out, according to this Talmudic legend, which has become an asset of Judaism, that there could be more than one truth within the oneness of God. This revolutionary idea can provide great support to the reinvention and renovation of Jewish religious and interpretive pluralism. I hope that Christianity and Islam also have such tools that enable a quantum leap forward into the next evolutionary stage of theology. Without such tools and breakthroughs we are bound to go backward. We may have to resort to the dark ages of spiritual darkness and religious wars that have proved fatal.

From the Shammai-Hillel dispute and other disputes from which God was kept out, for the benefit of human discourse, we can make God smile again. It is wrong to think that God is only satisfied when his altars are washed with the blood of sacrifices. The only times Jewish sources describe, in legend, God's satisfaction is when his children, namely us mortals, interpreted his intention differently from his will. When we force the human meaning on God's intent and its rules, he sits there in heaven and says, "My children won me over indeed, won me over,"[12] and smiles with satisfaction. In order for God to smile more often, we need to win him over and over again. We need to give a new human meaning to old sacred scriptures, lest those who aspire to represent the ancient original will sweep us into a war of religious confrontations and conflicts. Otherwise, it could be that absolutist religions will again take the place of the just-defeated human totalitarian ideologies and Hitler, Mussolini, and the rest of the world's villains will replaced by Elohim, God, and their colleague, Allah.

CHAPTER 12

I SHALL LIVE

HOW MANY TIMES SHOULD A MAN DIE? HOW MANY TIMES can he die? My father died many times. He died when his liberal Jewish Germany died. He died several more times when he was on the road. A Jew who does not die several times in his life does not have a life. My father died twice in the twilight of his days: the one before the last was on the eve of Independence Day. He was honored with the task of lighting a symbolic torch during an official ceremony at the Mount Herzl Military Cemetery in early evening, between Memorial Day and Independence Day. He was to stand on the stage and light the flame in front of the nation during a live broadcast, read five sentences that would sum up his nine-plus decades on earth. "In the name of…In the name of…And to the glory of the State of Israel." But Father was already very sick. He was busy dying and he was more on the other side. He was more unconscious than conscious and breathing irregularly.

Mother went to light the flame in his name. Proudly, with a shaking voice, she lit the torch to the glory of the state. This was poetic justice, as all her life she lived in the shadow of his intense light. Yet she lit the flame this time. Nothing was more Israeli than this torch on that night. She always was ahead of him in being Israeli, and by far. She is Israeliness and he is Judaism; he was in the hospital and she carried the flame.

After the ceremony, we crossed the street and sat around his bed. The old lion was leaving this world. We parted sadly, but feeling comforted and thankful that his suffering was over and that he was leaving the world in a dignified manner. His children and grandchildren came and said goodbye and thank you. Then everyone left and I was alone with him for the night shift, he and I and the silence. He shouted occasionally, scattering broken words like verbal dew. It was a night of senseless sounds. Once he shouted, *"Police, Policier,"* and shook with excitement. He was dying all night, but in morning he returned to life. Like the child of the Turkish woman in Hebron, the relentless survivor outsmarted grim death. Several more days passed with more medicines and then he came back to us for another half year of life. It was a productive six months, with the addition of two great-grandchildren and good news for all of us. When he woke up, I told him of his nightmares.

"What did you see, Dad?"

"Is your computer here?"

"Yes."

"Then get it out. I want you to write something."

This was his dream—word fragments that did not complete a story, something imagined, fantastic and not fully comprehensive. "I dreamed that I was in Paris and I was taken to a fancy restaurant...I did not want to eat because I worried about the prices. They took me out and laid me on a big mattress, and facing me were Israelis who were abroad on behalf of the health maintenance fund. I was afraid they were cheating the fund and I made myself a mental note to tell Ada [my sister]."

My interpretation of his dream was that he was in Paris, just like after the Shoah, when he worked three years for the Mossad, the Yishuv organization that smuggled illegal immigrants to Israel. Facing him were Israelis; not with him, not beside him—facing him. There, abroad, he meets Israelis. But they are probably sick, since they were sent there by the health fund. He thinks the worst of them, that they cheat. He deals with them with his brain, making a *mental note*. This is my father, pure brain-power. In his overseas arena, he is against the rest of the Israeli world. He is from there, wise and alone; we are from here with our shortcomings, sick and cheating.

"I was sitting alone, and a hard-shell suitcase like a Samsonite was near me, and I wanted someone to help me stand up and ask where we were, but none of the Israelis made a motion. So I started to shout at them and said, if someone does not come immediately, I will call the police, and I speak French, so don't get wise with me. Some of them left; they probably didn't have visas. The rest did not move. I don't remember exactly what I wanted, so I cried out 'Police, Policier.' Then none of the Israeli heroes stayed; they all fled."

In the first part of the dream they wanted to put him to sleep, to make him leave, but he refused, disobeying. He is a survivor. Once a Nazi officer told him, "Dr. Burg, every morning you come to our Gestapo headquarters and make deals on lives and Jews [my father represented his people at the Gestapo, negotiating daily for their lives]. Why should I not send you there as well?" My father, who lived by the sharpness of his tongue, replied: "Mr. Officer, you and I have the same goal. You want to free Germany of Jews, and I want the Jews out of Germany too. I help you and you help me. Therefore you have no interest in sending me there."

The Gestapo wanted him on a wooden bunk in a death camp, but my father is of the Heroes of Israel. He spoke French, was saved, and went on saving others. An authentic specimen of the People of the Book, and of the culture of persuasive arguments that made use of words that were eradicated in order to bring Israel and loudness into being. Only at this moment, on the threshold of his death, in the passage between this world and the one to come, he forgot his three languages: German, his native tongue; Hebrew, which he knew how to read before he went to school; and Yiddish, with which he communicated with my mother and with the rest of the Jewish world throughout most of his life. In that particular last moment of his, he revisited Paris, in French. Yosef Burg was between two worlds, between the world that was ruined and the world that was yet to be built between Jewishness and Israeliness. He found refuge with French as the language of transition, not ruin and not resurrection. The dying Yosef Burg dreamed of postwar Paris, the city that was like a second womb to him and to my mother. This was where he became accustomed to the loss of the spiritual empire of Germany, where he would sever the cord with Europe as a place to live and where he would be born again into the established

Israel. How symbolic that it was in Paris he was informed of his election as member and vice speaker of the first Knesset. It was in Paris that my mother's life touched my father's expansive world for the first time. There they raised Tzviya, my late sister, as a happy young couple, not knowing that fate would claim her before their own deaths. My sister Tzviya was named after my grandmother, who died in misery at a camp. They did not know then whether Grandmother Tzivya was alive or dead, so they named the doomed child after her, but with slightly different spelling of the name, Tzviya, not Tzivya. Perhaps this is why she lived and then died so early.

My father was so lonely in his dream, he and his suitcase, like the Wandering Jew. Always traveling like a nomad. Always ready to flee to another place with his suitcase within reach. It would be a Samsonite, and he is Samson the Hero. Heinrich Heine once said that the Jew after the Ruin created for himself a mobile homeland that included his Pentateuch, his prayer shawl, and his phylacteries. My father's homeland was inside the suitcase. When he immigrated to Israel in the 1930s he brought with him a wooden crate in the style of nineteenth-century globe-trotters, a German crate, Kabinen Koffer, containing thirty-five ironed and starched silk, linen, and cotton shirts, and more than forty pairs of socks, all embroidered with his initials. There were other things as well that his Jewish mother packed for her son's one-way trip to the Holy Land.

He spent many months in Tel Aviv living in the Germany that he imported in his crate, postponing his bond with the old-new land that had become his safe haven from the new Germans. He desperately needed help, for years, from the Israelis who did not make a motion. Then something happened, he said. "I shouted at them."

This cannot be, Father. You never shouted in your life. Once you were angry with me when I spoke ill of the chief rabbi, and another time when I played with the toy Chevy that you brought me in your suitcase, because it was during the Sabbath, between two o'clock and four o'clock, in the winter. Except for these two instances, you never showed anger. And you did not call the police. It cannot be. My father would never inform the police, as in our prayers we say, "And for the slanderers let there be no hope."

This was in the dream. In reality, my real father spoke to them, regardless of the language, but he surely did. The Israelis, some of them, fled like Israelis. Some of them treated him, with his adherence to the rule of law and his full command of many languages, with indifference. Here comes the bitter truth about many people's dreams at the end of their lives, including my father's.

"I do not exactly remember what I actually wanted."

"What did you really want, Dad?"

Later my father described in great detail a jumbled fantasy of a technological innovation that included my sister and my brother-in-law and a petite French woman and her giant husband wearing a French hat, who wanted Father to sign something. The dream took place in Tel Aviv, Geneva, and Paris simultaneously. Father stands between two doors, not knowing which one to enter. Father, who was with one foot in the grave just the day before, was facing two doors. On that day he was rational again.

"Dreams should not be investigated. I see the café in Paris, and it turned out that there is a happy end. If you open one door, you are in this hospital; if you open the other, you are in the luxurious hospital with guards and everything." In other words, everything is sick. The world is a hospital and we are its patients. But there is a *hôpital ordinaire* and a *hôpital de lux.* "The simple interpretation," he said, "is that it depends. 'Two doors open to a man,' it says somewhere in Midrash. I don't remember where, but it occurred to me this minute. I know more than I know. It could be that I dreamed about an illustration of the two doors. Then it connects to the whole fantasy. You helped me find myself in this matter."

I had never heard this before or after from my father, the man whose light, along with my mother's, illuminated my life. He actually said this, on his sickbed, on the threshold of his grave. Before he passed through one of the doors to the next world, from this hospital to a world of luxury, he told me that I helped him find himself in the matter. The matter was the conclusion of his life, no less. My warm and self-restrained father, whose biggest compliment was, "I have no complaints," yet always had something to say—about a mispronunciation, a necktie off center, the wrong eye color—and I had to know if this was real criticism that should be pondered and acted upon, or just a reminder of humility, to ensure that I do not become arrogant. One rebuke as a compliment and another as education—but always criticism.

I turned off the computer, kissed him, left the room, and cried my heart out. I wept for my father who was going to die, and would not be comforted. For that one precious moment, my father, you returned to the living? Only to say those wonderful words that so few children hear from their parents, especially if their parents are *Yekkes* from Germany?

Now, years later, when I read my father's dream I can discern some secrets. I went looking for the Midrash and found two gates, not doors. A door, *deleth* in Hebrew, is an old biblical word, and our sages and their Midrashim did not favor it. The door became a gate. The Midrash says that Rabbi Abba bar Cahana said: Two gates lead to the Netherworld, one internal and one external. Everyone who was killed wrongly comes and sits his years by the external. The European Jews were killed wrongly, and my father was saved by the skin of his teeth. His life is half buried in the ash of Europe. The other half he lived in this world, which is also quite hellish. Many times I thought to myself that my father must have lived so many years on behalf of those who died ahead of their time. We once discussed life expectancy, and he told me that life expectancy means that for someone like me to live ninety years, someone like Tzviya, my daughter and your sister, has to die before the age of fifty. His longevity was a retaliatory strike against the Nazis and their collaborators.

In the remaining months of his life we spoke a lot, more than ever, about everything. The well-trodden stories, which every family has, found their way into our conversations. What is the meaning and what is the moral? This would be the last time these stories are told. Therefore they should be understood as they are and as they can be interpreted, as in the Talmud. My father's waking time was diminishing, as well as his voice, and his eyes became grayer and extinguished. In the end, at the very last of our conversations, in his last sentence to my ear, as if he knew it would be his last, he said, "Avraham, I'm worried. Who will take care of the Jewish people?" The bells were ringing, and I did not ask. They rang for me, Father. You helped me find my way in this matter.

Several days passed, my father was sleepy, preparing himself for his eternal sleep. He would sigh every once in a while, and we were there to interpret: does he mean "I am thirsty," or "It hurts," or "Plump the pillow under my head," or "This side hurts me, please turn me over?" He sighed and we interpreted. He sighed and we did our best. He sighed, and we sighed with him. There were no more words, just syllables and a few vowels.

The evening after Yom Kippur we found ourselves around his bed in a small room feeling much sorrow. Suddenly, we started humming a Jewish tune, a *nigun,* without the words. I do not recall that my father ever really sang. Now and then he would hum, but never sing. He was musical, though. His old violin's strings broke and were never reattached. I think that he stopped singing after the Shoah. Only on Sabbath eves, after Mother's chicken soup, did he sing from beginning to end, alphabetically, his father's *nigun, Kol Mekadesh Shvi'i,* meaning "whoever hallows the Sabbat as befits." These were the only notes that survived Avraham Burg of Dresden. I had not heard this melody at any other home, on any Sabbath, anywhere in the world. This is our tune, of Grandfather, my father and myself. The rest he would leave to Mother: "Zing Zmires," meaning "Sing songs" in Yiddish. When *klezmers,* musicians, played before him, when he heard his favorite melodies, he would smile to himself and nod his head, either responding to the rhythm or approving the beauty of the moment. Yet he did not sing. Now we were surrounding his bed and singing a *nigun,* a religious tune.

When one of the Rabbis of the Belz Hassiduth got married, the best composer of the Belz court composed a cheerful rhythmic melody to the lyrics of the "Days of Awe" prayer: *Avinu Malkenu,* "Our father our king, let this hour be an hour of mercy and goodwill from before you." My father loved this melody very much, and always asked us to sing it. On the evening after Yom Kippur, we slowed the melody's tempo. We turned this wedding song into a melancholic lamentation. Slowly, with beauty, with all our might, we sang and wept.

Then suddenly, from the shadow of death, as if revisiting our world for a moment, my father mumbled something and joined the singing with his blocked throat, his voice muffled by the oxygen mask. He muttered something twice, as if trying to speak just one last time, to utter those eight Hebrew words that would say it all: Let this hour be an hour of mercy and goodwill from you. He wanted to say it so much and yet could not, so we acted as his mouth. This is how my father departed this world, with a melody that has become our own hymn of sorrow and grief.

One day we will wake from our long nightmare and sing "End and Beginning," a poem by the marvelous Polish poet Wislawa Szymborska about the consequences of war. Perhaps someone will compose a melody to it, and it will become the second hymn of us all.

When we wake up, history will resume. Life will return to life and it will become clear that it is impossible to dig in, forever, in the trenches that stretch between the cemeteries. Someone will announce: "That's it. It's over." Another will declare: "We can defeat Hitler."

Because it is possible, we must do it. We must leave the Valley of Weeping, the shadows of death and climb up to the hills of hope and optimism. We will remember, but will be hale. Scarred, but whole, balanced. On the first day of normalcy, the new beginning after what happened to us in the middle of last century, we will begin the cleaning up of Israeli public life. "Someone must clean up," wrote the poet. How then will the cleaned up, cured Israel look?

Holocaust Memorial Day will not be commemorated on its present date, an artificial date, the day of the Warsaw ghetto uprising. This important date will be commemorated on a different occasion. With the perspective of time, it is clear that the sublime honor that we feel toward the ghetto rebels is not the Shoah's main lesson. Even Israeli independence and the rebuilding of Jewish force are not the most important consequence of the smokestacks. As time goes by it becomes clear that the value given to heroism, in relation to the extermination and destruction, was exaggerated. Heroism will reclaim a more modest place beside the main issues: the crimes against humanity and the ruining of the thousand-year-old relationship between the Jews and Europe. It was our destruction and theirs. Therefore, three times a year, not just one, Israel will commemorate the tragedies.

One time it will be with the rest of the world, on January 27. The international community designated the liberation day of Auschwitz to commemorate the Holocaust and World War II. On this day we will grasp the universal dimensions of that era. We will not think only of ourselves, but of humanity as a whole. This will be a day in which even Israel's Arab citizens will stand in solemn silence, grieving their own pain, as partners to the new human obligation. It will be a day of "No more": no more violence, no more xenophobia, no more discrimination, and no more racism. In school we will study other people's holocausts; we will understand the origins of violence and aggression and the ways to eradicate them; we will fight tyranny and commit to justice, equality, and peace.

We will vow again and again that "Never again" includes everything; it will not happen again to anyone, anywhere, anytime. It will be the day in which Israeli citizens will become aware every year of the other heroism of the Shoah, that of the righteous gentiles who were committed to their own conscience and defeated, with modesty and without fear, the beast of tyranny that was in them and among them. And first and foremost, we will stand together, with the civilized nations, at the forefront of the worldwide struggle against hatred wherever it is. We will convert our personal wounds into a cure for all humanity. This will be the day in which all Israel's prayers will be as those of my parents-in-law Lucien and Janine Lazar, who were first to teach us the alternative Passover Haggadah, and endowed us with the magic of their ways and the light in their soul. No more verses like "Pour your wrath on the nations that do not know you and on the kingdoms who do not call in your name"[1] but as in a sixteenth-century German Haggadah: "Pour your love over the nations that do know you and on kingdoms that call in your name on behalf of graces that they do to the seed of Jacob and their defending of your people from their enemies. May they see the booth of your chosen and rejoice in the joy of your nations."

A couple of months later, early on May 9, we will commemorate with the immigrants from the former Soviet republics the victory over Nazi Germany. During this day we will honor the heroes in the ghettos, forests, camps, and in the rank and file of the regular armies. These immigrants have changed the landscape of life in Israel. Many of them, if not most, feel that they were the ones who defeated Hitler. The massive, heroic partnership of Jews with the Red Army made them into the proudest of Jews. Many of them are not Jews according to Jewish religious law, but they are Jews because they share our fate. The day will mark the amazing international partnership that brought Hitler down. Therefore it will no longer be defeated Israel, the victims' sole heir, but Israel and Israelis in the family of victors who did not relent until the tumor was removed and the world began its healing. The fact that so many of the former Soviet Jews who live in Israel are non-Jewish is also an invitation to alter our own private identities. They are Israelis on account of fate. They are not bearded rabbis, but Israelis like Ruth the Moabite. Their definition of Israeli identity is through life: their studies, language, hard work, culture and service. Their absorption is our return to our ancient tradition of welcoming those who wish to join our people and our nation. As our Talmud tells us, the descendants of some of our worst enemies, Sisra, Sanherib, and Haman, studied the Torah and taught it in Jerusalem and Bnei Brak.[2]

With them and for all of us, Israel must understand that after the Shoah, genetic Judaism has to end. We have to connect to the Judaism that shares a common fate and values with others. There will be among us descendants of Abraham and Sarah, but we will all be the children of Adam and Eve. Unlike many rabbis among us, like Rabbi Yehuda Halevi and his predecessors and followers, who believed that a non-genetic Jew is not equal to us, we will adapt the medieval scholar Maimonides' astoundingly modern views and bold positions. This is what he wrote to Ovadia the Proselyte, his contemporary: "There is no difference at all between us and you in any matter…and do not underestimate your origins. If we are descended from Abraham, Isaac, and Jacob, you are descended from the Creator of the World."[3] Victory Day over Nazi Germany will also be the day of victory of the shared identity over the divisive religious law.

The third day to commemorate the Shoah will be on the Ninth of Av, the date on which both our temples were ruined. This day will be a time for our own private memorial, a family gathering, ours alone. It will be another link in the sequence of events of ruins that visited our people. Shoah is actually a new name for the traditional term of *Ruin*. The Zionist indoctrinization system considered it very important to open a new page of Jewish history and therefore called this ruin by the name Shoah. One purpose, among others, was to dissociate it from the Jewish historical continuum, to make it unique and to separate us from all that Mother Judaism had known until then. It is time then to restore the trauma to its natural place in the Jewish and Israeli calendar. Therefore the third day of Shoah commemoration will be marked late in the Jewish year, on the traditional Av Ninth. This way the Shoah and its lesson will not be alien events in Jewish and human cultural history. The Shoah will return to its traditional name: *Hurban,* one ruin among many. Indeed it was a colossal ruin, greater than all that we had known, but still ruin. Only thus we will be able to harness the tools of memory in the Jewish experience, as unfortunately rich as it is in these matters.

There are many explanations why Av Ninth is not a very meaningful date in the Israeli calendar. Some argue that we are busy building and therefore have no time to commemorate ruins; others say that it is not appealing, since the date marks something so ancient it is irrelevant to a people who live devoutly and compulsively in the present. Everyone agrees that redemption is in and exile is out.

Av Ninth, usually in July or August, is in the middle of the long summer break. No school, no homework. From kindergarten until military service, no one reminds us of this day. We are on the beach, vacationing from Jewish history. If five generations of Israelis have not studied Av Ninth and its lessons, it's no wonder that this day of mourning and fasting has become an unknown "holiday."

There will be no choice but to restructure the vacation calendar and to bring the Israeli students back to school to start the battle of memory and awareness. The summer trimester will be devoted to consciousness and remembrance. It is difficult to imagine much enthusiasm from the students for this enterprise—they will have to hear about the ruin instead of summertime play and trips—so we will have to be creative. I never made secret of my opinion that the commemorative, forced trips for Israelis to the death camps in Poland are ill-conceived and dangerous. Since the experience is emotionally overwhelming, we are cultivating a subconscious mental reality, in which all past horrors are reconstructed, cloned, only to be renewed and perpetuated by future generations. It is like collective reincarnation. Instead of breaking the cycle of pathology, we perpetuate it. Instead of healing, we re-infect ourselves. Instead of forgetting, we scratch our wounds and bleed again. Israeli national separatists find in the heaps of ash—which once were smiling, creative people—fertilized ground for tortured souls.

Therefore, in my awakening Israel, the days of the annual summer break will be dedicated to a much more meaningful journey. Instead of a one-way trip to a time and place of pain, humiliation, and ruin, I wish to propose a multidimensional journey to hope and trust. Groups of Israeli students, Jewish and Arabic, will visit Spain: Aragon, Castile, and Andalucía. There they will become familiar with the golden age, when Islam and Judaism had mutually beneficial relationships. Each one of them will see and understand that there was time of spiritual alternatives to military service, suicide bombing, and terror. From Spain they will travel to Germany and Eastern Europe, will study the European Jewish millennium, of which only the last dozen years were that horrible.

They will visit immigrant Muslim concentrations in the heart of Europe, where a new European Islam is attempting to exist. From there they will return home to Israel and tour the confrontational history of Jews and Arabs. In the end, they will sit down to draw their own conclusions of the historic tour. I hope and believe that the unequivocal conclusion of many of the children will be that violence, racism, and extermination are not an alternative. Extermination has no building value and it lacks imagination and creativity. They will understand by themselves that only cultural cooperation, with the acceptance of the other as an equal to be appreciated, will yield for us an optimistic future and a second golden age for the benefit and the glory of the entire world.

Israel's education system should arrange another trip for its students: visiting and staying with Jewish communities in the West, and especially in the United States. There we can learn what it means to live a life free of threats. We can learn about solidarity, and how life with national meaning can be lived without an external enemy, and with full trust between Jews and the non-Jewish environment.

Without listing what needs repair in Israel's public life and jurisdiction, I wish to point out three areas that deserve careful attention: the *Law of Return*, the *Law of Punishment of the Nazis and their Collaborators* and the relationship with Germany.

Every state in the world determines its identity and how residents and immigrants are naturalized. In Israel, the direct path to becoming a citizen, at least for Jews, is the Law of Return. In Israel's early history, so says the parliamentary legend, the law was enacted as a mirror image of Nazi Germany's Nuremberg Laws, which defined Jews for their future persecution. I have never found confirmation of this in the Knesset records, but in all parliamentary discussions of the law, everyone, whether a minister or a house member, who took to the podium claimed that the Law of Return was our answer to the discriminating race laws of Nuremberg. Almost everyone who would have been defined by Hitler as a Jew and was sent to his death must be granted a protective Israeli citizenship. So even if this was not the legislators' intent at the time, it has become the working assumption of its successors. Until the link between Israeli citizenship and the Nuremberg Laws is severed, Hitler will in effect continue to decide who is Jewish. A modern definition of citizenship, according to a genetic or religious code, is by itself an enormous ethical problem, especially for Jews.

The problematic definition of a Jew according to the Law of Return—"A Jew is a person who is born to a Jewish mother or who converted and is not of a different religion"—should be abolished, along with the old-fashioned concept of the nation-state. Israel should become the democratic state of the Jewish people which belongs to all of its citizens, and the majority will decide on its character and essence. I am afraid that if the association between our traumatic past and our schizophrenic present continues, our acquired immune deficiency will continue for a few more generations. It would be a shame, because I believe that all issues of identity of the modern human in general, and of the Jew in particular, have completely changed, and therefore there is no choice but to redefine who belongs to the state of the Jews.

Israel must disengage from both the Nuremberg definitions—which define a Jew as anyone with a fourth-generation connection with Jewish blood—and from current policies and practice, which recognize only the strictest Orthodox conversion as admissible. I am sorry, but this does not define my identity and my Judaism. A multifaceted culture cannot be squeezed and defined by orthodoxy only. For me, the only valid test is if someone identifies with the human and universal aspects of the Torah and the dreams of our prophets, someone who identifies with the achievements of past Jewish civilizations, and someone who identifies with contemporary Jewish culture.

The strict man-made rules, which my friends, the majority of Israelis, and I do not even think of observing, should not be the standards imposed selectively on our newly converted only. Only the fundamental position of the mother of all the Jewish converts, and the ultimate mother of the Jewish Kingdom, namely Ruth the Moabite, is the position to which we should return. The Bible story tells us of Naomi, a widow from Bethlehem, who returns from the field of Moab with her young daughter-in-law, also a widow. The two of them were poor and bereaved, returning empty-handed from exile. The young Ruth promised the old Naomi thus: "Where ever you go I shall go and where ever you lodge I shall lodge, as your people is my people and your God my God."[4] Ruth first expressed her identification with Naomi, then with her belonging to the collective, and only then with the spirit and with God.

With us, the order is reversed. God's rabbis received from the heads of government in the early state a monopoly over civilian identity, and all they demand is external superficiality. They demand submission before a blurry God, hidden and severe, without really building the internal structure, the solidarity of those joining the Israeli collective. I say solidarity first, and all the rest, if at all, later. This line is not my own; it is written in our Talmud. "A proselyte who comes to convert at this time should be asked: What did you see that you came to convert? Know you not that Israel at these times is pained, pushed, downtrodden and maddened? And they are tormented? If he says, I know and I do not mind, he is received at once."[5] For me, a convert to my people is someone who came to share my destiny, or someone who is partner to my human and cultural values, whatever are his origins.

Once the Israeli identity debate opens and we are able to base Israeli identity on foundations of self-confidence, openness, and acceptance, we can also discuss the deletion from our legislation of the term "crimes against the Jewish people." If the Jewish people and the Israeli state are not an integral part of humanity, but are an independent, separate entity that does not belong to history, then such a law is essential. But if our eyes are turned to the expanses of the world, to human history, then this law, even as a monument to our past torments, perpetuates our un-historic being and condemns us to separate ways of life and conduct.

We should no longer be strange exhibits in a preserve for creatures in danger of extinction, but must integrate with the whole of human society, in which a crime against the Jewish people is naturally a crime against humanity. There is not, and there must not be, a separate Jewish humanity. Humanity is humanity, without compromises and exceptions. Not even us. With the annulment of this notion from our law books, we will be free and liberated.

In the detention cell of humanity there is only one detainee left from the dark days, and it is Germany. There will be those who will justify it and claim that they deserve it forever. But others may understand that the best interest of the human race requires the unshackling of the problematic relationship between the Jewish guard and the German prisoner. A wise person once described the future relations with Germany like those between two Siamese twins that will never be separated, as their fates are intertwined. In my view, Israel and Germany are two nations that live by a sea of common torments. They are very different, but are always neighbors. As long as Israel was in the pole of seclusion, Germany was bound there as well. In the day we leave Auschwitz and establish the new state of Israel, we also have to set Germany free.

True, we must not forget, but at the same time we should not be forever held hostage by memory. We should not live in the past, but be cured of it. When Israel releases Germany, the world will be better. This will be our contribution to the sufferers of the world and those currently persecuted. Today Germany and Israel are synonyms of one experience, the Shoah, which unites the two and creates for us and for them an impenetrable private space. As a result, Germany cannot exercise its full power in the international arena. On the day that we are set free, we will set free. When the Jewish people recognize that the Shoah is much bigger than us, and that it is not only ours and we have no monopoly over it, that it is our disaster but it belongs to all humanity, and that we are but part of one expanding family of nations that is not willing to accept any harm to any people—then and only then will the Jewish people be able to "donate" its Germany to the effort. Germany's economic capability, together with profound awareness and the will to atone for the crimes of the past, can change the picture of world evil and paint it with goodness. A statement by Israel's prime minister with Germany's president, a common humanitarian treaty, or any other practical step that will spur both countries to cooperate in the repair of the world will constitute an almost prophetic fulfillment of the vision of sublime humanity of the Jewish people at the hand of "modern Persia." The last two verses of the Bible express it.

> Now in the first year of Cyrus king of Persia, that the word of the LORD spoken by the mouth of Jeremiah might be accomplished, the LORD stirred up the spirit of Cyrus king of Persia, that he made a proclamation throughout all his kingdom, and put it also in writing, saying, "Thus saith Cyrus king of Persia, All the kingdoms of the earth hath the LORD God of heaven given me; and he hath charged me to build him a house in Jerusalem, Is. 44.28 which is in Judah. Who is there among you of all his people? The LORD his God be with him, and let him go up."[6]

Haman's Persia was about destruction and hatred, but there was another Persia, of Cyrus, that was about tolerance, restoration and building. There was a Germany of Hitler, and it is up to us if there will be a new

Germany, a generous one. Perhaps a Jewish-German vision for a better world is possible, a vision that will continue the wonderful German Jewry from the point of its extinction. This was the most amazing Jewry we had ever had, its dreams were as long as the knife that slit its throat. It was a Jewry whose ideals are missing here, whose prophets, writers, and artists have never received much recognition in Israel. It was a Jewry that was based on peacefulness, reconciliation, high culture, identity, and integration, roots and modernity, Judaism and universalism, and faith in man and endless innocence until its end. And now, when Germany is different and can absorb the ideas of its Jews, they are gone. They are lost and forgotten.

On the day that the Shoah is no longer part of our daily lives, we can recite the Kaddish for its victims and for ourselves. The prayers will transition from the mournful years of bereavement, suspicion, and anger to the age of memory, optimism, trust, and hope.

Sometime in the state's early days, my parents moved from Tel Aviv to Jerusalem, from the outdoor chess games of Ben Yehuda Strasse to the *Yekke* respectability of Sderot Ben Maimon in Jerusalem.

For many years I thought that my parents wanted to raise us in the heart of the secular Israel, the one open to the new Israeli trends. During many years I loved my neighborhood, where I learned to integrate identities of religiosity and Israeliness. Our home was an Israeli home. Mordechai Bar'on, the IDF's chief education officer and a peacenik, lived downstairs. Next to him lived the Sidon family, whose father was a waiter from Morocco. They immigrated to America and left me a scar, the sorrow of my first childhood separation.

Across from us lived senior officers, such as Moshe Dayan and Chayim Herzog and all their successors. Above us, in a spacious apartment, lived Eliezer Kaplan, the first minister of the treasury, and his wife Dr. Kaplan, the scary doctor. Above them lived the Kidrons, the mother Shoshana and her daughters Michal and Naomi, my childhood friends. Their father, Avraham, was a military judge who sentenced the soldier Meir Tobianski to death as a spy for the British in the War of Independence, and was later a diplomat and the director-general of the Ministry of Foreign Affairs. Can you imagine a better home to be born in? Today I think that home chooses you more than you choose it. It wanted me to be born in it so I could understand my identity through its memories, the stories of others that became the history of my home. This is a home with a name and a stunning history.

If it depended on me, I would ask that all the children born from now on be guests, if just for a moment, at the house in which I was born. The home's family name is the Avikarius Residence, and its first name is Villa Lea. The stone tablet at the entrance to the single non-Jewish home in Rehavia says: "Villa Lea, 1 May 1934." Avikarius was an attorney of Armenian ancestry who arrived in Israel with British General Edmund Allenby, who conquered the land in World War I from the Turks. Avikarius fell in love with Lea, a Jewish girl from the ultra-Orthodox neighborhood of Me'a She'arim, married her and built a home for her in Rehavia, which was very distant, geographically and spiritually, from her native neighborhood.

This is the only home in all Jerusalem that publicly carries a narrative of faiths. Urban legend says that for his lover, Avikarius went to pray at our synagogue, Yeshurun. This is the synagogue where I read the Torah on my Bar Mitzvah, and the only synagogue where the cantor Meislish sang the melodies of the German Jewish composer Lebendowski, convinced that these were the melodies that the Levites had sung in the Temple.

Lea then broke his heart, running away to England with a British officer, whom in turn she dumped for an Egyptian senior official, later disappearing without trace. Avikarius did not want to stay there any longer, and the house became the property of the British Mandate. At the end of the 1930s, the British gave the home to the Ethiopian emperor Haile Selassie, who fled Mussolini's troops when they conquered his country. This is a true story. Nobody believed me when I told my friends in school that I lived in a royal palace. But one day I saw the African king on our porch under a parasol to protect him from the blazing Jerusalem sun. Well, not with my own eyes, since I had not yet been born, but in the Israeli television series *Pillar of Fire*.

Is it only a coincidence that my parents chose that house to be their home? My mother was an Arab Jew from Hebron and my father was a German Jew from Dresden. If more of us knew the stories that our house walls know and remember, there would be more peace in the world, in the way of my father, and much more love in the way of my mother. With peace and love, the world is so much better. It was from this house my mother left for her last journey. On a rainy night in Jerusalem, an old Turkish gentile woman who worked for us had said to me her very last words ever, "Avraham, all of you fill me with happiness." Then my mother went to bed and left us forever, calm, reconciled, loving and loved. Her love won.

NOTES

CHAPTER 1

1. Yevamot 65b

CHAPTER 2

1. Isaiah 60:2–3
2. http://en.wikipedia.org/wiki/March_of_the_Living

CHAPTER 3

1. Proverbs 13:24

CHAPTER 4

1. Ofer Schiff, *Assimilation in Pride: Anti-Semitism, Holocaust and Zionism as a Challenge to the American Jewish Reform Ideology* (Tel-Aviv: Am-Oved Publishers, 2001).

CHAPTER 5

1. Friedrich Nietzsche, *The Pity of it All: German Jews before Hitler* (Hebrew) (Israel: Devir, 2004)
2. Hannah Arendt, *Eichmann in Jerusalem* (New York: Penguin Books, 1963)
3. An official press release by Netanyahu's spokesperson from http://www.netanyahu.org/uvtiucizqvgvq.html
4. Thomas Gauly, *The Future of Liberty* (Hebrew) (Tel Aviv: Am Oved Publishers Ltd, 1999)
5. Frantz Fanon, *Black Skin, White Masks* (Hebrew) (Tel Aviv: Maariv, 2004)

6. Ian Kershaw, *Hitler 1889–1939: Hubris* (Hebrew) (Tel Aviv: Am Oved, 2004)
7. Hannah Arendt, *Eichmann in Jerusalem* (New York: Penguin Books, 1963)
8. Yeshayahu Leibowitz, *People, Land, State* (Hebrew) Keter

CHAPTER 6

1. Tom Segev, *The Seventh Million* (New York: Hill & Wang, 1993)
2. Ibid., *Davar* was a Hebrew language daily newspaper of the labor movement.
3. Judith Loyis Herman, *Trauma and Recovery* (New York: Basic Books, 1992)
4. Talmud Bavli, Baba Metzia, 62:71
5. Alain Finkielkraut, "The Religion of Humanity and the Sin of the Jews," *Azure* 21 (2005)
6. Ibid.
7. Genesis 18:25
8. Talmud Bavli, Gittin, leaf 57, ii
9. Genesis 32:7
10. Mekhilta dRabi Ishmael, Mishpatim, Dnezikin Mishpatim, Parasha 18

CHAPTER 7

1. Barak, Ehud, Lt. Gen., Auschwitz-Bierkenau, 1992
2. Ibid.
3. http://kibbutz.org.il/welcome.htm?page=http://kibbutz.org.il/orchim/050602_mihtavim.htm
4. Israel Air Force, the official website, http://www.iaf.org.il/Templates/Journal/Journal.In.aspx?lang=HE&lobby ID=50&folderID=1126&subfolderID=1127&docfolderID=1133&docID=22213
5. Hannah Krall, *To Steal a March on God* (New York: Routledge, 1996)
6. Marek Edelman, *Resisting the Holocaust: Fighting Back in the Warsaw Ghetto* (New York Ocean Press, 2004), 101
7. Ibid.
8. Marek Edelman, *Resisting the Holocaust: Fighting Back in the Warsaw Ghetto* (New York: Ocean Press, 2004)
9. Marek Edelman, *The Fighting Ghetto* (Tel Aviv: Hakibbutz Hameuhad, 2001) 103
10. Natan Alterman, *HaTur Hashvi'I* [The Seventh Column] (Tel Aviv: Hakibbutz Hameuhad, 1955)
11. Natan Alterman, *HaTur Hashvi'I* [The Seventh Column] (Tel Aviv: Hakibbutz Hameuhad, 1955)
12. Bereshit Rabba 42,13. R Yehuda "plays" with the unique Hebrew word "*Ivri*"—the "Hebrew." Genesis 14: 13, which sounds like "ever," "over there," "the other side."

CHAPTER 8

1. Chronicles of the Knesset, page 9
2. Idith Zertal, Moshe Zuckermann (eds.), *Hannah Arendt: A Half-Century of Polemics* (Hakibbutz Hameuchd, 2004)

CHAPTER 9

1. Yair Oron, *Denial, Israel and the Armenian Genocide* (Tel Aviv: Maba, 2003)
2. Ian Kershaw, *Hitler 1889–1939: Hubris.'* (Hebrew) (Tel Aviv: Am Oved: 2004)
3. R.J. Rummel, "The New Concept of Democide," in *Encyclopedia of Genocide*, ed. Israel W. Charny (Santa Barbara: ABC-CLIO, 1999), 18–34, also in in *The Pain of Knowledge*. Yair Oron, (Tel Aviv: The Open University of Israel, 2003)
4. The Banality of Indifference: The Attitude of the Yishuv and the Zionist Movement to the Armenian Genocide, Dvir (with Kibutzim College of Education), Tel-Aviv, 1995, 395 pp. (Hebrew) p 325
5. Galed Margalit and Yifat Weiss, *Memory and Amnesia—The Holocaust in Germany* (Tel Aviv: Hakibbutz HaMeuhad, 2005)
6. Yehuda Elkana, "In Defense of Foregetting," *Haaretz*, March 2, 1988 (Hebrew)
7. Boaz Evron
8. Genesis 18:25
9. *Haaretz*, August 2004
10. *Haaretz*, August 2004
11. Ian Kershaw, *Hitler 1889–1939: Hubris* (Hebrew) (Tel Aviv: Am Oved: 2004)
12. AvivaPage: 4 Aviram. "Defendant Germany, Charge Annihilation," *Haaretz*, August 2004.
13. Knesset Minutes 27-01-04
14. Isaiah 2:2–4
15. Isaiah 56:3–5

CHAPTER 10

1. Jonathan Garb, *The Unique Will Become Herds* (Hebrew) (Carmel: Shalom Hartman Institute, 2005)
2. Yitzhak Ginzburg, *Kingdom of Israel* (Hebrew), private edition.
3. http://www.ynet.co.il/articles/1,7340,L-3138771,00.html
4. Genesis 38:2
5. Talmud Bavli, Masekhet Shabbat, 33
6. Numbers 16:3
7. Talmud Bavli, Masekhet Brakhot, 52

8. Yehuda Halevi, *Kuzari: An Argument for the Faith of Israel* (Tel Aviv: Schocken Books, September 1987)
9. See Gevuroth Hashem, *God's Mighty Acts,* for the holiday of Passover, The Passover Hegada, http://www.daat.ac.il/daat/vl/tohen.asp?id=241. Netzach Yisrael, *The Eternity of Israel;* Netzach (eternity), has the same root as the word for victory, on Tisha B'Av (an annual day of mourning about the destruction of the Temples and the Jewish exile) and the final deliverance, Derech Chaim, *Way of Life,* (1589) a commentary on the Mishnah tractate Avoth.
10. Hakuzari 1. 11–115
11. Avraham Kook, Yitzhak HaCohen, *The Holy Lights* (Hebrew), 14
12. *Haaretz,* November 27, 2005
13. "They Are not Poor, They Are Arabs," *Haaretz,* November 19, 2005

CHAPTER 11

1. Zvi Yanai, *Yours, Sandro* (Jerusalem: Keter Books, 2004)
2. Genesis 32:8
3. Deuteronomy 30:11–14
4. Maimonides, *Guide for the Perplexed*, Part A, Chapter 26 (Tel Aviv: Tel Aviv University Press, 2002)
5. Ephraim Meir, *Memory Act, Society Man and God after Auschwitz* (Hebrew) (Tel Aviv: Resling, 2004)
6. Exodus 14:31
7. Samuel II 12
8. Psalms 115
9. Emmanuel Todd, *After the Empire: The Breakdown of the American Order, European Perspectives: A Series in Social Thought and Cultural Criticism* (New York: Columbia University Press, 2003)
10. Exodus 1:10
11. Talmud Bavli, Masekhet Eruvin, 13, 72
12. Talmud Bavli, Masekhet Baba Metzia, 59, 72

CHAPTER 12

1. Psalm 79
2. Talmud Bavli, Masekhet Sanhedrin, page 96b
3. Maimonides. *Letters.* (Jerusalem: Mosad Harav Kook, 1989)
4. Ruth 1:16
5. Talmud Bavli, Masekhet Yevamot, page 47a
6. Chronicles 2 36:22–23

INDEX